THE DERRYDALE PRESS

Treasury of Fishing

Edited by J. I. Merritt

THE DERRYDALE PRESS

Treasury of Fishing

Edited by J. I. Merritt

THE DERRYDALE PRESS
Lanham and New York

THE DERRYDALE PRESS

Published in the United States of America
by The Derrydale Press
A Member of the Rowman & Littlefield Publishing Group
4720 Boston Way, Lanham, Maryland 20706

Distributed by NATIONAL BOOK NETWORK, INC.

Copyright © 2002 The Derrydale Press
Library of Congress Control Number: 2002103578
ISBN: 1-58667-077-8 (cloth: alk. paper)

∞ ™ The paper used in this publication meets the minimum requirements of American
National Standard for Information Sciences—Permanence of Paper for Printed Library
Materials, ANSI/NISO Z39.48–1992. Manufactured in the United States of America.

Contents

CONTENTS

A Brief History of Angling, Angling Writing, and The Derrydale Press

This anthology of fishing stories draws from books published by The Derrydale Press, founded by Eugene Connett, a sportsman, author, and editor whose titles set new standards for content and typography. Nick Lyons, a distinguished outdoor writer and editor in his own right, calls Connett "the ultimate sporting-book publisher," not only of his time and place but "the finest of all time, anywhere."

Connett had great instincts as an editor, and most of the fishing authors he published during the period he directed Derrydale (1927–1941) were skilled story tellers whose writings reflect upon a tradition that is ages old. We will never know when one of our hunter-gatherer forebears had the novel idea of shaping a piece of bone into a hook and lashing a line to it to catch a fish. Nor will we know what sort of pleasure he (or was it she?) derived from his invention beyond the eating of what he caught with it. Fishing with a hook, or "angle" (a word rooted in Anglo-Saxon) connects fisher and fish in the most tactile and immediate way, and that first angler must have run through the same gamut of feelings—the anticipation of a bite, followed by the excitement of hooking and playing a fish and the satisfaction of landing it—experienced by uncounted millions down the millennia. And he surely felt the same sense of disappointment over the ones that got away.

Stone Age hooks made of bone and antler gave way to copper hooks forged by Neolithic smiths seven thousand years ago. At some point, someone figured out the advantages of attaching the line to a pole, an innovation depicted in Egyptian tomb art of three thousand years ago. Confucius fished for carp with a silk line and thornwood rod fourteen hundred years ago while working out his moral philosophy, and by eight hundred years ago the Chinese were storing the line on a reel (a piece of equipment that did not catch on in Europe until the 1700s).

Catching fish and telling about the catching—and maybe embellishing the tale a bit—are inseparable. The first fish stories, doubtless, were told around the campfires of preliterate clans. Written accounts of angling appeared as early as the second century A.D., when the Roman naturalist Aelian described Macedonians fishing for trout in streams, using hooks dressed with wool and feathers. This is the first, oft-cited reference to fly fishing, but Aelian also wrote about Mediterranean anglers employing hooks dressed with seabird feathers to catch ocean fish, presumably by trolling the hooks behind a boat.

The first book devoted exclusively to fishing, *A Treatyse of Fysshynge Wyth an Angle*, appeared in England in 1496. It is reputedly the work of a nun, one Dame Juliana Berners, the prioress of Sopwell Nunnery. The *Treatyse* is a how-to book about fly fishing, complete with recipes for a dozen flies. The churchman William Samuel, vicar of Godmanchester, wrote *The Arte of Angling*, published in 1577. Its structure is narrative, built around a dialogue between a tyro and a master. Izaak Walton followed the same literary convention with his *Compleat Angler* (1653), an extended pastoral celebrating the charms of English country life.

The British brought angling to America, and as a recreational pursuit it flourished among the merchant elites of Philadelphia and other colonial cities. By the 1830s, articles about fishing were appearing in sporting publications like *The Spirit of the Times* and *The American Turf Register and Sporting Magazine*. The first American book devoted to angling, *Frank Forester's Fish and Fishing in the United States and British Provinces of North America* (1859), by the English expatriate Henry William Herbert, was followed by Thaddeus Norris's *The American Angler's Book* (1864) and Genio Scott's *Fishing in American Waters* (1869).

The booming post–Civil War economy spawned a new business and professional class. Many of its members embraced fishing and hunting as healthy antidotes to the stress of urban life, and for both practical advice and vicarious pleasure they turned to the pages of *Forest and Stream*, *American Angler*, and other publications launched during the Gilded Age to serve the sporting public. One of their avid readers was a boy living in the suburbs of New York City named Gene Connett.

* * *

Eugene Virginius Connett III was born in 1891 in Orange, New Jersey. His father and grandfather were "ardent sportsmen," as he recalled them, and he shared with them a passion for fishing and hunting. Soon after graduating from Princeton, in 1912, Connett began writing for the outdoor press, but only as a sideline to the serious business of making a living. He worked for the family firm, which made hats in a factory in Newark, New Jersey. Except for stateside service in the Army during World War I, Connett stayed with the company for thirteen years. For much of that time he managed the hat factory, working on the shop floor with hatters whose labor-intensive craft had not changed appreciably since the Civil War. The care and fastidiousness that went into the making of fine hats were also qualities that applied to the making of fine books. Stephen Ferguson, the curator of rare books at Princeton's Firestone Library, where the Derrydale papers are archived, suggests that Connett's "experience in the plant while working with the hatters no doubt served as a comprehensive preparation for later dealing and working with printers." Connett enjoyed supervising hatters, and one senses he could have been equally happy working as one, for like them he was by nature an artisan and hands-on perfectionist who cared deeply about the details of his craft, whether it was writing, editing, or printing.

While immersing himself in the family business, Connett continued to nurture his literary side. A member of the Anglers' Club of New York, he founded its quarterly, *The Anglers' Club Bulletin*, in 1920, and remained its editor for six years. He wrote his first book, *Wing Shooting and Angling*, published by Charles Scribner's Sons in 1922. Three years later he sold the family business for what one assumes was a tidy sum, since he did so at the height of the post–World War I economic expansion. By then Connett was married and the father of three children, but he seems not to have worried about supporting a family, for he took off several months to go fishing and contemplate his future. "During those happy days on various trout streams," he later wrote, "I made up my mind that I wanted to publish fine sporting books."

Undaunted by his ignorance of the publishing business—"I didn't know enough to be afraid"—and the craft of printing, he set out to master both. He talked the printing firm of J. N. Johnston & Company, which had produced hat catalogues for the family firm, into hiring him as a salesman. He also studied the technology and history of printing at the New York Public Library and the Morgan Library and spent a summer fishing and studying in England. In the study of his Manhattan home he set up a small press and produced for the Anglers' Club limited editions of *American Trout Streams*, by Henry A. Ingraham, and *Magic Hours*, a collection of his sporting essays with the charmingly discursive subtitle "Wherein We Cast a Fly Here & There as We Wade Along Together." Connett set the type and did the bindings for both books, and for *Magic Hours* he even drew the illustrations.

Magic Hours was the first book to bear the imprint of The Derrydale Press, and along with *American Trout Streams* it was listed in the first Derrydale catalogue, published in 1927. The name Derrydale played off on the Merrymount Press of Daniel Berkeley Updike, a typographer and book designer admired by Connett. Derrydale went on to make its mark as a sporting press. Connett recruited some of the era's preeminent outdoor writers, including Russell Annabel, Kip Farrington, Roderick Haig-Brown, Preston Jennings, Jack O'Connor, Edmund Ware Smith, Burton Spiller, and Howard T. Walden; to illustrate their works he relied on equally gifted artists like Lynn Bogue Hunt and Milton Weiler. Derrydale under Connett published 169 titles, most of them in slipcased editions limited to fewer than fifteen hundred signed and numbered copies. Handcrafted deluxe editions such as Charles Phair's *Atlantic Salmon Fishing* (1937) were limited to forty or fewer copies and featured actual flies and their materials mounted on display cards bound into a companion volume.

Today, original mint-condition Derrydales can go for five figures on the rare-books market. Bibliophiles indifferent to hunting and fishing (or even hostile to blood sports) admire and collect them for their superb design and craftsmanship. Connett, a staff of one, designed every book himself. He once wrote, "I also edited, read all the proofs, rewrote some of the texts, and checked all the facts in every sporting book we did." His attention to detail was singular. Once, when fact-checking a book on equestrian jumping, he took the manuscript to the author's farm on Long Island "and asked him if he had a reasonably peaceful horse I might ride. Then we read the manuscript out loud and I attempted to carry out his teachings in the saddle. The horse and I went over the jumps without mishap, and I published the book." With fishing and shooting books, he added, "I was spared such grueling investigations, as we discovered I usually knew as much as the authors."

Connett insisted that his books be published exclusively on fine paper imported from European mills. Foreign sources of high-grade paper dried up after the outbreak of World War II, and America's entry into the conflict in December 1941 ended its domestic availability. When the U.S. government restricted publishers to small formats and cheap paper, Connett took the draconian step of shutting down entirely rather than producing books beneath his exacting standards. It is also possible that his interest in publishing had begun to wane. Nick Lyons recalls discussing Connett with the late Alfred W. Miller (better known by his pen name of Sparse Grey Hackle). Miller knew Connett well, for they were both members of the Anglers' Club. According to Lyons, Miller characterized his friend as "a man of great enthusiasms, most of which eventually bored him; Sparse thought Connett simply tired of the press."

Whatever his reasons for doing so, Connett in early 1942 sold the business and its inventory and publishing rights for approximately $12,000 to Nat Wartels, the founder of the Outlet Book company, a remainder and reprint house that later became Crown Publishers. Random House acquired Crown, and in the late 1980s sold the Derrydale name to the Buckingham Mint, of Lyon, Mississippi, which published some of the original Derrydales in facsimile editions. The business was subsequently sold to Rowman & Littlefield, a publisher in Lanham, Maryland.

During the war years Connett became a bureaucrat, serving as executive assistant to the commissioner of the New Jersey Highway Department. In 1947 he returned to publishing, taking over the sporting-books division of Van Nostrand, where he edited seventy books before his retirement, in 1964. His last title was *A World of Fishing*, by Joe Brooks. In the postwar period Connett also wrote three books: *The Small-Boat Skipper and His Problems* (W. W. Norton, 1952), *Duck Decoys: How to Make Them, How to Paint Them, How to Rig Them* (Van Nostrand, 1953), and *My Friend the Trout* (Van Nostrand, 1961). He died in 1969.

In Nick Lyons's estimation, "Connett built a press unequaled in its excellence—perhaps dependent upon its time and the small and upscale market it published for, though not nearly as much as it was dependent upon the moment in a great publisher's life when taste, talent, time, patience, and perhaps capital, combined to produce the remarkable Derrydale Press."

Although Derrydale books are prized by bibliographic connoisseurs, Connett remarked that he took "much more" pride in their content than in their appearance. Lyons notes that "Quality begins with choice—and Connett's judgment was superb. He chose for literary excellence as well as authority." The following selections reflect that assessment. Some of them are stories in the conventional narrative sense, with characters and plots. Others are descriptive essays mixing narrative, natural history, and practical advice on tactics and tackle (most of it now dated, although still of interest). They are products of their time, and readers used to the faster pacing of contemporary writing may have to adjust to their measured rhythms, but it is worth the effort. In one sense or another, all of them are timeless discourses on the angler's art and what Walton called "this pleasant curiosity of fish and fishing."

—J. I. Merritt

This introduction draws mainly on the following sources:

Eugene V. Connett, "Some Random Notes on the Derrydale Press," *Princeton University Library Chronicle* XVIII, 1 (Autumn 1956), pp. 11–14.

Nick Lyons, notes for "The Ultimate Sporting Press," an address delivered October 21, 1998, at the Anglers' Club of New York.

Henry A. Siegel, ed., *The Derrydale Press: A Bibliography* (Goshen, Conn.: Angler's and Shooter's Press, 1981), especially biographical chapters by Stephen Ferguson and Siegel, pp. 1–16.

INSHORE AND DEEP-SEA

ONE

The Channel Bass

Van Campen Heilner

Most of us, I suppose, have a first love, and without doubt this writer's is the channel bass. Perhaps because this fish was associated with my early youth or perhaps because he was the first large fish I ever caught (a 41 pounder by the way), the place he occupies in my heart is a very near and dear one.

Memories of autumn days with the snipe trading down the beaches and the first flock of wild geese etched high against the sunset above the golden marshes, seagrass on the dunes bending against the hiss of the first northwester, spring days with the miles of rolling breakers creaming in across the bar and the nesting terns and laughing gulls setting up their ceaseless clamor in behind the thoroughfare—these all mean but one thing to me, that lovable old coppery warrior of the tides, *Sciaenops ocellatus,* the channel bass.

From Barnegat Light to the Gulf of Mexico I have pursued him down the years with a relentlessness that has amounted to a mania. Other fish have I caught which proved gamier; other fish have I caught which were more spectacular, more deserving perhaps of their place in the sun (or sea); but none gives me a greater thrill or a greater desire to repeat sensations which each year seem as new and exciting as they seemed when first I experienced them.

He goes by many names. From Jersey to Florida he is the channel bass or red drum. But the name red drum should be discouraged because it only confuses him with his cousin, the black drum, an oafish fellow with a beard, a hump on his back, stripes like a convict and the fighting abilities of a sack of potatoes. From Florida south he is the redfish and as you wend your way around the Gulf coast and approach Texas and Spanish America he becomes the red horse or the *pez colorado.* But he's still the channel bass to me, no matter under what name he masquerades.

The sportiest way to take him is by surf fishing. Surf fishing is to salt water angling what trout fishing is to fresh water. It is a one-man game from start to finish. You are the one and only factor. It is the same as still-hunting is to deer driving. Here you are and there he is. If he runs out all your line you can't pick up the oars or start the engine and follow him. No cushion or comfortable seat or chair supports your fundament, no thwarts against which to brace your feet, no companion to assist you or guide you. You must find your quarry yourself, you must rig and bait your hook yourself, you must become proficient in the art of casting so you may reach him, and you must bring him through a line of foaming breakers and surging tides until at last, whipped to a standstill, he lies gasping on the wet sands at your very feet. Then you must let him go because he deserves it.

Some bright morning in early summer you pack your duffle and rods and hie yourself to your favorite inlet. You have been mulling over that tackle all winter. Your rod is two-piece split bamboo,—maybe one piece—and the tip is from 6'6" to over 7'. It has a "spring butt" or a straight one, 24" or longer. Maybe you've rewrapped it during the winter and given it three or four coats of varnish. You've certainly oiled and cleaned your 2/0 reel and filled it with new 12 thread line. You've sharpened your hooks which may run from 5/0 to 9/0, put on new leaders, cleaned your fish knife and sharpened it to a razor edge, re-riveted your rod belt, molded some new sinkers of your pet shape and weight, cleaned out your bait box.

This season you have a couple of new gadgets. You've put a throat on the inside pocket of your beach bag with a drawstring, so the blowing sand can't get inside. You've made a disgorger out of a copper tube with a handle 18" long so you can get that hook out of the tummy of the bass without cutting your hands to pieces. And you have a finger gaff which is a big strong 10/0 hook drilled into a small barrel-shaped piece of wood so you can grasp it with your fingers. It only weighs a few ounces and you can hang it in one of the buckle holes in your belt where it's easy to reach and weighs nothing.

At the fish-house you've picked up a dozen fresh bunkers. They are nice and fat and fairly ooze oil. If you're beach camping or on your boat you have them already iced down, or you've made arrangements for some one to supply you with fresh ones every day.

At last you arrive at the inlet. You've judged it about right. The tide is some two hours down, the wind is onshore and while there isn't a heavy sea running, there's plenty of "fight" to the surf. You first make a survey to determine the most likely place. The formation has changed since you were here in the fall. Where is that beautiful pocket that lay just north of the point? It's gone and the beach there is as flat as a flounder. You walk on and pretty soon you find what you are looking for. A good cast from the beach lies a long bar over which the sea is breaking with diminishing intensity. It will be nearly dry at low water. Between it and the beach runs a long narrow slue, maybe half a mile long.

Another hour or less and you'll be able to wade it. Thousands of broken clam shells strew the beach in all directions. You can see lots of small bait in the undertow. You drop your beach bag near the high-water mark, take out your sand spike and stand your rod up in it. You heave a big sigh. "This is the place!" you say; "if they're anywhere, they ought to be here!"

While you're waiting for the tide you cut some bait. You find a board and lay your mossbunker on it. First you scale him. Then you cut off his head and split him down the side, keeping the knife just this side of the backbone. Then the other side. Now you have two nice scaleless, boneless slabs of bunker. If he was a big one, cut these diagonally in half and you have four baits. Cut just enough to fill your bait box, as fresh cut bait is much better. Later when the bunkers are a couple of days old, if you can't get any more you will have to wrap them on the hook with thread or they'll fall to pieces.

Now you're all set. If the water and weather are warm you'll discard boots and wade in. If it were late in the fall you'd probably be wearing boot-foot waders. Waders are better than boots, because sometimes the slues are deep. It's almost waist deep in the slue and you climb out on the outer bar which is nearly dry. A short cast to wet your line, bait up, swing back and heave her out.

For a long time nothing happens. Then your heart skips a beat. Something moved in with your bait. You wait. There it is again! This time the line runs slowly out. You set the hook but instead of the expected rush, something flies to the surface and flaps the water furiously about. A skate! You reel in disgustedly and spend five minutes stabbing and sawing the grotesque nuisance into several pieces before you can recover your hook.

Cast again. What a peach of a cast! Your form was perfect! If some of your friends could have seen that one! Maybe you had better enter the tournament this summer. You are so busy congratulating yourself that before you know it your line is whizzing out in long steady surges that you know can mean but one thing. You clamp down your thumb and the fight is on!

Out he goes, then the tide catches him and he goes with it. You have him almost in and out he goes again. But each rush is shorter. In fifteen minutes you see him on the surface twenty feet away. He's swimming slowly but still headed out to sea. The tide has changed now and the waves are getting larger. The bar is starting to cover. You bring him slowly to your feet and a receding wave leaves him flopping in a few inches of water. Luckily he's hooked in the mouth. You work the hook loose and with the next wave kick him back. About thirty-five pounds you guess. A good fighter.

It's getting pretty deep on the bar now and it's time you were leaving. You wade back across the slue and take up your station on the main beach. There's lots of movement in the surf now. 'Way to your left you see the gulls working over something that is breaking all over the surface. Blues! You're sorely tempted but you're after bigger game. Then you have a strong slashing strike and in a minute or two beach a beautiful weakfish, five pounder at least. Well, you'll take anything that comes. But you won't move from this spot, because— ah! that unmistakable pull! You'd know it anywhere, anytime. He drops it, he's picked it up again. Let him have it, let him have it, let him have it . . . NOW!

Thus the mechanics of surf fishing for channel bass. But to me the fish are but incidental. The miles and miles of lonely beaches stretching from Montauk to the Florida Straits. The dunes, shading from white to golden brown. The sedge grass blowing in the wind. The little "teeters" scurrying up the beach just ahead of the waves and right-about-facing just as quickly, to stab their long little bills in the moist sand behind the retreating surge. The confused clamor of hundreds of terns "working" over a school of blues. The wild fury of a "northeaster" pounding down on a deserted coast, with the whole beach under water and the flash of the distant lighthouse showing faint and blurred through the driving rain. Autumn, with the first crisp tang of a northwester, blue skies and blue surf and the first blackducks coming in at sunset to the marshes behind the inlet.

These are what I think of when I think of channel bass. And for myself I can think of nothing better.

Song of the Old Timers

Famous wherever surfmen gather.
Tune: "Watermelon Hanging On The Vine."

Oh, the weakfish am good
And the kingfish am great
The striped bass am very, very fine;
But give me, oh give me,
Oh, how I wish you would!
A channel bass a-hangin' on my line

SLIDE RULE FOR CHANNEL
BASS FISHERMEN

SCIENTIFIC NAME: *Sciaenops ocellatus,* channel bass, red drum, redfin, redfish, red horse, *pez colorado.*

DISTRIBUTION—Atlantic Coast from New Jersey to Texas.

FAVORITE GROUNDS—In the vicinity of all inlets from Barnegat to the Rio Grande. Bass are found next to the beach in slue and channels between the bars. In boat fishing, fish as close to the break on the bar as you can.

TACKLE—Great difference of opinion. No two anglers will agree and each one is right. The author uses the standard surf tackle, tip 6′6″ to 7′ in length, 12 thread line, 4 oz. pyramid or cone sinker (5 or 6 ozs. if strong current or heavy surf) and 7/0 Harrison White Label Sproat hook with 2′ wire gimp leader. A 2/0 reel, thumb stall, rod belt, sand spike, belt gaff, bait box, knife, disgorger and towel complete your equipment. But every surfman you meet will have a new gadget or wrinkle to show you.

BAIT—Cut open nearly any channel bass and you will find crabs in his stomach. Undoubtedly the best bait for all bottom-feeding fish of any species wherever found. But the old standbys are "bunkers" (menhaden) and mullet in the fall. Scale and split. Squid, fresh, frozen or salted, will do if the others are not obtainable. In trolling in Southern waters I have had redfish take 'most any moving lure.

BOATS—The writer prefers surf fishing above all other methods. It is the one way from start to finish where you are the sole arbiter. If you insist on boat fishing, get a boat and guide at any of the places where they specialize in this sport, go out the inlet and fish as close to the "break" on the bars as you can. Fish right in the "break" or in any little slue going through it. You should have a strong stomach, however, as it's sometimes quite rough.

HOOKING, PLAYING, LANDING—Channel bass will bite in any of three different ways. They will "fool" with the bait, picking it up and dropping it several times, they will grab it and run, they will pick it up and run in with you. In either case, wait until the fish starts off and you feel the weight of him—then set the hook. At all times give the fish his head, allow no slack line and don't, under any circumstances, "horse" him. When you get him in the undertow and he seems all in, watch your chance and as a wave comes lift him just ahead of it. This will shoot him up on the beach where you can gaff him or get your fingers in his gills.

WEATHER—TIDES—The last two hours of the ebb and the first three hours of the flood. Sometimes on the falling tide the point of the inlet is excellent. Find a "rip" if there is one and fish there. At dead low water, if you can wade to the outer bar, do so, and cast out beyond it. Back up as the tide comes in and fish in the slue and pockets as they commence to fill. The writer's experience has been that an onshore wind is best. It blows the warm surface water onto the beach. With the wind offshore, the warm surface water is blown out and the cold water wells up from underneath. Onshore wind, water warm; offshore wind water cold will always hold.

WHERE TO GO—North and south sides of inlets from Barnegat to the Rio Grande. Barnegat is best in the autumn which after all seems to be the best time, certainly the weather is most pleasant then. Chincoteague and Wachapreague, Va., specialize in channel bass fishing. Also Oregon Inlet (town of Manteo) and Ocracoke, N.C. Good fishing around the jetty at Mayport near Jacksonville, Fla., and Melbourne on the Indian River good also. All the North and South Carolina inlets excellent. Mid-June to mid-July and mid-September to mid-October best north of the Carolinas. April and October best for big fish from Oregon Inlet south. Barnegat is the northern limit. You will be more sure of fish from Beach Haven south. August appears to be a bad month everywhere and during this time the fish either drop off the beaches or go up in the big sounds and bays to eat oysters. Never heard of good bass fishing in August anywhere.

RECORD FISH—For many years the world's record was held by Joseph Cawthorn, the famous comedian, with a fish of 63¼ lbs., taken at Corson's Inlet, N.J., on July 17th, 1910, which was a famous hang-out of all the old timers. Then the record shifted to New Inlet, N.J., where Charles H. Smith chalked up a 65-pounder caught on Sept. 24, 1919. In 1935 the record stood at 74 lbs. with a fish taken by Charles D. Beckmann at Chincoteague, Va., on June 27, 1929. This fish was caught from the beach. The average channel bass will run on one side or the other of 30 lbs. Forty pounds is a gold button fish and if you catch a 50-pounder bring on the refreshments. You'll need them. "Puppy drum" of 8 to 15 lbs. literally swarm on the beaches of the Carolinas at all times of the year. The largest channel bass ever taken by any method was a fish of 75 lbs. reported by Jordan & Evermann, so there's still hope.

TWO

Marlin Off Cuba

ERNEST HEMINGWAY

Marlin and broadbill swordfish have been caught by commercial fisher-men off the north Cuban coast for more than seventy years. Commercial fishing for marlin and broadbill was introduced by men from Manila in the Philippine Islands who brought the method of drifting with the current of the Gulf Stream in small but very seaworthy skiffs fishing a dead bait with from four to six heavy handlines at depths varying from seventy-five to one hundred and fifty fathoms. The Cuban fishermen—there are as many as seventy boats fishing marlin regularly within a distance of thirty miles each way along the coast from Havana—set out each morning during the season two or three hours before daylight and drift with the current of the Stream to eastward. When the northeast trade wind rises about ten o'clock in the summer mornings, they row their skiffs into the wind to keep their lines straight down from the limber sticks to which they are looped and which by their sudden dipping will show a fish taking the bait.

Marlin and broadbill, when they are swimming deep, take the bait in much the same manner, first, perhaps, picking off a few of the sardines with which the point of the hook is covered, then seizing the whole fish used as bait between their jaws to crush it a moment before swallowing it. When the fish-ermen feel the weight of the fish solidly on the line, they strike hard on the handline, double handing it in as fast as possible to take up the slack. The fight the marlin or broadbill puts up depends on whether it is a male or female fish and how it has been hooked. Sometimes a marlin will jump as many as forty times and will tow the skiff behind him while he jumps with as much as two hundred and forty fathoms of heavy handline out. A fish putting up this type of fight will be a heavy male fish that has been hooked in the mouth or through the bill. Again, you will see a blue marlin of more than four hundred pounds pulled up to the skiff in less than ten minutes, making no runs and only breaching feebly, his whole stomach hanging out of his mouth when he has been hooked deep. I have seen a female broadbill, weighing more than three hundred pounds, from which forty-three pounds of roe were removed when she was butchered out, caught in six mintues on a handline, and I know of a male broadbill that weighed more than six hundred pounds that four men, working in relays on the same sort of handline, fought for five hours before he was landed. Once a fish is brought close to the boat, it is invariably harpooned before being gaffed.

Because commercial fishermen have been taking these fish for so long off the Cuban coast with hook and line, more is known there of their feeding habits and fighting ability than perhaps anywhere else. I first heard of the Cuban marlin fishing seven years ago when, on a trip after big kingfish at the Dry Tortugas, I met Carlos Gutierrez then in command of a fish smack which had put into Tortugas to catch bait. Carlos went smack fishing in the winter months and fished marlin, and broadbill, for there are always a few mixed in with the marlin run, from mid-April until the first northers of October ended the hurricane season and sent the smacks out again to the red-snapper grounds.

He told me how the Cubans fished for marlin, described the different fish and the time of their runs, and said he was sure we could catch them trolling, as the fish which feed deep in the early morning come to the top when the trade wind blows. The commercial fishermen, he told us, hoisted a sail on their skiffs and ran in when it became too rough for them to fish, and it was then they would see the marlin travelling to the westward, riding the swells. He had frequently hooked these fish trolling with a handline.

It was not until 1932 that we were able to put in a season after marlin in Cuba, but since April twentieth of that year we have fished two hundred and eighty days for them in the period of their run off the Cuban coast and have taken one hundred and one fish. Off Cuba the marlin travel from east to west against the current of the Gulf Stream. No one has ever seen them working in the other direction, although the current of the Gulf Stream is not stable; sometimes, just before the new moon, it is quite slack, and at others it has a westerly set as far as forty miles out from Havana. You will sometimes see marlin circling on the surface when they are feeding or when they are breeding, but you never see them travelling other than to the westward. Marlin will bite when the current has a westerly set, but they do not cruise or travel on the surface, and they never feed as well as when there is a heavy current to the eastward and a fresh east or northeast breeze. At such a time they come to the top and cruise with the wind, the scythe tail, a light, steely lavender, cutting the swells as it projects and goes under; the big fish, yellow looking in the water, swimming two or three feet under the surface, the huge pectoral fins tucked close to the flanks, the dorsal fin down, the fish looking a round, fast moving log in the water except for the erect curve of that slicing tail.

The heavier the current is running to the eastward, the more marlin you will see travelling along the edge of the dark, swirling current from a quarter of a mile to four miles off shore; all going in the same direction; seeming to travel at a uniform speed of six to eight miles an hour. We have been fighting a fish, on a day when they were running well, and seen six others pass close to the boat in half an hour. Some idea of how plentiful they are in a good year is shown by the official report of the Havana central market, which showed eleven thousand small marlin, i.e., fish that dressed out under one hundred and twenty-five pounds, and one hundred and fifty large marlin as brought to market by the fishermen of Santa Cruz del Norte, Jaruco, Guanaboa, Cojimar, Havana, La Chorrera, Marianao, Jaimanitas, Baracoa, Bañes, Mariel and Cabañas during a period between the middle of March and the eighteenth of July of 1933. All of these fish were taken by hook and line. Between the tenth of April and the eighteenth of July of that same year we caught fifty-two marlin and two sailfish trolling with rod and reel. The largest black marlin we caught was 468 pounds, a long, thin fish, 12 feet 8 inches long; the largest striped marlin weighed 343 pounds and was 10 feet 5 inches long. The biggest white marlin weighed 87 pounds and was 7 feet 8 inches in length. On the twentieth of May of that year I caught seven white marlin and we saw twenty-six fish. It was a wonderful year for fish.

The white marlin run first in late March, April and May; then come the immature striped marlin with brilliant stripes which fade after the fish dies. These are most plentiful in May and run on into June, and both are marvelous light and medium tackle fish. After these smaller fish are gone comes the run of striped and black marlin together. The biggest run of striped marlin is usually in July and as they get scarce the very biggest black marlin run during August and September and until the first northers come in October. A few very large striped marlin come early in the season with the white marlin, but if they appear they are gone in a day or two; but the possibility of encountering them complicates the tackle problem. The so-called blue marlin, too, are liable to appear at any time during the spring and summer.

There is no definite time when the fish appear each year. The white marlin may be running heavily in late March of one year and another not appear until toward the end of April. Everything seems to depend on the amount of current in the Gulf Stream. When there is much current off the Cuban coast, fish will be plentiful as long as the current lasts; when the current slackens fishing is invariably poor. The west wind puts the fish down just as the east wind brings them to the surface. They will also bite on a north wind unless it is a backing wind. On a backing wind the fish seem to stop feeding altogether. No fish feed off the north coast of Cuba with a south wind blowing. Few of the commercial fishermen will even go out with a south wind. I believed this might be superstition or due to the difficulty of sailing in with a land breeze blowing, because south and southeast winds are sometimes excellent biting winds for fish in the Gulf Stream off Key West, although the southwest is the worst fishing wind there; but no matter how strong the current, or how well the marlin had been running, we never caught any marlin with the south wind blowing. But after a south wind, with the start of the trade wind again, fish would start feeding at once.

As regards the moon, marlin seem to feed best after the first quarter on through the full moon and to drop off during the last quarter. They usually drop off in feeding for a day or so when the moon is full. We have never caught many fish during the last quarter of the moon, or on a new moon, although in the 1934 season, when least expected, there was a heavy run of blue marlin during early September on the last quarter of the moon and on the new moon. I missed the run, having left to attend to some work, positive that the fish would not run during that phase of the moon; and thus learned not to put too much confidence in lunar data.

Anyone wanting light tackle fishing for white marlin, which are one of the most spectacular of all sporting fish, should plan to fish Cuba in late April or in May when these fish are usually the thickest. Because of the heavy sea that often comes up in the afternoon when the trade wind is blowing against the current, and the possibility of having to work a fish in really heavy, breaking sea, I do not believe in using any line lighter than 15 thread. With 15 thread line, an 8½ or 9 ounce tip and a reel large enough to hold enough of the line so that if you hook a really big fish you will have time to turn the boat to go with him before he strips the reel, you have tackle that will permit any small marlin to make a brilliant fight and yet enable you to deal with a moderate sized fish in rough weather, and a big fish if there is no sea running. I do not believe it is sensible ever to use any reel smaller than a 9/0 in the Gulf Stream off Cuba as you can never be sure that you will not hook a very large fish. It is about twenty to one that the fish you will hook in May will be a white marlin and that you will hook no fish larger than 125 pounds. But on the always present chance of a big fish, you should have enough line to give you time to get around and head into the northwest when the big fish makes his first run and, since you are fishing in deep water, you must have enough line to handle the big fish when he sounds.

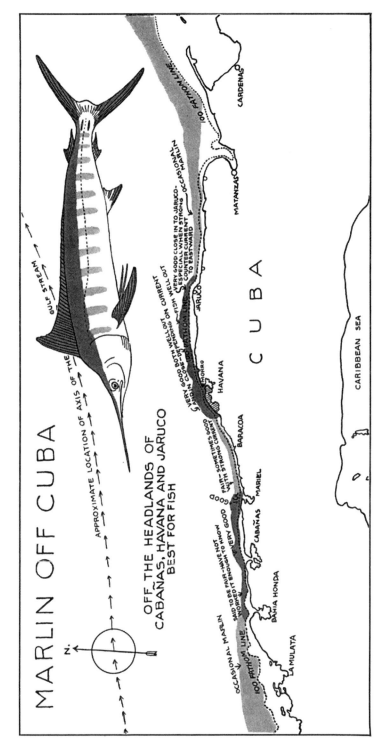

Drawn by Lynn Bogue Hunt from information supplied by Ernest Hemingway.

In June, when the first of the big striped marlin are due, you can use standard heavy tackle. June is not a month of much current usually, therefore it is not so rough and you can handle a really big fish on 24 thread line. June, with its heavy rains and possible slack current, is the marlin month to be least recommended. But in July, August and September, when you will only see a white marlin by accident and the fish will be running from 250 to over 1000 pounds in weight, you need 500 or 600 yards of 36 or 39 thread line, and a good big reel whose working you are absolutely familiar with, the drag of which can be loosened instantly no matter what pressure is on it, and a husky but limber tip of eighteen to twenty ounces.

For white marlin we use 10/0 Sobey or O'Shaughnessy hooks, which will also deal with any marlin up to around 250 pounds. They both have advantages and disadvantages. The Sobey is stronger, cannot open and will hook better in the tough part of the upper jaw, but its sharp, triangular cutting point keeps on cutting after the fish is hooked and is jumping, and I believe many fish throw the hook because the Sobey hook set in the juncture of the bill and the roof of the mouth often cuts such a long gash that it is flung loose by a leaping fish. Many times you will bring a fish to gaff and have the hook fall out when the fish is lifted aboard. The O'Shaughnessy is thinner, lighter in a strip bait so that the fish does not feel the metal and jump to throw it as you are slacking to him before he is struck, as white marlin will often do with the heavier Sobey. But they are so thin that in a long fight with a heavy fish, and a marlin has terrific strength in his jaws, they may either open or be broken. Fishing for large fish with a big bait such as a whole cero mackerel, bonito, barracuda or kingfish, we use a 14/0 Pflueger Sobey, 13/0 Pflueger Zane Grey or 14/0 Vom Hofe Grinnell swordfish hook. I have had very good luck with the Hardy Zane Grey swordfish hook. It is a wonderful hook, not too thick in the shank for driving it in as the Grinnell hook sometimes seems, yet strong enough never to have broken on big fish, and it is slightly offset, a great aid in hooking a fish. Being offset, though, it has a tendency to make a bait spin in the water so we only use it on a very big bait which is skipped along the surface. For white marlin we use any sort of strip bait; dolphin, bonito, mullet or whole mullet, goggle-eye, pilchards hooked in tandem, small mackerel, or a small fish called a guaguancho.

For white marlin we use number 13 tinned wire as supplied by Vom Hofe in quarter pound coils, 94 feet to a coil, retailing at $.45 a coil. The stainless wire is not as strong as the ordinary and it is best to make leaders new every day. We use a fourteen foot leader with Hardy number one, "sildur" swivel. This same wire will hold any size marlin and in three seasons of fishing we have never broken a leader; when fishing for big marlin you can use steel cable wire of 500 or 750 pound test, and feel safer since there is little likelihood of this size cable catching around the marlin's bill when you are slacking the bait to the fish. Light cable wire of the 220 or 150 pound test variety, suitable in size for white marlin and small striped marlin, and admirable to fight them once they are hooked, is absolutely unsuited to hooking the fish as at least fifty per cent of the time, in our experience, it will coil around the bill when the fish takes the bait and make it impossible to set the hook properly. This is the explanation of the great part of the marlin which jump free after a few frantic leaps. A white marlin when he takes a bait does *not* go down head first. His head comes up and his tail drops and if you can observe him from a high enough place on the boat you will see that he seems almost to be standing on his tail, straight up and down in the water. It is at this moment when the line is being slacked to enable the fish to get the bait well into his mouth that the very flexible cable, when slacked, will coil and loop around the bill. The fish feels the wire on his bill and starts off to one side or another, the wire comes taut, wound around his narrow bill like a coiled spring and the fish goes into the air to try to get rid of it. He may jump as many as twenty times and on a taut line the wire will hold; but on a slack line he will throw it, or when he sounds and changes his direction, or circles, he will get rid of it. Usually he throws it in the first few jumps. Fishing early in the 1933 season we once lost twelve marlin in two days using the cable, all of them after from three to twelve jumps. Figuring out what the trouble was, we shifted back to the old style piano wire and hooked and landed six out of the next eight fish that struck. This, of course, is an abnormally high average of hooked fish to strikes. On a strip bait marlin are easy to hook, but on a whole bait to hook one out of three fish that strike is a very good average.

Of course one cannot say that all marlin go tail down and head up to take a bait in; sometimes they come from the side and take the bait off sideways in their mouth and you cannot see how they take it in when you slack off. But one thing I can say—that I have never seen or felt a marlin tap a bait. Since their upper jaw is immovable, when they come behind a bait to take it they must shove their bill and upper jaw out of water to seize the bait with their lower jaw. Swimming with tail deep in this awkward position, their heads wobble from side to side and the bill wags and can easily be entangled in the leader when you slack the bait into their open mouth. Fish that see the bait when they are swimming deep often surge their whole length out of the water when they smash at it. Sometimes their rush takes them so far that they seem to lose the bait or they feel that they have missed the bait and do not come back after it again. It may be difficult, too, for them to see the bait when they have to go into the sun for it. We have also found that when we have a strike while going to the eastward with the current and miss the marlin, if we turn at once and head to the westward over the same piece of water, we will often hook the fish.

Marlin hit a trolled bait in four different ways. First, with hunger; again, in anger; thirdly, simply playfully, last, with indifference. Anyone can hook a hungry fish who orders the boat stopped when the fish seizes the bait, gives him enough line to get the bait well into his mouth, orders the boat put ahead, as the marlin is moving off with the bait, screws down hard on the drag and sets the hook with four or five good hard strikes. If the fish moves off slowly, strike him again three or four times, as the hook may not be set yet. If you pull it out of his mouth, reel in and speed up the boat and the marlin, if he is hungry, will usually smash at it again.

A white marlin will usually jump immediately when he feels the hook and may make his run in any direction. A striped marlin, too, will usually jump instantly when hooked and may run in two or three directions before heading for the northwest. A big black marlin may jump at once if he is hooked in a tender place, but if he is not being caused any particular pain he will move slowly and heavily, almost like a big shark, circling deep or even swimming toward the boat, and you can often bring him close to the boat before he realizes he is being led or even, possibly, that he is hooked at all. But when he does realize it he heads straight out for the northwest like an under-water speed boat. He may fight an hour or more before jumping or he may jump early in the fight. A blue marlin is so voracious that he will often swallow the bait; then he will jump, showering blood, his stomach will hang out of his mouth after two or three jumps; he will circle stupidly, wagging his bill out of water in agony, try to sound but give it up if you hold him, and you should make every effort to work him as fast as humanly possible without smashing tackle to get him in to gaff before the blood calls up sharks. Until we had a run of blue marlin off Cuba in 1934, I had never hooked a marlin in the belly or even in the gullet. Out of four blue marlin we caught last season, three were hooked in the belly while trolling. They swallow a bait as fast as a jewfish, whereas striped or white marlin will go into the air the minute they feel either hook or leader in their mouth. They go into the air the first time deliberately to throw out the bait and often you will see the bait thrown and a shower of flying fish come out of the marlin's mouth at the same time. The white and striped marlin are dainty feeders with electric quick reflexes; the blue marlin, at least off Cuba, is a voracious feeder which takes a bait in like a shark; and where the white and striped marlin are so fast that you can hardly follow their movements in the water when they are unhooked and at speed, the blue marlin seems comparatively slow and logy. I have no great respect for black marlin in comparison to the striped fish, except for their size, but I believe no fish could possibly give an angler greater sport than the white and striped marlin.

To return to the way in which marlin hit a bait, the really hungry marlin smashes at the bait, if he comes from the side, with bill, hump, dorsal fin and tail out of water. If you pull the bait out of his mouth he will come for it again as long as there is any bait on the hook. The fact that the hook may prick him does not seem to upset him if he is hungry. Remember that he is used to swallowing fish with spiny fins whole. If he is a black marlin and you have two baits he will sometimes take one and then come after the other. We had one fish hit one bait, slam back to take the other and with two baits in his mouth, come into the wake of the boat after the teaser. Luckily one of the leaders was caught around his bill, and wagging his bill he threw the bait and a few seconds later the leader came loose, so that when he went into the air for his first jump, he was on only one of the rods. But I can still see that fish charging back and forth at the baits, bill, fin and tail out, and then coming toward the boat after teasers, paying no attention to the fact that he was hooked until he felt the pull of the leader on his bill as we were both pumping line on him and striking.

"I've got him," said Joe Russell.

"Hell, no, I've got him."

"We've each got one."

"No, we've both got the same one. Look at him. He's big as a horse!"

Then Joe's reel going zing! zing! zing! as the marlin wagged his bill out of water.

"He's going to jump," Joe shouted as the lines slanted out and straightened, then rose. "He's off," Joe yelled.

"I've got him," you yelled and you remember how he nearly jerked you forward out of the chair as he rose full length clear of the water on a tight line, not thirty yards astern, you loosening the drag, the fish long, purple-black and making a splash like a horse falling off a cliff when he hit the water to come out again and again and again and then go down deep to head for the northwest.

The angry fish strike puzzled us for a long time. He would come from below and hit the bait with a smash. But when you slacked line to him he dropped the bait. Screw down the drag and race the bait in and he would slam it again and drop it. The only way to hook a fish that strikes that way is to screw down on the drag and hit him hard when he smashes. Speed up the boat and strike back at him when he hits the bait. There is too, an outside chance of foul hooking him. That sort of fish will hit the bait to kill it as long as it seems to be alive. I believe they are male fish in breeding season who kill any small fish they see.

The playful marlin, possibly a fish that has fed well, will come behind a bait with his fin high, shove his bill out of water and take the bait lightly between his bill and pointed lower jaw. No matter how fresh the bait may be he drops it. Speeding the boat up may make him take the bait better but you should hit him as soon as he turns with the bait for he is almost certain to drop it. The instant you see it go into his mouth, hit him. If you jerk it away from him it may make him take it harder the next time.

The indifferent fish will sometimes follow the boat, if you are going to the westward, for as many as three or four miles. Looking the bait over, sheering away, coming back to swim deep down below them and follow, indifferent to the bait as food, yet curious. If such a fish swims with his pectoral fins tucked close to his sides, he will not bite. He is cruising and you are on his course. That is all. The instant a marlin sees the bait if he is going to strike or even play with it he raises his dorsal fin and spreads his wide, blue pectorals so that he looks like some great, under-sea bird in the water as he follows.

The black marlin is a stupid fish. He is immensely powerful, can jump wonderfully if you have not hooked him in the belly, and he can ruin your back sounding but he has not the speed or the stamina of the striped marlin, nor his intelligence. I believe the black marlin are old female fish past their prime and that it is age and sexual change that gives them that black color. When they are younger they are much bluer in color and the meat, too, is whiter and of better quality. The meat of the very big old black fish is almost uneatable. If you fight them fast without resting, never letting up on them, you can kill them quicker than you can kill a striped marlin of half their size. Their great strength makes them very dangerous for the first forty minutes. I mean dangerous to tackle; no fish is dangerous to a man in a launch. But if you can take what they give and keep working on them, they will tire quicker than any striped marlin. The 468 pounder was hooked in the roof of the mouth, was in no way tangled in the leader, jumped eight times completely clear, towed the boat stern first when held tight, sounded four times, but was brought to gaff, fin and tail out, in sixty-five minutes. But if I had not lost a much larger striped marlin the day before after two hours and fifty minutes, and fought another the day before for forty-five, I would not have been in shape to work him so hard.

Fishing in a five-mile-an-hour current, where a hooked fish will always swim at least part of the fight against the current, where the water is from 400 to 700 fathoms deep, there is much to learn about tactics in fighting big fish. But one myth that can be dissipated is the old one that the water pressure at

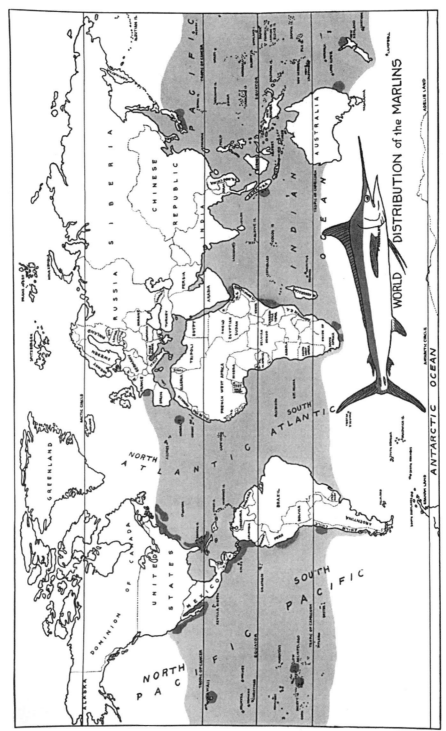

Drawn by Lynn Bogue Hunt from information supplied by Ernest Hemingway.

one thousand feet will kill the fish. A marlin dies at the bottom only if he has been hooked in the belly. These fish are used to going to the bottom. They often feed there for we find bottom fish in their bellies. They are not built like bottom fish which always live at the same depth but are built to be able to go up and down in any depth. I have had a marlin sound four hundred yards straight down, all the rod under water over the side, bend double with the weight going down, down, down, watching the line go, putting on all pressure possible on the reel to check him, him going down and down until you are sure every inch of the line will go. Suddenly he stops sounding and you straighten up, get on to your feet, back into the chair, get the butt in the socket, and work him up slowly and heavily, but steadily. Finally you have the double line on the reel and think he is whipped and will be coming to gaff, and then the line begins to rip out as he hooks up and heads off just under the surface to see him come out in ten long, clean jumps. This after an hour and half of fight; then to sound again.

The 343 pound striped marlin jumped 44 times. Every one has a fish in favor of whose qualities he is prejudiced. I am frankly prejudiced in favor of the striped marlin as we meet him off the Cuban coast. All marlin have stripes and as yet the various marlin have not been properly classified by scientists, so I will not put my theories on them here. But what is called a striped marlin off Cuba is a marlin that runs in weight from 125 to more than a thousand pounds, with a small, depressed head, long, finely shaped bill, bright silver coloring when the fish dies, and broad violet stripes from one and a half to nearly three inches wide which remain clearly visible after the fish is dead many hours. A true striped marlin is never plum-colored as the blue marlin shows in the water and when he jumps the broad stripes are clearly visible. The female counterpart of this fish is the silver marlin, shaped the same, bright as a freshly minted dollar and with very pale stripes which fade out entirely. This is also a wonderful fighting fish. The commercial fishermen who handle them on hand-lines and know how they pull will catch a 400 pound blue marlin, hooked deep, in a quarter of an hour or less. A striped marlin of the same size, hooked in the same way, will often take the same man three or four hours to bring alongside his skiff. The striped marlin fights with his mouth tight shut on the leader and nearly always after the first jump, when he vomits what is in his belly or in the top of his belly, jumps with his mouth tightly shut, while the blue or black marlin almost invariably jumps with his mouth wide open. The commercial fishermen say the only fish that will outpull the striped marlin is the male broadbill and that no fish can out-jump him. They say the fastest thing in the water is the first run of a big tuna or a hundred pound wahoo. But they claim that on a handline, once a tuna's head is turned, when he is towing a skiff, he is whipped and will only circle. The wahoo makes one great run at the start and another excellent run when you get him up to the boat and the market fisherman's lines are really too heavy for him to show how fast he is. But no one can say what will happen with a big male broadbill or a big striped marlin. These same fishermen call the blue and black marlin "bobos," or fools. They swallow the bait, get rattled and sometimes quit, and their main problem is to keep them from going down deep to die. Of course, to a rod and reel fisherman who has not line strong enough to deal with the weight of the fish, or is inexperienced in handling heavy fish, the mere size of blue and black marlin can make them a problem. But as a sporting fish they can never, at least in waters where I have fished them, rank with the striped marlin. Although, if hooked in the mouth, they can put up spectacular fights before they tire.

The mako shark is caught off Cuba all through the marlin run. They are as strong as a broadbill, can leap marvelously, but have no heart. They will sometimes make a terrific fight for a short time, but when they find they are still hooked, will come to gaff docilely with all their strength intact. But when you gaff them, look out. And when you take them in the boat afterwards, look out. I believe they are the only fish in the sea that will deliberately attack a man while they are hooked. I know of numerous cases of this among the commercial fishermen and was lucky enough to get a cinema picture of a mako jumping twice at a fisherman in a skiff who was playing him on a handline. Of course, what really makes a spectacular fight in a fish, if we do not try to deceive ourselves, is panic. A mako has no panic. He probably feels little pain from the hook, too, and that is why he comes in so easily sometimes.

Considering the size the fish attain, the present Atlantic records on marlin taken with rod and reel are ridiculous. The largest fish we have taken weighed 468 pounds. The largest taken in Atlantic waters on rod and reel weighed 502. Yet the commercial fishermen of Cuba do not consider a marlin which dresses out 750 pounds of salable meat with the head, guts, flanks and tail removed, a phenomenal fish. The largest marlin ever caught by commercial fishermen dressed out 1,175 pounds of salable meat; several have been caught which dressed out over a thousand pounds of meat. The head, guts, flanks, blood, hump, fins and tail, which are cut away before the fish is sold, will weigh from a quarter to a third of the weight of the whole fish.

The difficulty is to have the tackle and the knowledge of the fish to handle such a one when he is hooked. To catch a really huge marlin a man must be prepared to spend several entire seasons in the Gulf Stream. Some years exceptionally big fish run, in others there seems to be a top limit of four hundred to five hundred pound fish, as there was in 1934, and no giant marlin running. I caught the biggest fish I had a strike from in 1934, a 420 pounder, so I have no apologies for that season, but in 1933 through lack of experience, unsuitable tackle and some bad luck, we lost marlin whose size I would not dare to estimate in print. The next year we had more experience and the proper tackle and the biggest fish were not running. Happily, in fishing, there is always a season ahead.

Tactics, as I see them now, with very big fish consist in this; first be certain you have really hooked the fish. It would not be exaggerating to strike firmly and solidly at least a dozen times on a really big marlin with all the strain the tackle can stand. His mouth is very hard and, at the start, he may have his jaws shut tight on the leader so that you cannot set the hook.

When the fish is first hooked if he fights deeply and slowly, work him as hard and as fast as you can. The slower he works the faster you should work. The faster he works the easier you must take him. When he is slow never give him an inch of line unless your refusal to let him have it would break it. It is the ability to work always close to the breaking point of your tackle and never break it that makes a real fisherman with heavy tackle. You cannot do this with a drag alone as you cannot feel the strain you put on accurately enough. You must use your hands on the reel to know what drag you are safe in applying. When your fish is jumping have a very light drag on, stand up if you can, and hold your rod high to get the belly of the line out of the water and have the boat follow the fish, keeping him on the quarter and watching for a shift in his direction when he goes down. As soon as the fish goes down, tighten up on your drag and get every bit of line back that you can. When you have run up on the fish, try to lift him by pumping. Any time you can hold him you can get line on him. If he is sounding straight down you must put every bit of pressure possible on the line without breaking it. Make him bend the rod as far as it will go without breaking it, and start raising him instantly the moment he stops. Don't let him rest or have time to make any plans.

Try to take the play away from him at all times and never simply defend yourself against the fish. More big fish are dominated and convinced by heavy tackle and led to gaff than ever are killed by the tackle. It is better to convince him than to try to kill him. The ceaseless bend of the rod putting the utmost strain on him to lead him is what convinces him. When you get him coming, work as hard as you can to keep him coming and you may be able to bring him alongside on that course without having him start circling. If he starts to circle, as most tired fish will do, first try to turn him by holding him as hard as you can with the spring of the rod. If you cannot hold him, keep the boat well

ahead of him and be content to let him take out line each time on the circle
but try to get a little more back than he takes out each time he turns toward
you. When you have shortened his circle, try to turn him again. The first time
you turn him try to bring him alongside on the course he is on. As soon as the
boatman takes hold of the leader, stand up and loosen your drag and watch
one thing—that your rod tip is clear at all times and that there is no loose line
to catch around the guides or anywhere else in case the boatman cannot hold
him to the gaff and has to turn him loose. Make your boatman understand
beforehand that he is only to gaff the marlin in the head and that he is not to
try to gaff him unless he is absolutely certain that he can reach him. In gaffing
always reach over the fish, see the particular part on the head that you are aim-
ing for, and then bring the gaff toward you with plenty of force. Unless you gaff
for a definite place it is like trying to hit a quail by shooting at the covey. When
the fish is gaffed, let the boatman hand the gaff to the huskiest man on board
to hold while he grabs the fish's bill with a gloved hand, pulls upward on it
and clubs the fish between the eyes until his color changes and you know that
he is dead. You can put a line through his gills and shift him astern and using
the gaff and his bill to lift, get him over the roller on the stern and bring him
aboard head first.

The essence of tactics—after the fireworks over which you have no control
are over and the work commences—seems to me to be to know that the fish,
down deep, wants to go either one direction or another and to handle your
boat accordingly. This is not to fight him with the boat but rather to avoid
fighting the weight of the boat against the fish. The ideal to be achieved is to
have the boat a neutral yet mobile point from which to work the fish. No angler
can match a big marlin in strength when he is going away from you, against the
current, so if you pull against him with the boat thrown out he must take line
until you will have to run up on him again to get the line back. It is for this
reason that you have to manoeuver the boat. Discover which way he wants to
go and then keep a little ahead of him. As long as he is strong he will usually
want to go to the northwest, i.e., out to sea and against the current. When you
get him rattled he will change his course. When he begins to tire he will usually
go with the current. If you cannot bring him up one way try to make him turn
and often he will come up steadily and easily in the opposite direction. Put the
boat ahead enough to get him astern, then throw out the clutch while you try
to raise him. Try never to put any strain on him with the boat. If he is coming
toward the boat you will have to get ahead of him again. Usually you will have
to do this a great many times.

When there is a heavy current, remember that if you fight a fish with your clutch out and the fish heads into the current, that current will be carrying your boat, which weighs several tons, away from the fish at the rate of four to five miles an hour if the fish only maintains his position. Of course if you are in a light boat you can shut down on the drag and let him tow the boat. But if you do not work him to get him up and keep him up, the chances are he will go down deep to die. They always try to go down, and you must hold them.

Remember that what you want to do with a big fish is pull his head sideways and upwards. If you work him so that he is going straight away it is as big an advantage to him as for a man to be able to pull on a line over his shoulder. Remember the more a big marlin jumps at the start the better chance you have of landing him, if he is still on after he jumps. Repeated jumping, that is twenty or more jumps, tires the fish greatly and also fills the sacks along his backbone, which take the place of an air bladder, with air which prevents him from sounding deeply. If he jumps enough he cannot sound at all. He will try to, but the air will hold him at a certain depth. If you fight him fast there is no time for his pressure apparatus to adjust itself, if it is ever able to adjust itself after such effort. If you see a marlin, after the very first part of the fight waggle his bill out of water, it means he is hooked deep and is a whipped fish. You should put on all pressure and work him as fast as possible. At the end of a fight, if a fish begins to jump wildly it is almost certain that sharks are after him. Stand up, loosen your drag while he is jumping and if he is on a very short line ride with the jumps with your rod, that is dip to them, to keep the line taut and at the same time keep from smashing the tackle. The instant he goes down, tighten up your drag, sit down and see how fast you can bring him in.

A twenty foot bamboo pole with a sharpened file on the end is the best thing I have found for keeping sharks off a fish when he is in close. Shooting at them with a rifle is useless. Try to hit them in the head with your lance, but hit them. Have a line on the pole so you can retrieve it if one carries it off.

As I see big-game fishing with rod and reel it is a sport in which a man or woman seeks to kill or capture a fish by the means which will afford the fisherman the greatest pleasure and best demonstrate the speed, strength and leaping ability of the fish in question; at the same time killing or capturing the fish in the shortest time possible and never for the sake of flattering the fisherman's vanity, using tackle unsuitable to the prompt capture of the fish. I believe that it is as bad to lose fish by breaking unsuitable tackle in an attempt to make a light-tackle record as it is to allow animals to escape wounded in an attempt to get a record bag or a record head.

Talk of giving the fish a sporting chance on excessively fragile tackle seems nonsense when one realizes that the sporting chance offered the fish is that of breaking the line and going off to die. The sporting thing is to kill your fish as promptly as possible on suitable tackle which does not prevent him running, pulling or jumping to the best of his ability, while you fight him as rapidly as possible to kill him as quickly and mercifully as possible.

Any good heavy-tackle fisherman who would be willing to fish drifting for three or four seasons off the Cuban coast would undoubtedly, by hooking fish in the belly so they could not fight, be almost certain sooner or later of breaking the world record for marlin. But all he would demonstrate would be that there are huge marlin to be caught off Cuba by drifting and letting them swallow the bait, and the commercial fisherman have been demonstrating that for seventy years. There are also huge fish to be caught there trolling—just as big as have been caught drifting—and that is something that interests a sportsman to prove.

When there is little current in the stream and no east breeze so that the fish do not come to the top, marlin may still be caught drifting. In this form of fishing a whole cero mackerel or a kingfish is put on the hook, head downward, the hook being introduced into the body of the fish at the tail, while the fish is held curved in the hand, and run along the backbone until the point is brought out through the skin a little behind the gill opening; shank of hook and leader being inside the mackerel which hangs head down with the curve of the hook and the barb projecting. The tail of the fish is then tied fast to the leader so it cannot be pulled down; another thread is tied around the fish where the hook projects and all the projecting part of the hook is covered with sardines or pilchards hooked onto the projecting curve and barb by passing the point of the hook through both their eyes. This bait is lowered over the side and allowed to sink with its own weight and that of the leader to a depth of from seventy-five to a hundred and twenty-five fathoms. Usually four baits are put out on four different rods at seventy-five, ninety, one hundred, and one hundred and twenty-five fathoms. The baits float deep with the current and the engine is manouevered occasionally to keep the lines as perpendicular as possible. A strike is signalled by line running off the reel, perhaps slowly at first in a series of jerks, then steadily and rapidly when the fish has taken the bait in his mouth or swallowed it. As the fish moves off he will usually hook himself against the pull of four to six hundred feet of line moving through the deep water.

Occasionally a white marlin will come to the top and jump with the bait before the fisherman's rod or reel give intimation of a strike. He has taken it from below and come straight up with it. As soon as the fisherman knows he has a fish on, the boat is headed toward the northwest and the fisherman reels and pumps while the boat is going ahead to straighten out the deep belly in the line. Once he has a taut line on the fish, if the fish has been hooked in the mouth, the problem is then the same as with a fish hooked trolling except that as a big fish always heads out against the current, the boat has the advantage of heading out with the fish from the start without the necessity of making a turn while the fish is making his run, as would be necessary when hooking a fish while trolling against the current. This eliminates the most difficult and most exciting manoeuvcr in trolling. Striped marlin and white marlin are sometimes hooked in the mouth when drifting, but blue and black marlin are almost invariably hooked in the gullet or stomach.

To me it is a method of fishing to be employed by a sportsman only when the fish can be taken no other way due to a lack of breeze or current, or when, due to there being a great quantity of feed in the lower strata of the current, marlin keep down and will not come to the top; or when the expenditure of gasoline for trolling is a dominant consideration. A fish hooked in the mouth while drifting can put up as good a fight as one hooked trolling, but you miss the excitement of the strike and you have a definite advantage over the fish from the start.

Mr. H. L. Woodward, whom we met in 1933 and who is a pioneer rod and reel fisherman for big marlin off Cuba, does not agree with me on drifting. We have had many discussions about it during the times we have had the pleasure of him fishing with us in the 1934 season. In a letter he writes: "I shall give you such pertinent information as I can regarding my fishing, but it is the sport that counts and not the individual. Therefore, *where not absolutely necessary*, please leave my name out of the text of the article. Now for the information.

"I began my salt water fishing in 1915. I have been fishing for marlin since 1921. I cannot tell you how many marlin I have caught because I have not made it a practice to record in writing any fish except large ones. Last season I caught 8. Probably 6 or 7 per season would be a fair average. The largest marlin I have caught was the 459 pound fish, photograph enclosed, showing Mr. Hugo Lippmann and Mr. C. H. Ford with fish. Photograph was taken of myself with fish but turned out very poor. The largest fish I ever caught in the Gulf Stream was a 522 pound mackerel shark.

"The best fighting fish that I have ever hooked and landed in the Gulf Stream was a 360 pound striped marlin. This fish was hooked while drifting, the hook being set well forward in the mouth, just under the eye. This fish fought for one hour and fifty minutes and was at no time over 200 feet deep. The 324 pound marlin which was hooked by Dr. Hernandez, fought for two and a half hours by myself and landed by you on your boat, was one of the best fighting fish that I have ever hooked on the surface. The unfortunate part was that this fish fouled the leader with his tail within the first hour. He made a very spectacular fight for the first forty minutes on the surface and moved so fast that at times we had a double bag in the line.

"You and I have never agreed about 'drifting' and fishing between 450 and 700 feet down. As I have done a great deal of it, I think my opinion is more valuable than yours. Unusual care has to be exercised in striking fish early so that they are hooked in the mouth. If that precaution is taken, fish hooked in this fashion will come to the top immediately and put up just as good a fight as fish hooked on the surface. The 459 pound blue marlin caught in 1934 was hooked at about 550 feet down. However this fish, like all of that species, put up a very poor fight. It is true that I gave this fish a little more time than I usually do when I felt it take the bait. This resulted in the fish being hooked in the back of the mouth. However, my experience coincided with your own when it comes to the ordinary large-headed blue marlin. They are stupid, generally slow in action, and put up a very poor fight.

"Havana men who fish each summer for marlin in the Gulf Stream are: Esmond Brownson who has caught eleven and Thorvald Sanchez who has caught twenty-four, Frank D. Mahoney has caught a number of small and medium sized marlin. Mario Mendoza used to be a great peto (wahoo) fisherman and also caught a few marlin. There are a number of other Cubans and Americans who have been trying their hand for the last one or two seasons. Nearly everybody is handicapped by lack of proper equipment. Boats are not adapted and the beginner generally starts with cheap and ineffective tackle.

"Now about broadbill swordfish. The large ones do not get this far south. In all the time that I have fished the Gulf Stream I have only seen one very large broadbill and I have only caught two small ones. One weighed 262 pounds and the other weighed 212 pounds.

"I will close this letter by saying that from my own personal experience in fishing here and elsewhere, and from all that I have read, I think that no place in the western hemisphere can equal the marlin fishing in the Gulf Stream along the north coast of Cuba during the summer and early fall months. Your own experience in 1933 corroborates my own idea. Eventually the men who love this sport will acquire the habit and come here each year. The local people do nothing of consequence properly to advertise this marlin fishing."

The 324 pound fish Mr. Woodward refers to was hooked by Dr. Hernandez in a small launch without a fishing chair, was fought under impossible conditions by Woodward until, as it was getting rough and the sun was going down, our boat which had been standing by in case they would be caught out in the dark with the fish, took both anglers on board to let them work the fish from a proper chair. The fish was finally brought up, dead, tail tangled in the leader, from a depth of 500 yards. At least there were five hundred yards of 30 thread line out, straight down, when the doctor, whose first marlin it was, suggested that a third angler have a try at the fish. The bringing-up process took one hour and three-quarters. It was interesting to see that a dead 324 pound fish could be raised from that depth on 30 thread line, but it is an experience the repetition of which is to be avoided.

If a fish tangles his tail in the leader jumping he will have to die at whatever depth he is at the time as, if you hold him, pulling his gills open against the water as you try to lift him, will drown him. You can use the currents to lift him by heading against the current for a little, while you try to have it start him lifting. Then go with the current and try to keep the fish coming, even if it is only a quarter of an inch at a time. If you can raise him a quarter of an inch you can get him up. Thirty-six and thirty-nine thread line will take an unbelievable strain when it is wet, and a good twenty ounce tip, when your chair is high enough so you can brace your feet and pull, acts like a derrick.

A fish that is hooked in the belly will go deep to die if allowed to; but he should not be allowed to. Such a fish, once he comes to the top, should be fought on as short a line as possible; try to get him on the double line as soon as you can, hold him hard when he starts to go down and gaff him at the first chance. Many people have gotten into trouble with heavy marlin by being afraid the fish was too fresh to gaff when they brought him close early in the fight. A fish is never too fresh to gaff if you gaff him in the head. If you cannot gaff him in the head, do not gaff him.

As to the advisability of using outriggers to skip bait for marlin I am not competent to judge. When marlin were on the surface feeding, we were always able to get as many strikes as we could handle without them. Fishing without outriggers we have had strikes from seventeen marlin in a single day. A hungry marlin will come right into the wash of a propeller after a bait and one of the greatest pleasures in fishing, to me, is seeing the fish come and feeling him first take hold of the bait. Also, when marlin are plentiful and striking well I should imagine outriggers would be a nuisance.

Thorvald Sanchez, who is a fine sportsman and very faithful fisherman of the Gulf Stream, always uses outriggers and several days last season when fish were scarce he had marlin strikes when we raised no fish. On other days we would raise fish when he would have a blank day. But I believe that out of an equal number of days fished he raised more marlin with the outriggers than we did without them. We intend to give them a thorough trial this season (1935). There is no doubt but that they save much fatigue, but there is no better training for using a big rod and heavy reel than holding that same outfit day after day.

In the winter months when marlin are absent, the Cuban sportsmen fish for wahoo, locally called *peto*, which run to a great size off Cuba. Mario Mendoza with his brothers Raul and Adrian Mendoza, I believe hold the record for having caught the greatest number of wahoo in one day with 14. Their largest on rod and reel weighed 75 pounds. Adrian Mendoza has also taken a white marlin of 136, the Cuban rod and reel record. Dr. Jorge Muniz, one of the first rod and reel fishermen in Cuba, and Julio Cadenas are other Cuban sportsmen who have caught marlin and for many years specialized in wahoo. There are many other excellent Cuban fishermen whose names I do not know, but Julio Sanchez and his brother Emilio have caught many big marlin at Bimini.

Wahoo are trolled for along the hundred fathom curve either way from Havana harbor with Tarp-orenos, heavy metal Tarp-orenos, feather jigs or strip baits. Running to as big as 140 pounds, they are a marvelous sporting fish on medium tackle. They have wonderful speed as well as strength, and making a very slashing fight they do everything but jump. There are certain patches of bottom like the so-called tuna holes of Tahiti, which they frequent and these are known to all the local fishermen. Just off Cojimar, to the eastward of Havana, off Bacuranao in the same direction, straight out from the Morro Castle, and off Jaimanitas to the westward are all famous wahoo spots. I believe the record for one man in a day is held by Julio Hidalgo with nine taken trolling with a handline. The largest I have ever seen weighed 105 pounds, but they have been caught weighing 125 pounds by the commercial fishermen and are said to run much heavier. They have great strength when they are really big, with no loss of speed, and they smash much tackle.

In the summer they live in the cool deep water and do not come to the surface unless the wind should shift into the north when you are liable to get a strike from one at any time. They ruin many big marlin baits, cutting them off as sharply as with a knife just behind the hook. You do not know it is a wahoo so you slack when you feel the strike; then when you reel in there is the bait chopped in two. We catch them by fishing a feather on a light rod and long line between the two big baits. This feather makes a good teaser for big marlin. Anyone fishing it is instructed to strike hard if they feel anything hit and if they do not hook the fish to race the feather in.

Frequently a marlin will chase it in and then switch to one of the baits which are usually fished about forty feet astern. With the baits we use two teasers; one green or blue, the other white. These you can make yourself in any size. We have found one about twice the size of Pflueger Zane Grey teaser painted green with a red head to be very effective at raising big fish. To keep it from breaking off the line, it should be fitted with a heavy swivel in the head. Teasers get water-logged with constant fishing and need to be replaced and dried out or, when their line happens to break or be cut away by a wahoo or other fish, they will sink and be lost. When a fish charges the teasers never pull them all the way out of the water or he will go down. But keep them dancing out of the water and pull them away from him until you can pass him a bait. The minute the bait is into him or slacked out to him and he turns toward it, jerk the teaser aboard. Always have the teasers tied so some one can reach them instantly if a fish shows behind them.

Lines if fished every day are much better not dried, but when first put on should be wet their entire length and then reeled back on without the boat going ahead very much while you are reeling, so the line will not be packed on so tightly that later on the heat may rot it altogether. Reels need lots of oil and grease. Any time after fighting a big fish, oil your reel again before putting out another bait.

The principal points about a boat are that the larger and heavier it is the better it must be able to be manoeuvered if you are not to break fish off; that the stern must be low enough so that you can get a big fish aboard; that the man at the wheel must have an unobstructed view of the line in the water when a fish is hooked, and the fishing chair must fit the fisherman so that he can brace his feet and pull when the fish is astern, broadside, or on the quarter. The chair too, should be high enough so that when a fish sounds straight down the bent rod will not strike the gunwale. Twelve to fourteen miles is as fast as a fishing boat needs to go with marlin, but you should always be able to get forward with the rod and up into the bow if necessary to chase a jumping fish. When he sounds you can get back into the stern again.

White marlin breed off Cuba in May. They breed in the same way that the grouper does, except that as they are a fish of the current they breed in the current instead of on a reef. The female marlin heads into the current while the male heads in the opposite direction, and while they are side by side the female expels the eggs and the male the milt; the male then catches the eggs in the basket-like opening of his gill covers and lets them pass out through his mouth. We hope, if the fish run well next year, to find the young marlin in the sargasso weed where it would seem logical that they would take refuge along with the young fish of so many other species. The broadbill too must breed off Cuba for the fish are often taken in pairs full of milt and spawn and I have seen female broadbill so full of roe that the eggs would be expelled in the boat when the fish was moved.

The fishermen say that the striped and black marlin breed during July and August but that the very big fish that appear in September and October are usually without fully developed roe or milt and must have spawned some time before. Marlin when they are paired seem very devoted. The fishermen claim the male fish always hangs back until the female fish has taken a bait, but since the male is often only a fraction of the size of the female this may not be pure altruism. I know that we have frequently hooked the female fish of a pair and had the male fish swim around all during the fight, staying close to the female until she was gaffed. I will tell an incident that anyone is at perfect liberty to doubt but which will be vouched for by Captain Joe Russell and Norberg Thompson of Key West who were on the "Anita" at the time when we hooked one fish out of a pair of white marlin. The other fish took a bait a few seconds later but was not hooked. The hooked fish was brought promptly to gaff and the unhooked marlin stayed close beside it, refusing a bait that was passed to it. When the hooked fish was gaffed the unhooked fish swam close beside the boat and when the hooked marlin was lifted in over the gunwale, the unhooked fish jumped high in the air close beside the boat as though to look and see where the hooked fish had gone. It then went down. I swear that this is true but you are quite at liberty to disbelieve it. The hooked fish was a female full of roe.

At another time in the 1933 season my wife caught a 74 pound white marlin which was followed by three other marlin all through the fight. These three refused bait but stayed with the female fish until she was gaffed and brought aboard. Then they went down.

I have never caught a really small marlin but I have seen them jump in the summertime looking not much longer than three feet, and have had strikes from them when we were fishing the big baits, looking not much bigger than a good sized garfish. All marlin seem to suffer much from sucker-fish which sometimes get into their gill openings and get as white and bloated as toads in a well. The native fishermen say that a marlin that follows the baits sometimes and will not strike, is afraid to open his mouth because the position of the sucker-fish worries him so that he is afraid that if he opens his mouth they will get into his gill openings. I believe the sucker-fish must eat a vast quantity of eggs during the spawning season. They should always be killed rather than thrown back into the water.

Aside from their breeding movements, and it is quite possible that they return to the same part of the coast where they were bred as salmon do, marlins' migratory movements may be controlled by the movements of their feed which, in turn, must follow the movement of the plankton. It may be that the blue marlin follow the squid which could fatten and coarsen them and give them the darker color. Again, the striped marlin and the white marlin may move with the flying fish which might account for their greater speed. Marlin, during their run, sometimes stay several days in the same place. Off the monastery down the coast between Havana and Cojimar, where there is a great tide swirl when the current is strong, we several times raised what appeared to be the same fish in the same spot. Carlos Gutierrez told me that when drifting he had once seen a huge marlin in the same place for four different days, recognizable by a harpoon scar on his head. This fish was either circling, or holding himself steady in the current.

Another possible theory on the blue marlin is that they are from the spawn of the degenerated old black fish, while the striped and silver marlin are bred from fish in their prime. But this is all conjecture and is only put in to start more sportsmen wondering where their fish come from and how and where they go. We know very little about them yet; the sea is one of the last places left for a man to explore; and there is wonderful exploring yet for any fisherman who will travel and live for months on the ocean current in a small boat.

Excellent fishing guides with whom I have fished and whom I can recommend as putting on first-rate bait and understanding our methods of fishing even though they do not speak any English, though being thoroughly trained by Captain Joe Russell of Key West and myself, are Carlos Gutierrez of Vives 31, Havana, and Angel Prado, known as "Bolo," of San Ignacio, 24. Highly recommended men with whom I have not fished personally are Jorge Cuni who can be reached through the Havana Yacht Club, care of Julio Cadenas for whom he works but who, if he was not fishing, might cede his services; Justo Gallardo, San Ignacio, 24; Raimundo Quinto of Cuarteles No. 1; and Manuel Paredes, also of San Ignacio, 24. These last three are recommended by Carlos who vouches for them, but I do not know how much rod and reel experience they have had. If he recommends them they are good fishermen.

The usual arrangement is to pay a fixed sum, say $2.00 a day, to the guide and have him buy your bait for you. If you catch a marlin let him dispose of it so that it will not be wasted, and if he sells it let him buy the bait himself the next day and share the remaining money among the crew who worked on the fish—in gaffing, handling the wheel, taking him aboard and later cutting him up. You will also soon have a great many people to whom you will have promised fish whether you know it or not; but always see your principal fisherman gets some for himself. They are all keen and conscientious and get up at three or four o'clock to get bait at the market, but a little blood money freshens anyone up.

Launches available for fishing are the "Caiman," belonging to Dr. Charles Roca, a very keen fisherman and good guide himself, address Cero 597 or care of the Havana Yacht Club. The "Caiman" is not fast but can be fished from successfully and has excellent chairs. She is something over 30 feet and you sit in the open under the sun. On the other hand, Charley Roca is a marvelous amateur cook and can mix very good drinks.

The "Corsario," owned by a very enthusiastic fisherman and yachtsman, Claudio Fernandez de Velasco, who can be reached from 12 to 6 o'clock at A8028 and in the evening at U6326, is a fairly fast cabin cruiser that has been fitted up by her owner as a party boat. When we are not fishing in Cuba he will probably have Carlos Gutierrez as guide.

Julio Hidalgo of the Port Pilots, reached at their office in the Calle Caballeria, has a small boat the "Eva" built especially for marlin fishing. A very big fish could be handled from her easily as she is only 24 feet, is light and at the same time seaworthy. You could cut her engine out and let a hooked fish tow her. If Julio had installed a proper chair, she would be a good boat for anyone willing to fish in the sun and her lightness would simplify tactics.

Of the following boats I have only Carlos' information that they have been fitted up as charter boats. All these boats should charter for the same rate as boats of equal size in Florida waters although gasoline is nearly ten cents higher a gallon in Cuba.

"Manjuari," owner José Elias Nobo, G and I Vedado; a 38-foot Matthews cruiser, 65 hp. motor, 4 berths. All information from Fernando Panne, pilot of the port. Same address as for Julio Hidalgo.

Launch "Lena," owned by Aurelio Rocha, Calle 27 and Lima, or the Motor Boat Club; Yacht "Cachita," 41 feet, owned by Oscar Lavin, the Fisherman's Club, 24th St. and Lima, telephone F2400; launch "Adela," owned by Luis Coto Leiseca, a 34-foot cabin cruiser, also at the Fisherman's Club, telephone 2400.

Anyone coming to fish in their own boat should bring their card of membership in a recognized yacht club, which is necessary to obtain a 45-day yacht permit enabling you to fish for sport. This is obtained of the Captain of the Port by application through the American Consulate, and should be applied for as soon as the yacht has made entry. It is renewable on application. The best procedure after that is to obtain a local fisherman as guide and make arrangements with him along the lines that I have suggested. If you are only fishing a few days the rates may be a little higher. It is customary to give a tip, say, ten to twenty dollars to the fisherman at the end of the trip.

Fishing is good either way from Havana Harbor, to the eastward as far as Jaruco; to the westward as far as Bahia Honda. Fish the edge of the current. If it is out, go out; if it is in close, you can fish right in to the hundred fathom curve. A few barracuda will bother you, but there are not many. The biggest marlin are as liable to be close into the edge of soundings as to be far out. Often the current will be well out in the morning and in close in the afternoon. You will find plenty of sharks around the garbage that is dumped out in the current from lighters, but the marlin avoid the discolored water. Stay clear of it or you can foul a propeller badly. There are good beaches to swim about twelve miles to the eastward; you can anchor off and swim into the beach. Don't swim in the Gulf Stream. Sharks really will hit you off the north coast of Cuba no matter what you hear. There is very little feed and and few small fish in the Stream; that is probably why the marlin come there to spawn; and the sharks are very hungry. We have had them hit feathers and teasers and they will hit a bait even when you are trolling fast. You do not need to troll any faster than just enough to give your teaser a good lively motion.

White marlin are called *aguja blanca,* by the local fishermen; striped marlin are called *casteros* or *aguja de casta;* black marlin are called *pez grande,* or *aguja negra.* Blue marlin are confounded with the black but are called, sometimes *azules* or *aguja bobos.* Dolphin are called *dorado;* wahoo is *peto;* barracuda is *picuba.* Tarpon are called *sabalo.*

The different bait fish are *pintada,* the cero mackerel; *guaguaucho* a pike-like fish; *lisa* or mullet and *chicharros,* goggle-eyes and *machuelos,* pilchards. Bonito, albacore and small tuna are called *bonitos* or *albacoras.* The broadbill is called *imperador* and the mako shark is called *dentuso.* I hope you catch them all.

THREE

Giant Bluefins of Jordan Bay, Nova Scotia

S. Kip Farrington

Forty miles west of Liverpool lies a tiny hamlet known as Jordan Ferry. The houses of the residents are widely scattered and the dock is reached after a drive through what is known as Nine Mile Wood. When you get through this wood—it seems particularly long at three-thirty in the morning—one of the loveliest bodies of water on the Atlantic seaboard will lie before you. The bay is practically landlocked, with a small entrance to the ocean, and is surrounded by a beautiful wooded countryside, dotted here and there with the houses of fishermen.

The Jordan River flows into the bay, and, though you may find this hard to believe, the tuna go into the river itself. All day long the tuna are seen rolling here but although Tom Gifford and Herman Gray have tried every trick in their bag, they have had no success in catching them except around the nets. The nickname which I have given this bay is the "Jordan Bathtub." With a depth of water ranging from four to ten fathoms, most of it with an average of about six fathoms, it is the realization of the tuna fisherman's dream. Without a doubt, it will become the place where ladies, elderly gentlemen, and young boys and girls may catch their tuna—and there won't be many midgets among these fish. I feel that the world's record tuna caught by a woman, which was taken in Jordan Bay in 1936, is not likely to be exceeded or, at least, that it will not be beaten by a fish taken in any other place. I believe fourteen fish were caught in Jordan Bay in 1936, and twelve of them stayed in the harbor. It is evident, therefore, that not many of them get into deep water. It was in this bay that Zane Grey caught his world's record tuna of 758 pounds, a catch which remained high until 1932.

The methods followed in tuna fishing here are exactly the same as those used at Liverpool. However, there are fewer nets to bother the angler and the fish is hooked in four fathoms of water. As they do at Lunenburg, the tuna seem to come into Jordan Bay before they visit Liverpool, and August the first finds the season in full swing. Not many of these fish have been taken at Jordan for the past few years though most of the Liverpool guides have been at Jordan Bay when the tuna were not at Liverpool. In 1936, Joe Penny took Dr. Brinkley to Jordan Bay and they caught two fish, one of them a 525-pounder, caught in twenty minutes, and the other weighing 650 pounds. The first fish must have struck his head on a rock, so shallow is the water, and thus was killed.

Captain Herman Gray, of Palm Beach, who that year was acting as generalissimo of the tuna guides of the province for the government of Nova Scotia caught a fish for Elliott Campbell, a government official. He then proceeded to startle the fishing world by bringing Mrs. Francis Low, wife of the well-known New York and New Jersey tuna fisherman, and guiding her to the world's record held by a woman.

Mrs. Low had only three days in which to fish. On the first day she caught a 600-pounder in six hours and twenty minutes. Not bad for a beginning! This was on a Saturday, August 15th, and as the Jordanites do not fish on Sunday, she had to wait until Monday to resume her record smashing. Probably, after looking over the shallow depth of the water and the landlocked bay, Mrs. Low came to the conclusion that her 600-pound fish would not stay "high" very long, and immediately proceeded to catch what is the world's record fish taken by a woman. This tuna weighed 749 pounds and took two hours and five minutes to bring to gaff. Mrs. Low was really in stride now and fishing in earnest. The best her husband could do was to follow her with a fish of 620 pounds. It was a job well done, and Mrs. Low deserves no end of credit.

Captain Gray realized Jordan's possibilities and got the commercial fisherman, George Bush and his three able sons to equip their boats and build fishing chairs. Some of these boats were re-built overnight, practically, and these men learned the rod and reel game almost as rapidly. There is only one other guide at Jordan, Cecil Baptiste.

Jordan Bay remained quiet for the week, after the Lows had left, until Friday when Mrs. Farrington arrived at Liverpool. We started our drive to Jordan at one o'clock on Saturday morning. At eight o'clock, a fine fish took the bait within three feet of my hand, as I pulled in the leader to throw the bait out to him. Mrs. Farrington drove the hook home and we then went on a ride which carried us under one mooring, through two nets, and into a market fisherman. After we were clear, the tuna got the line wrapped around a huge boulder— how many times I do not know. Three or four minutes elapsed in which Mrs. Farrington was powerless to do anything except keep a very light drag, and the line continued to run off at a terrific pace. When about 50 or 60 yards of line were left on the 12/0 reel, it untangled itself. Once more the Ashaway line proved its worth by taking all that burning and searing against a hard surface. Following an easy fight of one hour and thirty-eight minutes, I had the pleasure of gaffing the largest fish I had ever boated—a 720-pounder. This was the only tuna I have ever seen jump completely clear when hooked. This was due, I suppose, to the very shallow water. Mrs. Farrington was fishing from a dory rowed by Earl Bush, who did a splendid job.

A. Pam Blumenthal, who was with me, also landed one that morning in fifty minutes, a 510-pounder, and W. G. Curran of New York, took one which weighed 717 pounds. Although Mr. Curran's was not a legitimate catch, I feel that his story is worth telling. After having a large reel freeze up because of lack of lubrication, Mr. Curran cut the line and fastened it to another rod and reel. This rod he promptly broke and ended up by hand-lining the fish after a four-hour battle.

The following Monday we returned to Jordan and Mr. Blumenthal caught a 654-pounder in one hour and fifty minutes. This fish was more difficult to kill, as he went outside. At this time Michael Lerner arrived on the scene from Louisburg and quickly got into the Jordan spirit by catching a 720-pounder in sixty minutes and a 430-pounder in forty-one minutes. Not a bad morning's work! Thus, to his catch of 1,136 pounds of swordfish, taken off Louisburg, Mr. Lerner added 1,150 pounds of tuna three weeks later.

All the fish described were caught on 36- and 39-thread line, which is as large a line as one needs. I firmly believe that Jordan Bay is the one place on the East Coast where one may catch a 700-pound tuna on 24-thread line. The only difficulty would be in getting clear of the nets, and in that case 24-thread, naturally, would not hold very long.

Other fish were taken in 1936—one of them by Colonel Hugh D. Wise, of Princeton, New Jersey, which weighed 451 pounds. Under the circumstances the taking of this big tuna was a remarkable fishing feat. A woman, this time a Canadian, Miss Edna Jamieson of Truro, N.S., caught a fish weighing 725 pounds. This was taken in six hours fifty-five minutes, on 72-thread line.

In 1936 the only accommodations at Jordan Bay were at the house of Cecil Baptiste where rooms for about eight people were available. At Shelburne, however, which is only six miles away, there is a first-class hotel, the Atlantic House.

Rod and reel fishing also made a beginning off Shelburne, where there are herring nets, in 1936. The first tuna was taken by W. G. Lawrence of New York, and weighed six hundred pounds. The harbor at Shelburne offers tremendous possibilities.

If you expect to visit Jordan Bay, write George Bush at Jordan Ferry. You may depend upon him to give reliable information as to the tuna fishing conditions there. It is always best to know, at any given place, whether or not the fish are in. The information given as to the times when fish should be in, is based of course on records which have been kept for ten or fifteen years past.

FOUR

Montauk's Miracle Waters

S. Kip Farrington

Only 115 miles from the heart of New York City, a trip of two and one-half hours by train or motor, lies the quaint old Village of Montauk. It is surrounded on three sides by water; at its doors are Gardiners Bay, Block Island Sound and the Atlantic Ocean. In the last eight years Montauk has gained a well-deserved reputation as the leading rod and reel sport fishing center on the North Atlantic Coast.

From the tiny snapper and porgie to the mammoth mako shark and the gigantic broadbill swordfish, the eastern end of Long Island has as fine fishing to offer as almost any fishing place in the world, beginning in April and ending in December, and for accessibility to the big cities of the East, it is unequalled.

As late as fifteen years ago, Montauk, which was named for an Indian tribe, the Montauketts, was wild country, a wild fowler's and hunter's paradise with an abundance of deer, fox and all kinds of small game, not to mention a population of ducks, geese and shore birds. Besides the very small fishing village and the little inn resting on the shores of Fort Pond Bay, it boasted only three small houses where sheep herders lived. As the natives still say, it was almost impossible to "get on" by automobile, and there was only one train a day. All of the fishing was done by the commercial fishermen who harpooned swordfish, hand-lined sea bass, cod and other bottom-feeding varieties, and pulled their traps for a living. There was and still is a tremendous business in lobsters. In 1925, the construction of a concrete road across Neapeague Beach was begun, a hotel was erected, and Great Pond, now known as Lake Montauk, was dredged and a channel dug for a harbor entrance to Block Island Sound. Lake Montauk is now a landlocked harbor. Here a casino and the Montauk Yacht Club were built, and it is from the club dock from which many of the charter boats now leave.

In 1933, the Long Island Rail Road inaugurated the first Fishermen's Special, a train leaving New York and Brooklyn at five fifty each morning. On Saturdays, Sundays and holidays a second section leaves at eight thirty. The running time is two hours fifteen minutes. These trains are provided with refrigerator cars so that the returning fisherman can leave his catch on ice during the homeward trip, which is begun at five o'clock in the afternoon, the late train leaving at seven. The round trip fare is $1.50. The railroad company has built a clubhouse, equipped with locker rooms, shower baths and lunch counter, at Fort Pond Beach, where the fishing boats which meet the trains leave from a specially designed dock. The boat fee is $2.00, including bait. Many of those who make this trip come for surf-casting on the beaches or for fishing from the docks. On one side of the dock is a fine beach with bath houses and life guards in attendance.

The boats that meet the train are in charge of Captain Herbert N. Edwards, son of a famous skipper of Long Island's whaling days. The boats are especially equipped for fishing and range from 40 to 110 feet in length. Most of them are powered with Diesel motors. The run from the railroad dock to the fishing grounds is a matter of one-half to three-quarters of an hour.

Within a few hundred yards of Fort Pond Beach, and directly opposite the main railroad station, are the headquarters of the sport fishermen in the Village of Montauk, the Montauk Fish & Supply Company. All the charter boats which do not use Lake Montauk and the Montauk Yacht Club dock here. The fisherman will find here everything he needs—boats, tackle, bait—and the best of advice in all matters pertaining to the sport.

FLOUNDER

The fishing season begins early in April, when the winter flounder awakens from his long sleep in the mud and begins biting. Skimmer clams and worms are his favorite bait and he likes a sandy as well as a muddy bottom. Any kind of light rod and line, a 3- or 4-ounce sinker, with a small O'Shaughnessey hook on a gut leader is the rig to use. All of the Montauk captains are equipped with such tackle. The Montauk boats are ready for service the last two weeks in March. For this fishing, some of the boats make their headquarters at I. Y. Halsey's dock at Threemile Harbor, East Hampton, which is fifteen miles nearer New York than Montauk and there are also boats which leave from Sag Harbor. Off these points are to be found some of the best flounder fishing grounds.

POLLACK

In March and April there are still codfish and haddock to be caught off Montauk Point but they disappear about the first of May. However, their cousin, the pollack, or Boston bluefish as he is called by the Down Easters, puts in an appearance about May 15th and stays until the middle of June. The pollack run of six weeks gives the fisherman some of the finest sport of his season, a fact which but few of the angling fraternity appreciate.

The fish come to the surface and bite more freely one hour before and after the tide is at flood or ebb. Usually, they feed on whiting, butterfish or squid. Sometimes one sees hundreds of pollack in a small area, some four hundred acres, say, driving the small fry to the surface, to be chased in every direction by pollack of from ten to forty pounds.

This fishing takes place at the tip end of Montauk Point, directly under the lighthouse, and out as far as the Great Eastern Spar Buoy, a mile away. Pollack are taken by trolling very slowly with a line of about 100 feet in length. An 8-ounce vom Hofe tip and 4/0 reel filled with 12-thread Ashaway line is about the right size tackle to use, but, of course, 3/6 and 6/9 outfits make for all the more sport. The favorite bait of the pollack is the ever-popular Japanese feather jig, with an 8/0 hook rigged to a 4-foot piano wire leader. Usually, a piece of squid is put on the hook. As second choice, I prefer the heavy old-fashioned Block Island jig made of lead with hook attached. The piece of squid is even more important with this lure. The weight of the jig helps to keep the bait lower down in the water, a great help sometimes in getting more strikes, particularly before the tide has changed. If the fish are not on the surface, your boat captain will, no doubt, attach a drail sinker to the line, lowering it to ten feet or more, and there the strikes will be even more frequent. Of course, such fishing does not offer as much fun and is resorted to only when the pollack have gone down. Four or five rods can be fished at once—I have seen eight or more—from a beam troller. Thus, a day's trip can be made economically if expenses are divided. The usual charge is $25.00 to $30.00 a day, including tackle and bait.

The pollack is a much under-rated denizen of the deep. To me, fishing for pollack is far more sporty than blue or weak-fishing. A 30- to 40-pound pollack is not uncommon and I can vouch for his gameness from start to finish. The fish is one which, when served with a heavy egg sauce, tastes particularly good.

SEA BASS, PORGIES AND FLUKE

As Decoration Day approaches, the sea bass, the porgy, and the summer flounder or fluke arrive. This fishing continues until late October. There are many fine spots but the most popular is the famous Frisbee Ground, just around the Point, and about two miles offshore. This is the place where many of those who come on the special trains have their fun, with little risk of seasickness. A line of 150 feet and almost any kind of rod and reel with an 8- or 10-ounce sinker will do. Squid is usually the best bait.

MACKEREL

About June first sailing vessels in numbers appear at Montauk. This is the mackerel fleet out of historic Gloucester, returning from the Delaware Capes in close pursuit of the schools of mackerel and making tremendous hauls of these little green warriors with their purse seines. This common mackerel also schools up off the Point during the late pollack fishing and sometimes remains until the middle of August. Mackerel are also caught by trolling, using the tiny lead mackerel jig, but unfortunately it is almost always necessary to keep the lure well below the surface. However, these fish are fine fun on the very lightest of tackle and a delicious addition to the menu.

SWORDFISH

By the tenth of June the season's point of greatest expectation has been reached. That great gladiator of the sea, the broadbill swordfish, is now sixty to seventy miles offshore on the inside edge of the Gulf Stream. A good many of the commercial men who always start the season with a week's trip to the edge of the Stream, are returning with the first harpooned catch of the season. They will get from fifty to sixty cents a pound, so great is the demand at this early date.

On shore, the rod and reel men are in a state of great excitement, waiting for the swordfish to be reported within the 40-mile limit. New lines, leaders and hooks have been purchased, the big reels oiled and put in order, and the outriggers adjusted. The harpooners have put on their pulpits and are already out looking for fish. At last the fish are seen a little closer in and out we go.

Let me tell you now the difference between harpooning swordfish and catching them on rod and reel. When the commercial fisherman arrives on the swordfish ground, all aboard go aloft and begin looking for the telltale sickle fin and tail which clip the surface as a swordfish cruises about. Without a doubt, swordfish are bottom feeders and probably come to the surface when digesting their food and to get a little sun. Therefore, they are apt to show but little interest in the sport fisherman's baits. But the market fisherman has no such trouble; he sights the fish and bears down on him. The helmsman puts the striker, on his pulpit, directly over the fish. From this position he can easily drive in the dart or lily iron, which is fastened to 500 feet of line attached to a keg. This keg is thrown overboard and the fish pulls it about until he is exhausted, a matter of a few minutes at best. The dart is thrown from a 10-foot pole which detaches itself as it enters the fish. A good striker can harpoon a fish under water also. On the other hand, it is almost impossible for a rod and reel man to bait a swordfish that is not on the surface.

Finding his fish is a much more difficult undertaking for the sport fisherman, owing to the fact that only a few boats have masts as high as those of the marketmen. Once the fish is sighted, then begins the matter of presenting the bait in such a fashion that the broadbill will see it. It seems to me that the broadbill has the poorest eyesight and the worst sense of smell of any big fish I know, but if he does see the bait and strike, the fisherman gives him plenty of line and lets him have it, as we say, which means striking him hard three or four times to set the hook, which it is hoped, will find a good firm spot in the mouth or stomach. The big fish strikes so hard and with such a tremendous swirl that over half the broadbills caught have been foul hooked, that is, hooked outside of the mouth, mostly in the head, back or dorsal fin, or else the hook has pulled out of their soft mouths. The broadbill must be fought with a very light drag at all times and handled with the utmost care because of the extreme softness of the mouth. It is, of course, impossible to tell where the fish is hooked until he is in the boat, and it must be taken for granted that the hook is in the mouth.

The most important factor in swordfishing is to have a bait that is correctly rigged, that looks right and swims with a natural motion, and that will not be knocked up the leader when the fish strikes it with his sword. This is a difficult job and few anglers or, even, guides have the skill necessary to do it properly. My first two broadbills struck on baits of my own manufacture. They were promptly cut in two, one piece flying ten or fifteen feet over the ocean. That, of course, was the piece which the swordfish chose to pick up. The other bait, a mackerel, was knocked up the leader. If a fish is hooked it is a great advantage to keep any portion of the bait from running up the leader, as other fish or sharks will sometimes strike at it, cutting the lines and leaders and freeing the fish. This is a common occurrence in southern waters. I know of one instance, off Montauk, in which the squid bait was stuck at the swivel, fifteen feet up the leader, when a big mako shark came along and grabbed it. For about five seconds both were fast before the heavy aeroplane wire cable was bitten through.

At Bimini, an automatic cut-off for the bait is a necessity if you are to catch any of the fish which you hook.

After experimenting for two or three years, the late Oliver C. Grinnell caught the first Atlantic broadbill in 1927, with Captain Bill Hatch as his guide. Up until 1935, forty-three had been taken, all on squid or mackerel bait. They weighed from 105 pounds to the record of 505 pounds, a catch made by Rex Flinn, of Pittsburgh. In 1935, fifteen were taken, seven more than in any previous year, and the number of strikes and fish hooked was doubled. This increase is attributed to the practice, originated by Captain Howard Lance, of using a large piece, practically the whole belly of a small tuna. Captain Lance took six fish for his parties, twice as many as any one guide has taken in a summer's fishing, and ten of the fifteen were caught with this bait. This season also saw the first broadbill taken with a whole weakfish and the first one taken on an artificial feather bait. In this case, the fish rose to the trolling bait and hit; this was what is called a blind strike, the fish not being seen until he rose in the wake, when the boat was under full headway.

The reason for the attractiveness of the tuna belly, apparently, is its oiliness. It gives the bait a much stronger odor than squid which has sometimes been washed to make handling easier and therefore has lost much of its ink. Leaving the little ventral and anal fins with some of the tail attached to the tuna belly gives this bait the proper motion in the water. Whatever the reason for its success, I know of cases in which swordfish have passed up a squid for the tuna bait. Of course, if you get it across the fish, say, three times, and he shows no interest, then switch to squid. If you still have no luck, try mackerel which has been somewhat successful in getting strikes.

On the way to the fishing grounds two baits of each kind rigged and ready for use should be prepared, ready with hooks and leaders, and put on the ice. The change can then be made with rapidity by using the snap swivel and loops on the ends of the leaders, thus doing away with the nuisance of tying knots. The swivel should be seized to the line.

My experience with broadbill has been that a fish which does not strike the first three or four times you offer the bait will not strike at all. However, I once put the bait to a gigantic old warrior fourteen times before he went down, and to two others, eleven times each. A commercial man usually can "stick" the fish if you are satisfied that he is not going to strike. An economic arrangement which is made with some skippers allows the skipper to harpoon and keep the fish after giving the rod and reel angler first chance.

But all these matters are of little consequence if the captain or the angler does not know how to rig the bait or does not have the proper tackle. Most of the "commercials" who have had long experience in harpooning fish can get a bait to them in fairly good style; but knowing when to pull the clutches, when to throw them in again, as well as maneuvering the boat properly throughout the fight, are arts which, as a rule, they lack. I will say, however, that some of our best rod and reel guides on the Atlantic Coast were formerly market fishermen and I am sure that a great many more of them could develop the necessary skill.

Some captains present a bait slowly, others rapidly. But, whatever you do, don't change the speed of the motor as you come up to a swordfish, as this may distract him. If he starts following the bait without striking, it is then good practice to speed up the boat to excite him. He has shown his intention and if he then hits but does not pick up the bait, which happens frequently, pull the clutches out and let the bait sink of its own accord.

The best fishing captains claim, rightly, that whatever fish you are trying to catch, the bait should always fit the hook and *vice versa;* in other words, a small bait for a small hook. For broadbill swordfish I believe the 12/0 Grinnell made by Edward vom Hofe, is the outstanding hook, due to its great strength and thick shank, which will not pull out of the soft mouth of the swordfish. This hook, with the standard stainless wire cable and a 36-thread line on a 12/0 Edward vom Hofe reel, and their 20-ounce hickory rod, or the Hardy No. 5 Palonka rod, made of the very finest bamboo, is, to my mind, a heavy and well-balanced outfit to use, particularly when one is after big broadbill. Many of the leading fishermen have switched to 24-thread on a 10/0 reel, and are using the lighter leader wire, known as marlin rope, on a 9/ or 10/0 hook. The reason for the change is, some feel, that the heavier line, leader and big hook tear out of the fish much more easily. This opinion is shared by Captain Tom Gifford and Captain Owen Duffy who were the first to use this line at Montauk, though, of course, almost all of the Pacific broadbills taken at Catalina have been caught with this rig. Baits should always be kept on ice when not in the water, and a good ice box, which is found on almost all of the better equipped boats, is most important.

I cannot help feeling that a great deal of the success enjoyed by swordfishermen at Montauk in 1935 and 1936 was due to the use of outriggers. In most cases these are long poles which extend from fifteen to fifty feet on each side of the boat. Most of them are made of bamboo, and a few of spruce. Many of the longer ones have bases of aluminum. The line goes from the rod tip to a clothespin run up to the end of the outrigger. Thus the bait is trolled outside the wake and at any distance one may wish. My practice is to keep one bait for swordfish ready on the ice but attached to the outrigger on one side and a marlin bait trolling in the water on the other. In broadbill fishing the bait is never put over until the fish is sighted but marlin may be expected at any time so in this way I am prepared for either. Even broadbill, fastidious creatures that they are, have trouble restraining themselves from hitting the bait skipping from the outrigger. The greatest advantage of the outrigger is that it keeps the leader wire completely out of the water so that there is nothing to arouse suspicion in the fish before he strikes. The fact that the bait is out of the wake is also an asset, since getting into the wake of the boat often drives the swordfish down.

Swordfish always seem to be full of whiting, squid and butterfish, in the order named; therefore, I claim that a whiting would make a highly effective bait. Few men have tried whiting, the opinions being that their softness makes it almost impossible to rig this fish, but in this I do not altogether agree. Why mackerel are used I do not understand, as they are rarely found in swordfish.

Up to the season of 1935, when seven more fish were taken than in any previous year, and a great many more hooked than ever before, I placed the odds against catching a swordfish in the course of day's fishing as follows: ten to one that the day you go out will not be the right kind for fish to be finning or showing; ten to one that if the day is good you will not see a fish; fifteen to one that if you do see one, he will not strike or you cannot get the bait to him before he sounds. In 1935, I should say that the odds against his striking were down to about five to one; three to one that if he does strike, he will not pick up the bait; five to one that if he picks it up you will not hook him, and eight to one that you will not catch him if he is hooked. My estimates, of course, are based on my own experience. I worked hard at it for six seasons at Montauk before I caught a broadbill and this fish was the twenty-ninth to which I had presented the bait. In that time I had only three other strikes and the fish I caught was the first one that had ever picked up my bait. It was a small one, weighing 181 pounds, but it had the virtue of being the right kind of fish.

TUNA

Early in July the arrival, at Montauk, of the bluefin tuna, that little torpedo of the Atlantic, is announced by a few catches of some of his larger brothers, weighing from 75 to 100 pounds. The average school tuna taken during the summer off Montauk weighs from ten to sixty-five pounds, and it is the great schools of these fish which are responsible for most of the interest in offshore fishing in this region. A few giant tuna have been hooked and several harpooned at Montauk but to date, 105 pounds is the largest brought in on rod and reel. These big ones go by the Point in June, headed for the herring grounds off Nova Scotia, and return during October and November. The smaller school tuna, however, are here all summer and when in the mood, will strike at almost any lure put over; when not in the mood, and this is about one-eighth of the time, apparently nothing will make them strike. The usual procedure, and the correct one in school tuna fishing is to troll rapidly, at eight or nine miles an hour, with a very short line—the length of a 15-foot leader is sufficient—keeping the white Japanese feather, by far the most effective bait, within the white water raised by the propeller, as this white water is the chief attraction for these fish. Some captains have chrome-plated their propellers as an additional flashing lure. To disturb the water still further, a keg, fender, or the very large teasers are often towed close behind. The water, disturbed in this way, brings the tuna up very close and the angler fishing a very short line will catch many of these little speed demons. It is always hard to make beginners believe in the effectiveness of these tactics, and particularly in that of using the short line, though this practice is accepted by all the successful tuna fishermen and guides in northern waters for taking fish of this size.

A 9/ or 10/0 hook is large enough and a 12-ounce tip with a 6/0 reel filled with 900 feet of 18-thread Ashaway line, is about right for the beginner. The expert may use 6/9 or 3/6. You will find both extremely sporty, but at Montauk, where it is a simple matter to fish four or five rods at once, the man who tries very light tackle risks making himself unpopular with his fishing companions. Though he may catch tuna, he usually succeeds in keeping others from getting their share of the fish while he continues his long drawn-out battles. And he may even be the cause of losing the school which, in most cases, continues to follow a hooked fish.

Observation has led me to the conclusion that, off Montauk, small tuna act in three different ways. First, they may be biting furiously; you catch them from schools you may not even see and many blind strikes are made.

Second, the schools sighted are rippling the surface; the fish are not jumping, rolling or feeding. When you circle them, make certain you do not run them down and you will find that they strike at once. By keeping a hooked fish swimming behind the boat, you will be able to arouse the whole school and keep it there. The chances are that nine times out of ten you will catch all the fish you can possibly use. I have seen guides hold a school for miles by this maneuver. If keeping a hooked tuna astern does not work, try bleeding a fish into the wake, also put blood on the feather. This may draw sharks but will probably hold the tuna as well.

Third, the tuna may be jumping, breaking water, or playing on the surface.

In this case, they are either feeding or have just fed, and your troubles begin. I have stayed in schools all day long, tried every jig that is made and all the different baits; I have varied the length of the line, have run fast and run slow, but to no avail. Finally, one day, Tom Gifford and Owen Duffy showed me what is, to my mind, the only thing to do under these circumstances. Take a very small, shiny, metal jig, shaped like a heart, which is known at Montauk as the butterfish jig. Edward vom Hofe keeps them in stock. Tie the jig to the leader, which should never be over six feet long for these tuna. Put the boat as close to the school as you can and from the top of the cabin cast the jig as far out as possible and into the midst of the school. Then reel in fast and repeat the procedure. You should be rewarded with a strike within ten casts. As your hooked fish comes into the wake, some of the others usually follow and fishing begins in earnest. When acting in this way, tuna are feeding on small fry and bait in the water. Gifford claims that the jig described is an excellent imitation of their food. The fish are more afraid of the boat when they are surface feeding and go down immediately. Between July 1st and September 15th there are very few days when the well guided fisherman does not get as many tuna as he wants off Montauk.

Tuna which has not been canned does not appeal to me, but some people like it, including almost all the Florida guides of my acquaintance. They cut a very fine slice from the belly and this, I admit, is fairly palatable. You will, however, never be called a "fish hog" for taking too many tuna as your guide can always sell them to the canneries and receive fair remuneration.

WHITE MARLIN

Independence Day usually finds the white or common marlin, which has been described as the jumping jack supreme, arriving in the waters between Fire Island and Marthas Vineyard. There these marlin congregate in numbers. These fish are taken from one to twenty-five miles offshore. I have heard of one being caught at Great Eastern Buoy and I have seen them jumping and feeding fifty feet outside of the bathing lines off the Maidstone Club at East Hampton. They seem to like to be among the lobster pots and are often taken in and among the markers attached to the pots. A favorite spot off Montauk is the Gas Buoy, five miles due south of the light. Usually, marlin travel in pairs and they are almost always headed east. I have heard Captain Gifford, after catching one fish, announce to his party that he will get the mate, and have seen him make good his boast by running east for five minutes and there finding the other fish.

Marlin feed on squid, mackerel and small bonitas. I have seen them in schools of the last two fish named, slashing around with their bills, and have trolled into the surging mass and come out of it with a silvery marlin soaring aloft on my hook.

The first white marlin in this region was caught in 1924 by Julian Crandall, of the Ashaway Line & Twine Company. In the eleven years since then about 500 have been taken off Montauk. At least 150 of these were taken in 1935, the finest year on record for all kinds of salt water game fishing. White marlin jump repeatedly and when fairly hooked, greyhound and tail walk even more than they do in southern waters, it seems to me. Perhaps it is the effect of the cold water. Up here, many are caught on the Japanese feather which is understandable as so many of these are being trolled for tuna. Marlin seem to hit and seize this lure with one motion. I have never heard of anyone catching a marlin who dropped back with a feather, as is done with a cut bait. The fish are sure to feel the metal head and will throw it in a jiffy. Dropping the rod tip is quite sufficient if you see one cracking your feather; as he starts off with it, hit him hard three or four times. The fireworks will begin immediately. But luck will decide matters as the heavy-headed jig sliding up and down the leader is very likely to pull out the hook. However, I do not recommend fishing for marlin this way. If you see one behind your feather, reel it in close until you can get a cut bait or whole squid overboard. This advice is good, of course, only when you have such prepared bait on board. It is wisdom to keep a couple of marlin baits always ready to snap on in a hurry if necessary.

When outriggers are used, marlin will rarely get in at your feathers on the short lines trolled for tuna. I wish to emphasize the fact that one day, in the great marlin season of 1935, I saw boat after boat come in with from one to four marlin, all caught by the use of outriggers. And on the same day I saw boats which had no outriggers come in without marlin. That skipping bait which dances so merrily and so teasingly outside the wake has a great attraction for white marlin. Their big cousins of the black, blue and striped variety respond to an outrigger bait almost as readily.

The proper rig to use for marlin at Montauk is the same as that for tuna, the 6/0 reel filled with 18-thread on a 12-ounce tip. But make sure that you do not use a short tuna leader by mistake; a white marlin leader should be 12 or 15 feet long and of heavier wire. A 9/ or 10/0 Sobey hook should be plenty big enough. The light marlin rope is also recommended for leaders, but not the heavy swordfish cable, which they feel as they hit the bait. Marlin like all the different varieties of cut bait. Whole squid or small mackerel are second choice.

To my knowledge, the largest white marlin taken off Montauk was caught by Alois Menschik, with Captain Walter Clay as guide, and weighed 117 pounds. The smallest weighed thirty pounds and was hung by Pam Blumenthal, fishing with Howard Lance. As many as four to a boat in a day's fishing were caught in the 1935 season and in several cases eight or nine were hooked. In my opinion, the white marlin is the gamest and sportiest fish of his weight that swims and certainly on light tackle, he has no equal. As food, unfortunately, the marlin is not a desirable fish, although natives of the West Indies like them. Unless the meat is smoked, it has very little flavor.

BLUE MARLIN

In the past ten years three giant blue marlin have been harpooned and brought into Montauk but I am sorry to say that none have, as yet, been caught on rod and reel. A great many have been seen and conservative estimates place their weight at over one thousand pounds. In 1935, Charles Lehmann, fishing with Captain Bill Fagen, worked one of these great fish for over two hours. All kinds of bait were tried, but without a strike. The behavior was like that of most broadbill, and quite different from the behavior of this fish in southern waters, where he is usually very willing to take the bait. More than likely, he gets more food in these waters and the fact that he has just finished a long journey and is about to start another may have some bearing. I have seen a blue marlin battling a tuna weighing over twenty-five pounds as he fed in a school of these fish. The largest one brought into Montauk weighed 892 pounds dressed for the market, and was eighteen feet long. It was harpooned by Harry Conklin, who mistook it for a gigantic broadbill. This fish towed the keg under water for many minutes and two sharpies were required to tend it. The market price was not enough to pay express charges. The other two weighed 650 and 700 pounds. What a tragedy that they were not hooked by a rod and reel fisherman! In 1935 several more were seen, but despite all efforts with outriggers, none were taken.

MAKO SHARK

Almost simultaneously with the tuna—he seems to follow the tuna in—comes the only desirable member of the shark family, the great mako shark, which ranks as one of the four finest game fish. Zane Grey says that this shark jumps higher out of the water than any other fish. I have seen them clear the water by at least fifteen feet. Montauk bears the proud distinction of being the first place where these fish were caught on the Atlantic Coast. Savage as a tiger, the mako shark will strike at anything in the water. I once had the hook tear out after having one hooked on a feather for five minutes. The fish then returned and grabbed the hook again. My largest catch weighed 220 pounds and jumped seventeen times in an hour and twenty minutes. It is said that while hooked this fish will bite the heaviest aeroplane wire leader in half and this I believe. Few other fish have such sets of teeth.

The mako sharks will not always jump, but usually they put up a good scrap and after being gaffed they live for a long time. They are said to be the only creatures which a broadbill swordfish fears. Fishermen of Eastern Long Island are familiar with the story of the great fight which Captain Fagen broke up. A swordfish had had his tail bitten off by a mako which had evidently caught him from behind and when he was sleeping. Fagen harpooned the shark first and then got what was left of the broadbill. The mako weighed over five hundred pounds. After lying on the dock some twenty minutes, it went into a flurry, knocked the swordfish and another carcass overboard and almost wrecked the dock, endangering some of the spectators as well. This happened fully an hour and a half after the fish was struck with the lily iron.

The mako is a lovely blue on top and a creamy silver on the bottom. The nose is like that of a big Douglas airliner—the finest streamlining you could wish to see—and how they can turn on the heat! The meat has a delicious flavor and I doubt whether it can be distinguished from swordfish. It commands a good price. No doubt, a good many epicures sing the praises of the swordfish while enjoying a bit of shark. However, I do not mean to imply that this fish is common.

For mako shark you need a 10/0 reel and 1800 feet of 24-thread line or heavier. There were many little ones, weighing around sixty pounds in the season of 1935 and 1936, and these gave great sport on light tackle.

Almost all the other members of the shark family are to be found off Montauk and any one wishing to catch them can do so with ease. They are all there, hammerhead, blue, sand, and others too numerous to mention. They are much harder to harpoon than swordfish. I have never been able to understand why people who like harpooning do not devote themselves more to sharks. The answer may be that they are too hard to hit.

The big ocean sunfish and many finback whales are also offshore throughout the summer. Blackfish and the orca or killer whale are occasionally seen, and two or three giant basking sharks have been harpooned in recent years.

BONITO

By the end of July bonitos are found in great schools, which appear from one to twenty miles offshore. At times acres of them are in sight. Three species of these game little scrappers come into these waters and they run in weight from two to ten pounds. The common bonito, or skipjack; the arctic, or watermelon fish, as he is nicknamed; and the fat and chunky member of the family, the oceanic. These fish stay very late, usually well after Columbus Day, and are joined in August by the little tunny, or false albacore, which runs up to fifteen or sixteen pounds in weight. To my mind, little tunny are better fighters than tuna of equal size. In the south, this fish is erroneously known as the Florida bonito. As bait, it is excellent. Any kind of tackle from 12-thread line on an 8-ounce tip and 4/0 reel down makes trolling for these Four Horsemen off Montauk a real sport.

Now and then, the old timers claim, the false albacore school up at the Point, right under the lighthouse, on the pollack grounds. (I saw this happen only once, in 1929. As well as I can recall, feathers and the cedar jigs did the trick then.) Certain seasons find great schools of frigate mackerel offshore. These are the largest of the small mackerel family. I do not recommend any of these fish as first class for table use as their meat is rather strong and dark. However, a great many people eat bonito, particularly the arctic, but all varieties are shipped to the market.

DOLPHIN

The lovely dolphin, the fastest and most beautiful fish that swims, was abundant off the Long Island shore in August of 1935. School after school of small ones were found congregating around every floating board, log and box offshore. Never miss trolling your feather, which is their favorite bait, around any kind of flotsam or around patches of grass or kelp, no matter how small. There are sure to be dolphin around it if they are in the neighborhood. These little fellows weigh from three to five pounds but many weighing up to twenty-five pounds are brought in each year. There is no finer fish for eating and the roe, to my mind, is equal to that of the shad. I do not recall a single year in which dolphin have not been taken off Montauk.

BLUEFISH

The bluefish, more popularly known as the fighting blue devil, makes his formal bow, usually, in the first week of August, and remains until after Election

Day. The early catches are made in the Race between Fishers and Gull Islands, or Plum Gut, which separates Plum Island from Orient Point, or in the tide rips at Gardiners Point, off the old abandoned fort. At first, the bluefish is inclined to be particular and will not always surface. A great many are taken by the tedious method of jigging with a hand line, using a heavy lead jig for a lure. Attached to the line is the disagreeable device already referred to, the drail; heaving and hauling this for a two or three-hour stretch is not much fun. A great many of these fish are also taken trolling off the beaches, a practice which will be discussed later.

By Labor Day the bluefish are biting well in the spots mentioned and also at Cerberus Shoal, Shagwong Bell Buoy, and off the Point, again directly under the light in the ever-busy tide rips. They are caught on the turn of the tide, by trolling slowly with a line about 150 feet in length. Feathers are the favorite lure, with a white bone and the cedar jig second and third choice. A 5/ or 6/0 hook, a very short wire leader, and a 6-thread line on any kind of reel will give any angler a real thrill and an excellent dinner, for the bluefish has few equals on the table. Young bluefish, or snappers, are plentiful in all the bays and harbors from Fire Island to Montauk Point, furnishing delight for the children while their elders go offshore for tuna and swordfish. Palmer's dock, at Threemile Harbor, East Hampton, is one of the best spots for these little fellows. Any afternoon in August, twenty or thirty incipient big game anglers are to be seen with their bamboo poles tossing the little bluefish over their heads on to the dock. Any kind of small silversides, minnows or killies are ideal bait.

STRIPED BASS

The description of striped bass fishing at Montauk will be divided into two parts, trolling and surf-casting. The first appearance of this majestic fish is late in May. In July, striped bass are fairly plentiful but from August 15th to December 1st they are found in tremendous schools close to shore, for five or six miles west of the lighthouse, both inside and outside of the Point.

Trolling in the surf and rocks for these fish was first introduced at Montauk by Otto Scheer who built a small double-bottom boat, 18 feet in length and 8 feet in width. Her engine is muffled so as to lessen the noise, an important factor when fishing for stripers. The boat has a double bottom to protect her from the rocks and she steers from three different places. The helmsman stands on the bow and steers with a long, especially built tiller. Mr. Scheer's captain,

Bill Bassett, is a past master at bass fishing and knows every foot of the beach and all the rocks at Montauk.

A long line is usually trolled some 150 to 200 feet astern; 9- to 28-thread line may be used on a 3/0 or 4/0 reel, and a 6- to 12-ounce tip. Many a "strike" which startles the angler proves to be a rock on which the hook has caught. This is the chief reason for using the heavy line indicated. Also, a great many hooked fish will wind the line around a rock. It is fascinating to watch Bassett circle the boulders just outside the breaking surf as the boat goes up and down on the incoming rollers while he frees your jig or fish. Team work between captain and angler is most important in this fishing.

The feather is first choice as a lure, and one with a white eye should always be used. A 6/ to 8/0 O'Shaughnessey hook is strong enough, but if you have a Sobey, so much the better. Now I shall let readers into the secret of Montauk bass fishing. By using blood worms on the hook of the feather jig your catch of stripers, I venture to predict, will be at least tripled. A good many anglers paint their hooks red when they are unable to procure worms.

There are two or three boats at Montauk which are capable of getting in close enough for this fishing. A very able type of boat which is almost as practical as Mr. Scheer's *Pumpkin Seed* for this work, is the Jersey boat, Seabright dory, or sea skiff, as it is more commonly known. The most important thing is to have a native guide who knows the rocks, the beach and where the bass are living. Without this knowledge, trolling for striped bass is a risky sport and, sometimes, a decidedly dangerous one.

The largest bluefish and weakfish are usually caught when trolling for stripers. A day spent under the cliffs trying to outguess his majesty, the striped bass, will be one you will not easily forget. There is always action and plenty of fun as you ride the long rollers just before they break on the beach. There are a great many days when the striped bass will not strike at all. To me he rates among the first ten fish for fastidiousness in choosing bait. I am unable to agree in the opinion of most anglers that he is a terrific fighter. I should say that he is a hard striker, but unless he gets behind a rock the battle is an easy one. I have caught quite a few striped bass and I have seen my wife whom I consider no slouch as a fisherman, bring one of thirty-one pounds up to the landing net, in two minutes. This was on standard 6/9 tackle. The Ashaway line in use was at least two years old and so rotten that I was ashamed to have it on one of my reels. Catching striped bass from the beach is a much stiffer job and its difficulty is increased by the fact that a good many surf-casters use reels which are not as good as those used by offshore fishermen.

The best weather for bass is a light southwest wind. If it is blowing too hard from that direction the boat will not be able to get in close enough. A northwest breeze rates second but is likely, of course, to make the sea too calm. Northeast and easterly are not good, and you have to be very lucky ever to catch a striper when the wind is blowing from these directions. As a food fish, I rank the striped bass next to the bluefish. Catching one is almost the height of piscatorial good fortune at Montauk. The largest striped bass of which I have a record weighed forty-seven pounds, caught by trolling, and was taken by Mr. Scheer.

SURF-CASTING

Surf-casting is one of the sportiest ways of fishing. I often wish that I had more time to practice surf-casting and that I could improve my skill. No member of the angling fraternity, except perhaps the broadbill swordfisherman, works harder or needs more patience than do these enthusiasts. In all kinds of weather, they will stand knee deep in the rising waters off the beach, or on some slippery rock where there is hardly room to stand, casting their squid some 150 feet out into the white water. The surf-caster must be constantly on watch for a flush of bait or any telltale signs that birds may give him. He must know the beach, the rocks, the tide and wind, and must be ever on the move, up and down the shore, looking for fish.

At Montauk Point, surf-casting has been practiced for almost fifty years within five miles of the lighthouse both inside and outside. Commodore L. R. Hand of Riverhead, one of the pioneers in this fishing, caught his first striped bass in 1888. These fish were then taken by casting a hand line and sinker, the old heave and haul method, a far cry from the up-to-date rods and reels now in use. Most anglers prefer the long rod from six and one-half to seven feet in length. The butt is, of course, regulation for surf-casting. These rods have one or two guides, and the vom Hofe de luxe surf rod has a movable one that can be set at any point the caster desires. The Ashaway No. 21 surfman special line is the most popular, and a great many men use the standard 12-thread. A 2-foot leader made of piano wire is all that is required. The leading reels are the Islamorada, Beach Haven and Star, all made by vom Hofe. The Islamorada has the new star drag feature and the others vary in regard to width of spool and line carrying capacity.

Now we come to the highly important matter of bait. Many striped bass fishermen are almost as particular as fly casters. At Montauk, the most popular bait is the ordinary blue squid (jig) which, I believe, is known as the Belmar.

Yellow or red color variations are sometimes used. If these fail, eel skin is slipped over the jig and tied on. Second choice is the metal sand eel jig and if this does not do the trick, blood worms are resorted to, pieces of menhaden (moss bunkers), squid, clams or crabs bringing up the rear. An 8/0 hook is about the correct size. The only other equipment a surf-caster needs, besides his rubber boots, is a sand spike in which to set his rod when changing baits, a rod belt, lunch, a pleasant fishing companion and an inexhaustible supply of patience.

While casting for stripers at Montauk it is possible to pick up many fine blue and weakfish and almost all of the blackfish are taken in this manner. The last named, however, are caught only on the last five baits mentioned.

The East End Surf Fishing Club, a rapidly growing organization, with headquarters at Riverhead, erects four stands from which fishermen may cast. To make use of them one need not be a member of the club. These stands are particularly helpful for catching blackfish throughout the season and bass in the summer. This club has done a great deal for visiting fishermen at the Point and its members are always willing to advise the novice or newcomer. Fishermen visiting Riverhead would do well to stop at the club rooms in the Lee Building, where there is a fine collection of material dealing with striped bass.

As has already been stated, casters at Montauk frequently change location. Starting from the inside, about two miles west of the lighthouse, the best points for surf-casting are:

North Bar. East of Puritan's fishing shanty.
Jones. Best spot after easterly weather; also very good in fall.
Scotts Hole. Directly back of pond.
Point. Directly under light; three stands erected here each season.
Turtle Cove.
Browns. Directly under house with the windmill.
Stony Cove.
Kings Point. One stand here.
Cashiels.
Tea House.
Cocoanut. Very good in fall.
Morgans Cove.
Big Bend.
Cottage Point.
Ditch Plains. The last Coast Guard Station on Long Island is here. Very good in the summer.

Surf Club. The Montauk swimming beach.
Hither Plains. Next to the last Coast Guard Station.
Guerneys. From the inn east.

The last four points are particularly good in the summer.

The best tides for surf-casting at Montauk are the last of the flood and the first of the ebb, and I think that the best winds are the same as those favorable for trolling, namely, southwest to south, and west to northwest. There should always be some wind as white water is needed. If the water is clear, the bass is more suspicious of the bait. Most good casters get their squid out an average of about 125 feet, but I have seen many fine fish taken from hardly a quarter of that distance. Other fish that can be taken casting besides those already mentioned, are flounders, fluke, porgies and an occasional pollack.

Fishing for bass at Montauk in the fall of the year—the bass fishing is even better in November than it is earlier in the season—is an experience to treasure. The prevailing wind in the fall months is northwest, making for greatest visibility. The coloring is as beautiful as any that can be found in the East. On clear days, Point Judith, thirty-two miles away, is almost always visible to the naked eye and Block Island, half as far, can always be seen. Steamers offshore, fishing boats close in, and the ducks and geese winging their way to the west, add interest and variety to the scene.

Visitors to the lighthouse will receive a hearty reception from its keeper, Captain Tom Buckridge, who is one of the best surf-casters in this region. His assistant is the son of the late Captain Miller who was in charge of the light for some forty years. Captain Miller, I would be willing to wager, caught more stripers than any man in this country, and his hospitality to surf-casters at the Point will not be soon forgotten.

CODFISH

The cod, accompanied by the tom cod, returns to Montauk early in November, to remain all winter. These fish are caught on the sea bass grounds, using clams for bait, a 10- to 16-ounce sinker, with any kind of an outfit suitable for deep sea bottom fishing.

Boats for charter are available through Jake Wells who can be reached on the telephone by calling Montauk 90. Many of the captains live at Montauk all winter and are glad to make arrangements for chartering all season.

From various points in East Hampton Township, which extends from

Bridgehampton to Montauk Point, market fishermen put out five to twelve miles offshore in open Jersey boats to fish for cod with trawls. Seven or eight hundred hooks, baited with skimmer clams are used. These cod fishermen have my deepest respect. Their work requires days of preparation—digging the bait, cutting it, and baiting the many hooks. Then there is the long wait for fair weather that they may launch their boats through the breakers, a hard day off-shore, and another dangerous ride through the surf in the evening. Bitter cold, icy spray which freezes on their oilers and changing weather conditions, add to the trials of the life. All that stands between them and serious trouble is a little gasoline engine that was probably bought second-hand. In the old days these courageous men made a good living, but in these times it is hard to make expenses. They are a hardy group, many of them having gone offshore after whales in the old days when whaling was a flourishing business on the South Shore of Long Island.

All of the hake family are also taken in the winter, a good many ling, some pollack and a few haddock.

In closing, I venture the statement that there is no month in the year when fish cannot be caught off the eastern end of Long Island.

FISHING GUIDES AND BOATS

The guides and boats available for charter at Montauk should be divided into three classes: the men sailing from the Montauk Yacht Club, those sailing from the Montauk Fish & Supply Company, and from the railroad dock. In making a choice, the fisherman should take into consideration the following points: the type of fishing he intends to follow; whether he has his own tackle; and the record of each captain, which, nine times out of ten, tells the story of his ability. The type of boat is of the greatest importance, and consideration must be given the conveniences which the party considers essential in order to make the day a success. The boats and guides available have been known to me for some years and I shall try to give impartial information concerning them.

In the first group let us place all the guides sailing from the Montauk Yacht Club, on Great Pond, or Lake Montauk, its more modern name. These men are almost all Florida guides who bring their boats north; or else they run a boat for some private owner who wishes to charter fishing parties for the summer season. They do not arrive until late in June and by September 20th all of them have gone. I shall list the names of those who have made history at Montauk, though some no longer go there, having succumbed to the lure of summer fishing at Bimini. The native guides are permitted to pick up parties at the yacht club and they also take care of the overflow business.

I think it only fair to say, at the beginning, that all of the broadbill sword-fish, with three exceptions, have been taken by Florida guides, John Sweeting and Harry Conklin being the only Montauk skippers to catch them. These southern fishing captains pioneered the sport at Montauk and suffered many hardships and disappointments in helping to develop big game fishing at Montauk. However, it is also proper to state that the Montauk men have only recently begun to take an interest in broadbill fishing. No doubt, their showing would be better were it not for the fact that about ninety-eight percent of their parties want to catch only tuna and will not even try to find swordfish.

The Montauk Yacht Club is noted for the consideration which it gives the fishermen. The telephone number of the club is Montauk 105. Reservations can be made by calling this number. The dock telephone, which should be used in calling the guide in person, is Montauk 243.

In reviewing the fishing captains, let us begin with Bill Hatch, holder of the United States Atlantic Coast broadbill record of 505 pounds, taken by Rex Flinn, of Pittsburg [*sic*], in 1931. Captain Hatch has used the *Malobi* most of the summers he has spent at Montauk. Hatch also caught the first broadbill taken on rod and reel in the Atlantic. In all, he has ten broadbill to his credit. He has not been at Montauk since 1934, but has been fishing off Ocean City, Maryland. Hatch is popular with everyone and fishermen who frequent Montauk hope that he will return.

Captain Tom Gifford, with his *Lady Grace,* has been so busy pioneering at Bimini that he has not been at Montauk since the summer of 1933. When he left he had caught eight swordfish for his parties. For two years he held the record with a 430-pounder taken by Charles L. Lehmann. It is generally conceded that Captain Gifford did as much for Montauk fishing as any man who has been connected with the sport there.

Captain Bill Fagen usually fished the *Alibi,* which belongs to Charles Lehmann, in the seven or eight summers he spent at Montauk. Fagen has a total of eleven fish to his credit, and thus rates as high man up to 1936. He, too, has caught the Bimini fever.

Captain Douglas Osborne has served as mate for Gifford and Fagen and is one of the most capable of the men operating at Montauk. He has a 38-foot Elco, the *Judy,* which is equipped with twin motors.

Captain Howard Lance, in his boat, the *Cheerio,* caught six fish in 1935, three more than any other man ever took in a summer's fishing, and hung the largest one of the season weighing 460 pounds for Pam Blumenthal, making eight fish in all. Lance has a fine boat and is generally popular. In 1934 and 1935 he was high man at Montauk for broadbill and mako. He has ten broadbill in all.

Captain Owen Duffy, one of the most able men ever to round the Point, is another former mate of Gifford and Fagen. He is skipper of Landon Thorne's fishing boat, the *Twister*. Captain Duffy has eight fish to his credit and in 1935 with Mr. Thorne caught the third largest, which tipped the scales at 418 pounds.

Captain Walter Clay is an able skipper who comes north each year without his boat and is available for work with private parties. In 1935 he was skipper for Alois Menschik and caught two fish, one of 420 pounds, next to the largest catch of the year. He holds the Montauk white marlin record of 117 pounds. In 1936, he also caught two swordfish.

Captain Fred Wicht has taken one broadbill and is skipper of *Akela II*, owned by E. I. Low.

Captain Jack Kelley fishes the *Aunt Frances*, owned by Rolph Floyd, and has had great success with tuna and marlin during the seasons of 1934, 1935 and 1936.

Captain Charley Thompson who fishes the *Blue Shadow*, owned by Jay Holmes, has caught one broadbill on rod and reel. He is a fine harpooner and his unerring aim has been responsible for bringing in many giant sharks and sunfish. He is credited, also, with the catch of a baby whale.

The charge for these boats in this group is $50.00 on week days and $60.00 on Saturday, Sunday and holidays. All are completely equipped with outriggers, fishing chairs, ice and bait boxes, lookouts, steering control from two or three different places, twin motors and double rudders. Tackle, including leaders, hooks and all necessary bait, is provided at this figure. Considering the expense involved, the price is not high. My guess would be that gasoline bills amount to at least $20.00 a day. A good many of the men have added expense of shipping their boats back and forth from Florida and, of course, there are days when it is too rough to go outside. I must say that I have never yet found a charter boat captain who has grown wealthy in the sport fishing game and my feeling is that the men deserve every cent they get. The overhead on a boat takes most of the profit. Split between the members of a party, the cost of a day's fishing is really a modest sum.

In the second group I will run over the boats and their skippers who are natives from Montauk, and with the exception of Captain Harry Conklin, his son-in-law, Carl Erickson, and John Sweeting, who sail from the Yacht Club, the other party boats leave from the Montauk Fish and Supply Company's

Dock, Montauk Village opposite the railroad station, which as I stated early in this chapter, is managed by Jake Wells, and his telephone number is Montauk 90.

First we will take Captain Harry Conklin, whose personal telephone number is Montauk 245. Harry is one of the smartest fishermen and greatest fellows I have ever had the good fortune to sail with. He knows every foot of the Atlantic from Cape Cod to Fire Island. If you have a chance to go out with him, and the privilege of making his acquaintance, it is worth the trip whether you catch fish or not. He has taken three broadbill swordfish, including my own, and has caught as many marlin and tuna as any other man fishing out of Montauk. He has a brand new boat, built in 1937, named the *Duchess*. She is forty-one feet long and is completely equipped with outriggers, dual controls, a lookout, twin rudders and is powered with two Chryslers. The boat has four swivel chairs in its cockpit, which is a new idea. Captain Conklin is the only man at Montauk who carries two in his crew besides himself, which enables him to keep one man aloft looking for fins, all the time. Captain Conklin will be the first man to use a wireless telephone in 1937 at Montauk, by which he will be in constant communication with Captain Erickson, whose boat is also so equipped. They will be able to keep each other informed on fishing conditions, which should prove a great help.

Captain Carl Erickson is Harry Conklin's son-in-law, and he owns two boats, the *Lillian* and the *Vagabond*. The *Lillian* is a beautiful Wheeler, thirty-four feet long and completely equipped with outriggers, fishing chairs and dual controls. Erickson is a marvelous fisherman and has a most attractive, quiet personality and has fished out of Montauk all his life. He is one of the younger men, and I predict a great future for him. His other boat is a converted beam trawler, which makes a very good party boat, and is run by Captain Bill Dunn. Erickson's telephone number is the same as Conklin's—Montauk 245, and he has all the tackle.

Captain John Sweeting is a very able fisherman and has two broadbill swordfish to his credit. He has had great success with his parties and has all the equipment. His boat, the *Ranger,* is equipped with twin motors, and has a fine pair of outriggers. His telephone number is Amagansett 122.

Captain Budd King, also owns two boats, the *Lucky Seven*—a fine 38-foot Matthews, completely equipped—and a 40-foot cruiser, the *Norwest*. They are both completely outfitted, and Budd King is a very fine guide who I guarantee will give any party a wonderful day of sport. The *Norwest* is run by Captain Frank Edwards, when she is booked, and he is a very able man. I cannot recommend Captain King too highly, and his telephone number is also Montauk 245.

Captain Sheldon Miller fishes the *Ruth M.*, an extremely fast boat, 36 feet in length. She is equipped with chairs and outriggers. Captain Miller is exceedingly successful fishing off the Point. He, too, is reached by calling Montauk 245.

Captain Charles Tuma, Montauk 249, has a 32-footer, the *Dawn*. She has a high speed engine and is equipped with fishing chairs and dual controls.

Captain Harold Steck's *Rogue*, a 30-footer, is equipped with chairs. Many anglers have had great success with him. His telephone number is Montauk 14.

Carl Krieser and John Erickson both have converted beam trawlers for sport fishing which are equipped with all conveniences and have fishing chairs. Their telephone number is Montauk 90.

All of these boats are single-motored with the exception of John Sweeting's *Ranger*, which has two engines. But with the number of boats fishing off Montauk and the coastwise traffic, I feel that there is little occasion for fear in the event of being stopped offshore. The engines are first class and are consistently looked after, and I have never met a fishing captain who is not an able mechanic and a past master at keeping a motor in shape.

The men listed above charge from $25.00 to $40.00 a day, and are to be found at Montauk the year round.

In the second group is Captain Tom Rose, a free-lance fishing guide who is always glad to go offshore with a party in need of a skipper. He is one of the best navigators on Long Island and a fine fisherman with a long experience to his credit. In the last few years he has caught many marlin and tuna for his parties and he was one of the first native men to take an interest in rod and reel fishing. His telephone number is East Hampton 970. Captain Frank Edwards is another Montauk man available in the summer, who has no boat. His telephone number is Montauk 90. These men charge $15.00 per day.

In group three, we have the boats leaving from the railroad dock where the excursion trains arrive. This dock is in charge of Captain Walter Willis, with headquarters at the Fishing Information Bureau, in the lower concourse of the Pennsylvania Station in New York City, telephone number, Pennsylvania 6-6000. The following boats may be engaged by calling that number. Captain Bill De Waal's *Kneetop*, which is 40 feet long, completely equipped with chairs and outriggers; Captain Carl Derenberg's *Fortenate*, similarly equipped. These two, with Captain Lynn Simmons' *Mi-Joy*, and Captain Art Bengston's *Naomi*, complete the list of the better equipped boats for offshore fishing.

Other Montauk men sailing from the railroad dock who specialize in bottom fishing and inshore trolling are:

Captain	*Name of Boat*
Sam Edwards	*Montauk*
H. N. Edwards	*Mary A.*
Richard Edwards	*Robert E.*
Kenneth Edwards	*Magdalene*
Joshua Edwards	*Jennie*
Dan Grinshaw	*Viking*
Ed Vale	*Agnes*
Peter Burke	*Alice R.*
Gene Beckwith	*Peerless*
George Beckwith	*Fearless*
D. Lawson	*Helen L.*
Fred Pitts	*Mary*
Eli Pitts	*Nellie*
Peter Olsen	*Pollie*
Dan Racket	*Marjorie*

The boats owned by the Edwards brothers are converted submarine chasers, 110 feet in length, which are particularly comfortable for bottom fishing. The charge is $2.00 per person, including bait. The other boats are beam trawlers which go offshore, of course, and which are also used for trolling around the Point. They accommodate a good many fishermen. When chartered for a group, the rate is usually $30.00. However, they are not equipped with as many modern conveniences for fishing or for personal comfort, as are the boats leaving from the Montauk Yacht Club and the Montauk Fish and Supply Company.

WEATHER CONDITIONS AND PERSONAL EQUIPMENT

Naturally, weather conditions frequently play a big part in the day's catch. I have often said that the longer I fish, the less sure I am about the effect of weather on the catch. The man who makes bold to predict whether the fish will be biting or not is regarded either as a fool or a stranger to the game. However, I shall run the risk of venturing a few opinions.

For all the offshore fish, broadbill, marlin, tuna and the different varieties of bonito, I prefer first, a light wind from the southwest; second, a wind from the south and third, from the west. While some do not agree with me, I do not favor northwest as it usually makes the day much colder, even though it is sure to be very clear with fine visibility. My experience at Montauk has been that fish are not surfacing when the wind is in this direction. North, of course, is usually very cold, and while I have had some good fishing days on a southeast wind, they have been rare. East and northeasterly winds render conditions for swordfish hopeless and are very poor for all other varieties. In swordfishing, of course, it is difficult to pick up fins when it is blowing, but I have always felt that the percentage of strikes is greater if there is a good breeze, and one from the southwest suits me perfectly.

I have had fine fishing in the fog off Montauk; you are always able to pick up a fin near the boat, even though you can see but a short distance. A great many days when it is foggy at the Point you find weather beautiful ten miles offshore. And the variation between the weather at New York and Montauk is frequently striking; many days which are rainy and disagreeable in New York are fine at Montauk.

For inshore fishing, such as for pollack and bluefish, any wind, with the exception of east and northeast, is good.

As for clothing, aside from a heavy sweater or tee shirt and, possibly, an oil suit, one needs no warm clothing off Montauk in the summer months. In the late fall and early spring, a sheepskin jacket and sea boots, or the higher hip variety, are a great comfort, and a complete set of oilers is a necessity. In the list of accessories, I should certainly place a camera as photographs are the only thing you will have to show for your catches in the years to come, unless you have your fish mounted. Moving pictures are, of course, interesting. I like to have a good pair of field glasses; they are useful in distinguishing the difference between shark and swordfish fins at a distance, in sighting the many varieties of birds, and in discovering whether or not a brother angler is fighting a fish. The Zeiss Silverem 6×30 is the best all around glass, in my opinion, for use on a fishing boat; while the 7×50 has a larger field, and is much more powerful, being ideal for the yachtsman, it is a trifle large to use on a small boat where there is a good deal of motion.

A piece of equipment which serves any fisherman well is the long, peaked Block Island swordfishing cap, on sale at Abercrombie & Fitch, and Edward vom Hofe, in New York City, as well as at Montauk. For protection against the sun and wind and as an aid for picking up fins, I believe it the best hat that can be worn. And the cost is only thirty cents.

HOTEL ACCOMMODATIONS

The question of where to stay on Eastern Long Island is a simple one to answer. On the north fluke of the Island, the Henry Perkins Hotel in Riverhead, and the Greenport House at Greenport, are first class and there are several other desirable places in Jamesport, Mattituck and Southold. In Flanders, halfway between Riverhead and Hampton Bays, the Brewster House is frequented by fishermen, and Canoe Place Inn at Hampton Bays, is one of the best known and most attractive road houses in the eastern part of the United States. These hotels cater particularly to the fisherman and are glad to serve breakfast in the small hours of the morning. All of them are open the year round. Proceeding east from Hampton Bays, on Route 27, the Irving House in Southampton, is open only in the summer; and at Bridgehampton is the Hampton House, a delightful hostelry which caters to fishermen all year round. In East Hampton, the Maidstone Arms, situated on the main road opposite the pond, is open the year round. This hotel is an outstanding one in the fishing world. The Hunting Inn, situated on Main Street in the same village, is also an attractive place to stay.

Approaching Montauk over the old road, the fisherman will pass picturesque Guerney's Inn where the good striped bass fishing begins. It is an attractive spot and a convenient place for the surf-caster to put up. The prices, however, are high. A little further to the east, on the outskirts of Montauk, is Second House Inn. As the name implies, this was the second house built on Montauk. It is a charming place and its location is convenient for the fisherman.

On a high hill directly above the village of Montauk is Montauk Manor, one of the finest hotels in the East. You pay for what you get but you will find the hotel exceedingly well run. The Montauk hotels are open during the summer months only. The Maidstone Arms, at East Hampton, is the only hotel near Montauk which remains open all year. But wherever you stay on the eastern end of Long Island, you will find hospitality at its best.

WEAKFISH, PECONIC BAY

When the great hordes of yellow fin warriors, the weakfish, begin to arrive at Peconic Bay for their annual spring and summer visit, that lovely body of water and the country surrounding it are at their best. To my mind, the month of

May is the best time of the year on Eastern Long Island. It is possible for the angler who comes out from New York by train or automobile in pursuit of great tide-running weakfish to be at his fishing within two hours. At the following places, boats may be chartered and bait purchased: Riverhead, Jamesport, New Suffolk, Cutchogue, Mattituck, Southold and Greenport on the north fluke; and Canoe Place, Southampton and Sag Harbor on the south.

Peconic Bay which lies between these picturesque shorelines, is about twenty miles long and averages five to seven miles in width. It is famous for its oysters and shell fish the year around, for duck shooting in the fall and fishing in the summer. Directly off New Suffolk lies lovely Robins Island. No doubt you have eaten the famous oysters named for it and which are taken from the surrounding tide rips. It is from these same rips, known as the North and South Race, that some of the best fishing is to be had. Going east, we come to the famous Middle Ground, and three miles further is Jessups Point, probably the best known weakfishing spot in the country.

The usual procedure in catching weakfish is to throw over great quantities of shrimp for chum; the big weakfish follow the chum line right up to the boats. They are usually taken on the No. 1 Sproat hook, with a 3-foot leader; sometimes, when the tide is not exactly right, the very smallest lead jig is resorted to so as to get the line beneath the surface. The usual baits, besides shrimp, are blood and sand worms, and only the very lightest tackle should be used. Many anglers bring their fresh water outfits and a trout or bass rod makes for even more fun. Sometimes, when the fish do not surface, bottom fishing is practiced and many are taken this way, squid being used for bait. A great deal of this kind of fishing is done at night, in the body of water known as the South Ferry, lying between North Haven and Shelter Island. This spot is only ten minutes by water from Sag Harbor. Here, the fish, as they swim on their way into Peconic, always bite freely. The view at this point is a beautiful one; the fresh water fisherman sitting in his rowboat, which is all that is needed, might be on a lake in the Adirondacks or in some remote spot among the Thousand Islands. Eastern Suffolk County, it has always seemed to me, combines the characteristic aspects of a number of localities and it offers a great variety of outdoor sports.

Peconic is one of the best spots for the early flounder, and the kingfish is caught there all summer. Plenty of porgies and snappers are also taken. In the summer months, the common swellfish becomes the bane of a good many Peconic anglers, stealing the baits and hooking themselves. Swellfish are very good eating; a great many Eastern Long Islanders make salad of the meat. The swellfish is popularly known as blowfish, a name descriptive of their behavior when they are attacked. When boated, the same result can be obtained by scratching the belly. Children never fail to gain amusement from catching them.

The squeteague, as the weakfish is sometimes called, is a fair fish on the table and tastes best fresh from the water. I am sorry to say that, in recent years, there has been frightful waste in taking these fish in Peconic Bay and I am afraid that the supply will be seriously impaired unless measures are taken to protect them. I have seen as many as two and three hundred fish, weighing up to three or four pounds, thrown overboard from a party boat because the anglers did not care to have the small ones, and from reliable sources, I have heard stories of over five hundred of these fish being left on the docks at New Suffolk by a single boat. In part, the fault must, of course, be placed on the captain. The angler must remember that almost all of these fish come to the bay to spawn; if the present wastefulness continues, the fishing will not last much longer. The largest weakfish ever caught was taken from the Middle Ground by Fred Couzen, of Riverhead, and weighed 17 pounds 3 ounces, the world's record.

The average price for charter boats in Peconic Bay varies from $15.00 to $25.00 a day. Frequently, eight to a dozen anglers fish at once, so the cost of a day's sport is a small item if divided. The party pays for the chum, which is expensive, averaging from sixty cents to one dollar per quart, depending upon whether shrimp is plentiful or not. It is nothing for a boat to use a dozen quarts in a day. I might also add that blood worms are also an expensive item.

MORICHES INLET

In March, 1931, a terrific southeast storm with an abnormally high tide on a full moon, was the means of starting a new fishing center at Westhampton Beach, Long Island. The ocean broke through the beach and opened up an inlet opposite East Moriches. It is now deep enough for boats drawing up to six feet of water to go through, and there are one or two guides to be found and a good many party boats available at this place. An occasional swordfish is to be seen offshore and a good many tuna have been caught. The bluefishing and trolling for stripers in the surf off the inlet has been the best on Long Island outside of Montauk. On Shinnecock Bay, there is good flounder fishing and after August first the snappers are abundant from Fire Island east.

BLOCK ISLAND

No salt water fishing enthusiast should miss a trip to Block Island. The place has a charm all its own and literally smells of fish. Located sixteen miles east of

Montauk Point and about half that distance off the Rhode Island shore, Block Island gives one the feeling of being on an island out in the middle of the ocean.

There are two lovely landlocked harbors on Block Island. On the northwest side, with an entrance on Block Island Sound, is Great Salt Pond, called the new harbor. On the easterly side is Old Harbor. Here the fishing village, and most of the hotels, rest on high bluffs overlooking the Atlantic. Block Island is very similar to Montauk in general formation and the local belief is that Block Island was once a part of Montauk. There is an all year round population of some four or five hundred inhabitants, most of whom are engaged in haddock fishing during the winter months.

When you leave Old Harbor your fishing begins at once. Swordfish are often harpooned within half a mile of the shore, and white marlin are caught among the lobster pot markers off Southwest Ledge. Most of the rod and reel boats fishing out of Old Harbor usually join the Montauk fleet on grounds which are from twelve to twenty miles south of the Point. The fish, of course, move about and one day are closer in than the next, but it is always an easy matter to find the fleet if there is no fog. The Block Islanders have easy access to one of the best grounds, however, which lies to the east of Old Harbor and is called Cox's Ledge.

No better bluefishing grounds than those around Block Island are to be found. In 1930, while on our way to the America's Cup races, our party caught twenty-six fish in fifteen minutes' trolling off Sandy Point, on the northeast corner of the Island. The small cedar jig was used. The fish taken weighed from seven to ten and one-half pounds. Striped bass are also plentiful, and surf-casting is excellent. Naturally, all the varieties of fish found in Montauk waters are taken off Block Island. In view of the island's charm, it is surprising that more people do not make use of it. From Westerly, Rhode Island, the run by steamer to Block Island is only about one hour and a half, and some years a boat has been run from Montauk. There is also a flying field which is kept in good condition.

The four guides who have had most experience in rod and reel fishing are Harry and Ezra Smith, Mel Rose, and John Littlefield. Their boats are good-sized beam trawlers. These men are anxious to take parties and have shown willingness to learn all they can about sport fishing.

Block Island is the home of the famous Atlantic Tuna Club, whose attractive clubhouse is seen for many miles when approaching Old Harbor from the ocean. Many members come over every week-end in the summer months to compete for the club prizes in the various fishing competitions. The Atlantic

Tuna Club is the oldest fishing organization on the Atlantic Coast and has done a great deal for the sport. The author had the honor of being presented, in 1935, with the club's broadbill swordfish trophy, and he was the second member to receive this trophy.

MARTHAS VINEYARD

I venture the prediction that the place which will give Montauk the hardest competition for North Atlantic fishing honors in the near future is that historic and unspoiled old village, Edgartown, situated on Marthas Vineyard. For many years this quaint town has been the headquarters of a great fleet of commercial swordfishermen operating on two famous grounds, one only twenty-eight miles from Edgartown, and the other off Nantucket Lightship, some fifty miles further. As yet, no swordfish have been taken on rod and reel, and I doubt whether anybody has even put a bait to one. There are only two boats equipped to carry sport fishermen. But from the picture I am about to describe, you will sense the possibilities of the place.

From Edgartown, the course offshore to the fishing grounds is as follows: Run southeast for eight miles, to Wasque Point, on the southeast corner of the Vineyard; then proceed five miles more to the Southeast Corner can buoy where you will begin looking for fins and trolling for tuna. The course is now southwest by south, one hour and fifty minutes at an eight-knot speed, about fifteen miles. You will then be on the grounds, which are usually designated as eighteen miles southeast of No Mans Land. For fishing boats and yachts not drawing over twelve feet of water, a landlocked harbor, recently reconstructed and dredged, is available on the northwest corner of the Vineyard and is named Menemsha Bight. On leaving this harbor on the run offshore, you will pass close to the Devils Bridge Buoy, some five miles off Gay Head. Leaving No Mans you proceed offshore to the southeast for eighteen miles. The total length of this run is about twenty-five miles. Going inside, by way of Vineyard Haven Sound, the distance from Menemsha to Edgartown is just about the same.

Though I have carefully followed the statistics for the years between 1929 and 1934, I have made only two trips to Marthas Vineyard, but I believe that there are many more broadbill, marlin and tuna off No Mans after August first than at Montauk. A fisherman who goes offshore every summer has given me the following figures on his expeditions of 1935. He went out twenty-two times and was forced back only twice on account of bad weather. He saw twenty swordfish finning, harpooned sixteen, fourteen of them being killed. He counted fifteen more that breeched at short distances away. Thirty white marlin were sighted; sixteen of them struck, only three were hooked, and none caught. The answer, of course, is that these fishermen were trolling for tuna with feathers. Incidentally, they never returned without fish but they never attempted to use cut bait.

A 900-pound tuna was harpooned early in July, 1935, ten miles off No Mans and several big blue marlin have also been brought in by market fishermen. Most of these men go off for trips of two and three weeks to the Georges Banks. They take their catch to the Boston fish pier, New Bedford, or Woods Hole and if the price does not suit them, they proceed to New York and the Fulton Market.

As far as I know, the Georges Banks have not, as yet, been scratched by the rod and reel angler, but I am confident that this region will prove to be one of the greatest fishing places in the world. The Atlantic broadbill record of today may seem very small in the light of future catches. A blue marlin weighing 1230 pounds was harpooned on the Banks in 1932. From one vessel I know, twenty-eight swordfish were harpooned there in a single day, and over forty have been seen in the same length of time.

On the grounds off the Vineyard are to be found all of the varieties of fish caught off Montauk. From August 1st on, trolling for bluefish off Cape Poge

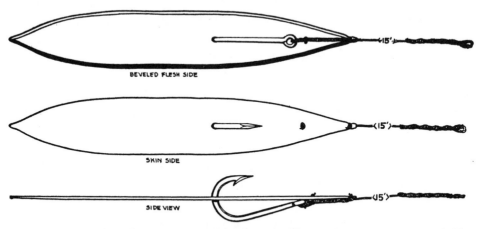

BEVELED FLESH SIDE

SKIN SIDE

SIDE VIEW

Broadbill swordfish bait as prepared by Captain Howard Lance from tuna belly for swordfishing at Montauk Point.

Light, or off Wasque Point, in The Rip, gives results equal to any I know. A great deal of surf-casting is done from Skiff Island. Plenty of striped bass are caught from various parts of the Vineyard and in July and August they are taken at night from the bridge between Edgartown and Oak Bluff, live eels being used for bait.

The two captains who are willing to take parties out from Edgartown charge $5.00 per person, with the understanding that they keep the swordfish. No doubt, a better arrangement can be made which would allow the party to present a bait to the broadbill. Captain Philip Norton has taken most of the tuna caught by trolling in his boat *Josephine II*, a staunch beam trawler which is equipped with theater chairs. Though Captain Norton may lack something in equipment, he more than makes up for the shortcoming with his knowledge of the vicinity and its fish. Captain Levi Jackson is the other Edgartown skipper who has had rod and reel experience. He has his own boat which is unnamed. Like Captain Norton, he has fished off the Vineyard all his life and has his eyes open to the possibilities of rod and reel fishing. If any readers go to No Mans, I should be interested in hearing the results of their fishing and to have their opinion of the possibilities of the region.

FIVE

Fighting Sharks

Hugh D. Wise

On Light Tackle—A White

C. Russell Bull, whom I call Charlie, lives when not out in his boat, at Townsend, near the point of Cape Charles, Virginia. He is a fisherman and he would rather fish than eat, which is fortunate; for, having to eat, he makes his pleasure provide for his necessity. He had regarded nets, traps, and lines solely as means of capturing edible and marketable fish until I came along and proselytized him to the shark game and so diverted considerable of his time from more useful employment.

At first he knew as little as I about shark-fishing, which was indeed not much, but he was an apt follower of an enthusiastic leader and together, he at the wheel, and I in the chair, we learned until we became an efficiently working pair of "nuts" and a menace to the asterospondyli, which is a "high hat" name for sharks.

Charlie's boat, a twenty-foot navy "barge," is seaworthy, well-engined, reasonably fast and handy, and it immediately caught my eye as just the boat for the sport. Its after third is an open cockpit in which I put my chair, but a few feet from the wheel, to have the angler be within easy communication with the boatman who in turn is within arm's length of the engine controls.

Forward of the cockpit is a little cabin in which are two bunks, a hanging table and cooking paraphernalia. All is simple and neat. It is just a little fishing boat on which two people can live comfortably and, if necessary, two more can live uncomfortably.

Charlie is not only a good fisherman and a competent pilot, but he is also an excellent cook. When we sail we stock up with staples, take plenty of eggs, butter, milk, fruit, and vegetables. The waters teem with fish, oysters, and soft crabs. On our trips we have no schedule and we are not slaves to the clock. In fact, the clock is of minor concern, for it is the tide which regulates our lives. When it is right for fishing, we fish; when it is not right for fishing, we eat and sleep. Meals are prepared when more important matters do not demand attention. If weather be good, we stay outside; if it be bad we come in for shelter and stay there until it is better.

There is always infinite variety in the sea and in the waters opening upon it—"Age cannot wither nor custom stale her infinite variety"—and, for the man who loves them, there can be no monotony. With good company, good air, good food, good rest, and good sport, knocking around in a boat can be just about an ideal existence.

We are not always after sharks and for a change, or to rest tired muscles, we may turn toward drumfish, bluefish, weakfish, or any other variety that will take our bait. Hence the assortment of rods and tackle which clutters the little cabin.

We usually get plenty of these fish, but on one of our trips we utterly failed, and it was a shark which saved us from being "skunked."

At that season the big weakfish, or "tiders," averaging from five to nine pounds, good sport on light tackle, should have been running strong; but they were not. So we went outside and chummed for bluefish. There should have been schools of them off Smith's Island and the Isaacs; they were not there. Having so spent Monday and Tuesday, we trolled on Wednesday for drums, but they too failed us. Thursday, a nor'easter put all fishing out of the question until Saturday, which turned out an ideal fishing day, with a light westerly breeze, but though we fished the channels and trolled along shore, our catch was nil. Sunday, my last day, with conditions perfect, found us two hours before sunset with but two fish—a pair of small weakfish.

We were then trolling for drum and had just come into Little Inlet, one of my favorite shark grounds, but it was six weeks too early for sharks and with a ten-ounce rod and No. 12 line, I was prepared for nothing heavier than drum. We were rolling along on the swell, hoping vainly for one of them to strike, when I spied a big fin. "Shark! Stop the Boat!" I shouted, and Charlie throttled the engine. "You don't expect to get him on that outfit, do you?" But I was already rigging a wire leader and a big hook onto my little line. "We'll try!"

The tide drifted us back, the bait, one of my little weakfish, trailing along beneath the surface fifty yards astern. When it reached the place where I had seen the fin, there came along the line the characteristic tug of a shark. He had firm hold of the bait but had not taken the hook so I slipped him a few feet of line, and Bang! he took the hook and I struck. "Whee-w-wee-w!" went the reel, and I seemed to be fast to a speed boat. "Follow him!" and I put on all safe drag. The little 4/0 reel seemed to howl with pain and I expected the rod to snap at any moment, for I was giving them more than reasonable strain. The boat finally got up full speed and we were following the fish, but he had out all but ten yards of my line when he ceased to gain on us. Then, with the resistance I could give him, we began to gain, and in the next two miles I recovered half of my three hundred yards of line.

Steering off on a course parallel to that of the fish, in another mile we were abreast of him and I had him yielding and beginning to turn. He circled nicely a few times, but then, changing his mind, he went off into another rush of several miles before I could turn him again. When the circling recommenced, the tide was carrying us out rapidly, so we went spiralling toward Spain. "Are you prepared to serve breakfast on this ship?" I asked Charlie. "I see no probability of catching this minnow tonight." "Not unless you and the fish will give me a chance to cook it," he replied, and the shark, unconcerned about our breakfast, spiralled out further to sea.

Land was almost hull-down when he sounded, and lay still and Charlie, taking advantage of this armistice, slipped the harness onto me. Hardly was I thus geared when the shark woke up and went off into another long and furious rush which, however, was his swan song for after it he grew rapidly weaker. The harness was now giving me relief and I saw to it that the shark got none.

Throughout the struggle this shark had puzzled me for he was faster than any species I knew, except the Mackerel Shark, but the fleeting glimpses I had had of a blunt nose and a massive body showed that he was not a "Mackerel." When finally he was brought alongside, his fins and fluke stiff, and his body motionless, Charlie struck with the gaff but, stimulated by the pain, the shark wrenched the gaff from Charlie's hands and went down for another half hour of struggle. Twice more was this repeated but when he came up the fourth time Charlie, leaning over the gunwale, finished him with a butcher knife in the gills.

Now we had our first chance to recognize him. The dark spots on his pectorals, his olive ventrals, his ashy-brown back, white sides, caudal keels and triangular serrate teeth identified him as a small though beautiful specimen of the Great White Shark.

On the boat side he measured nine feet and two inches over all, and we estimated his weight as well over three hundred pounds. He had cost me a sprung rod and a damaged reel but he was worth it. His vitality had been amazing, but the fool fish had helped to catch himself, for it was his frantic rushes and hysterical circling which exhausted him. For long stretches he was on the surface with spray flying over his bow like that from an aquaplane. Nevertheless, it took two hours and forty-six minutes, from hook to gaff, to subdue him.

Perhaps I should be satisfied that he was a modest edition of this largest and most ferocious species of our North Atlantic, for the Great White Shark is said to attain a maximum length of more than forty feet. Such a shark could not be handled on a cable and one of half that size would make the fight almost hopeless on rod for it requires a skillful angler with the best of tackle to land a ten-footer.

The Great White Shark is essentially a rover of the broad ocean though small members of the species do sometimes follow schools of fish into bays and estuaries. He must be credited or discredited with being the true "Man-eater," for it is against him that naturalists have most conclusively sustained the murder charge. Linnaeus even indicted him as being the fish which swallowed Jonah, exonerating the whale as being incapable of taking a man down his gullet, though we now know that certain whales could do this.

Before Linnaeus, 1758, sixteen other scientists had declared that Jonah's whale was a shark and one of the earliest of these, Heinrich Herman Frey, in 1594, devoted nineteen pages of his book, *Icthyobiblia,* to this subject.[1]

Even though one may not attach much importance to this question, it is interesting to learn how long and how vehemently this old controversy has continued though it is now probably of little importance to Jonah.

While but a minnow as compared with the prehistoric sharks, and much smaller even than the American Museum's megalodon, the largest White Shark of which I have heard in our times was enmeshed in the nets of the Ocean Leather Company at Cape Lookout, North Carolina, June, 1918.[2] This shark was credited with a length of twenty-two feet and a girth of eighteen feet and so would have weighed two and a half tons. Quite a fish for the nineteen hundreds!

It is a great temptation to go on writing about Whites and Mackerels, for there seems to have been an individuality in every one of them I have caught, but such a story would soon become simply "the same man caught another fish," and the reader, without the pitch of the boat, without the tang of the sea, without the whine of the reel, might be worse bored than I fear he now is, and besides I wish to tell about some other sharks.

DUSKY TACTICS

Duskies and Browns, which are somewhat like Duskies, do not fight in spirited rushes like Mackerels and Whites.

---

1. A copy of this book, published in Leipsic, may be seen in the American Museum of Natural History, N.Y.

2. Article by R. J. Coles in *Copeia,* American Society of Icthyologists and Herpotologists, May, 1919.

The Dusky *(Carcharibus obscurus)* is capable of considerable speed but he is more likely to base his stubborn defense upon his weight and power, and he thus deprives the angler of opportunity for making the fish wear himself out. If he simply sulks at the bottom and will not swim, the angler cannot make him circle. We might almost say that the Dusky does not work but makes the man work. If the angler does not force the fighting, the Dusky will simply offer passive resistance and apparently he could keep it up indefinitely. This calls for patience, skill, and strategy which lend interest to the fight with a Dusky though sometimes it recalls the old saying—"What's the use of kicking an elephant? You only wear out your shoe."

This shark is another suspected man-eater and certainly he is capable of being one for, averaging ten feet in length, he is stocky and powerful and his huge mouth is armed with dreadful teeth. Essentially a pelagic shark, he is nevertheless common to our inshore waters where he is not infrequently taken.

There is little trouble in identifying the Dusky because of his characteristic ashy-brown color, thick body, broad flattened snout, and extremely long falciform pectorals.

Among fisherfolk there is a tradition that he came to our shores during the Spanish-American War to avoid the gunfire in Cuban waters. Of course this is absurd, but he is often called the Santiago Shark.

One day, the Professor and I were chumming for bluefish fifteen miles off the New Jersey Coast and though we were not after sharks, our slick soon drew them. A sharp [*sic*] fin appeared, and then another and another until there were a dozen circling the boat at a respectful distance, close enough, however, to spoil our blue-fishing. I had aboard my tuna tackle, so baiting with a slashed bluefish, I began casting into the path of a large Hammerhead. He was, as usual, a very timid Hammerhead and he promptly drew off onto a larger circle. Attaching the rubber ball to the leader, I let it float out. When the Hammerhead came around he was mildly interested but sank out of sight. A moment later there came a savage strike which sizzled off a hundred yards of line and then a hundred yards more with all drags down. "The Hammerhead!" I shouted—"Up anchor!" for I knew what a lively time that big Hammerhead would provide. Then the fish sounded and I knew it was not the Hammerhead for I recognized the sullen drag of a Dusky.

He now had out about three hundred yards of line and he would probably try to go no further, so settling into the harness, I prepared to spoil his rest. He yielded grudgingly and after a half hour of pumping I had him at the surface fifty yards away. Then down he went and his resistance redoubled. I dared not put strain enough on the tackle to lift him; plucking the line, banjo-string fashion, and tapping the rod failed to excite him into a move. He simply lay back with a dull straight tug, satisfied, apparently, to hold his own and let the other fellow get excited. I could picture him there at the bottom—twenty fathoms down—nose in the sand—tail toward the boat, "weaving" to resist my pumping. Presently he went off into a short leisurely surge, then stopped again, and I resumed pumping whenever the tackle would bear it.

"Dusky tactics," I groaned to the Professor, "and we are in for a long sweat of it!" In another half hour the shark was almost beneath the boat where he was endangering the line by "keel-hauling" it. Then I got him almost into dart range only to have him dive again. Over and over this performance was repeated and again and again split bamboo and cuttyhunk were severely tested before he got the iron. He was not a big shark, perhaps only six feet long, and he had not worked hard—but how he had made me work!

These Dusky tactics do not provide excitement like those of Whites and Mackerels but they excel in requiring of the angler patience, judgment, and endurance. While I cannot really recommend the Dusky as a gamefish yet he does furnish the greatest test of self-control and, that failing, practice in language pardonable only to a fisherman *in extremis*. Also, a struggle with the Dusky should be good training for an oarsman or a stevedore. An angler friend of mine who asked why I wished to make a human derrick of myself must have seen a Dusky-fight.

ON HEAVY TACKLE—A GREAT BLUE

What was said of the Virginia Coast might almost as well apply to the entire Middle Atlantic Coast, and especially to the coast of New Jersey. There is a string of low islands and narrow sand strips standing off from the mainland as outposts against the onrush of the seas, and these separate from the ocean the almost continuous narrow sound which, in different places, we call by different names.

The water, too, has there the same gently rolling loveliness it has on the Chesapeake. There is a ripple, not a surge, to its movement and shadows from fleecy clouds, wafted by breezes laden with salt-marsh aroma, make myriad green tints on the surface. It is all so peacefully restful that even the gulls seem to dawdle in their flight. But through the inlets one bounds out onto the roaring blue ocean—What has all this to do with shark-fishing? Simply that the angler has his choice, as he had at Cape Charles. He may stay inside for little ones or he may go outside for big ones, but one of the uncertainties which go to make fishing interesting is that he may get the big one where he expected the little one, the little one where he expected the big one, or he may get neither.

I remember that, at the Virginia Capes, we had our angler lunching with John Smith, and the ships of the Jamestown settlers cut up his "slick." He will not meet John at Barnegat and the Indians killed most of those settlers long ago, but, musing, he may see explorers like Hendrik Hudson, Juan Caboto and others searching this coast for landing-places, or he may see founders like de la Warre sailing in to their new domains.

The altercation of the British and French fleets need not disturb him here though these waters are intimately associated with that fight he saw at the Virginia Capes. When de Grasse eluded Graves in the West Indies, Graves sailed along here hunting for him and then sailed back through these waters to meet de Grasse at the entrance of Chesapeake Bay and to be defeated there. Also, it was in these waters that Lord Howe played "puss-in-the-corner" with George Washington on land.

The fleet of transports which passed here en route to France from New York and Philadelphia is now replaced by a procession of peaceful coastwise merchant ships and frequently a Pacific liner bound for the Orient through the Panama Canal. Perhaps you could send shark fins on one of them to China.

We were out one day after tuna in these waters, trolling along over "The Ridge," an area of shallower soundings in the deep water off the Jersey Coast. My lure, flanked by the glittering splashing teasers, a hundred yards astern, skipped from crest to crest but it had failed to attract tuna, so at noon we had nothing to show but two large albacore.

A large Japanese steamer glided past, a quarter of a mile away, and across her white wake came cutting toward us a high triangular fin with rounded point. It ran so close alongside that its swis-s-s-h in the water was audible, while just below the surface, a long graceful form and a glint of blue suggested the species of its owner.

Dropping the tuna rod and seizing "Old Jim," my heavy tackle, I adjusted the ball close to the hook which John, the boatman, baited with half a bleeding albacore. When the shark came around in a circle he almost ran against the bait, floating on the surface twenty yards astern. He took it with a rush and headed straight out to sea. The whole thing was in plain sight. He had the hook. I did not need to strike, but I struck hard and, as we afterward learned, drove the big 14/0 Grinnell through the toughest part of the upper jaw where it held securely and where it interfered but little with the movements of the fish. The boat, too, was headed out to sea so we lost no time turning, and the engine "got the gun" immediately.

By heavy tackle, I mean that I was using heavy shark tackle, for any shark tackle might be called heavy, though it is not heavy for what it has to do.

Our three-ounce fly rods weigh a tenth as much as the trout we hope to catch on them and the lines will bear ten times the pull of a trout. If "Old Jim" were in that proportion it should weigh fifty pounds and the line should be a hawser.

I was especially glad that I was using what I have described as my "tapering line"; the first three hundred feet from the hook, No. 24; then six hundred feet of No. 21, and then six hundred feet of No. 18 to the reel; for this was an opportunity to test it. Notwithstanding our prompt start, and in spite of the resistance of the drags, the shark had out all of the No. 24 before we got up headway and when we had full speed he was out on the No. 18, a quarter of a mile away. Veering so as to take the fish over the starboard bow, retarding him with a fifty-pound pull, which also helped the boat, now forced ahead with open throttle, we held our own for five miles. Then we edged away to get a sidewise pull which finally turned the shark so that he began to circle as an amenable shark should do.

For an hour he raced around his course, covering more than a mile at each lap, in a surge of white foam, while we, at easy speed, followed on an inside circle. I had only to hold my end of the line against the resistance of the water to keep him circling. After about fifteen miles of this I tried to bring him closer but as he was not ready to come, I left him out on the big circle for more exercise. When he showed signs of weakening by slowing his pace, I pumped him in to the No. 21 line and then nagged him to greater effort and later brought him to the No. 24 where I "treated him rough." All through the fight this fish acted like a well-trained race horse, simply charging along his course with never an attempt to fly the track and I am glad that he never tried to sound for I did not know how deep the water was out there. When at last the iron was thrown, it struck in the vital gills and he died without undue commotion.

The aggressive and fearless way in which this Blue approached the boat and took the bait was characteristic of his species. The Blue Shark seems to have little dread of man and is the shark that gives most trouble to the whalers in their "cutting in" of the blubber for he is so bold in his dashes at the carcass that often he must be fought back with blubber-spades. Also, it may be mentioned as apropos of what has been said of ferocity and cannibalism among sharks, that those wounded by the spades are invariably killed and devoured by their companions.

The Great Blue, though a warm-water species, frequently cruises along our coast but he also ranges the wide ocean. It is usually this species that follows ships at sea; it is about the Great Blue that most of the sea shark-stories are told, and he is the source of sailor superstitions. Familiar among these is the belief that sharks follow a ship on which there is a dead sailor—perhaps they do, for in all probability they would be following it anyway.

HAMMERHEAD TRICKS

It may be remembered that it was a Hammerhead on the Chesapeake which literally towed me into this shark-fishing game, but it is not that alone which is responsible for the thrill I always experience when fast to a Hammerhead. He is a wary suspicious fellow who is hard to outsmart and he has gamefish qualities equalled by few other sharks.

This strange fish may have come down from some member of the Requiem group of sharks (Sand Sharks, Blues, etc.) whose slender body and pointed snout he exhibits in exaggerated form, while his flattened head extends to both sides in thin vanes that give him exactly the outline of a blacksmith's hammer on its helve.

Nature, always with a purpose in what she does, has given the fish this freakish head to be used for making his dives and loops, as ailerons are used on an airplane, and so erratic are his gyrations that once—I hesitate to tell it—a Hammerhead tied a knot in my line. I hasten to explain, however, it was a simple knot, not a bowline.

In contrast to other sharks, most of which have rather small, staring, amber eyes, the eyes of the Hammerhead, located in the outer edges of the vanes, are large, dark, and bovine, but please do not imagine that I am trying to make out a case of gentleness for him for he is, as his bladelike teeth indicate, as savage as other sharks, and as mean a devil as any of them.

Hammerheads are said to reach a length of eighteen feet though ten feet would be perhaps an average length for a large one. Because of their slender build, they are, however, lighter than other sharks of the same length.

They are top-swimmers, live-fish feeders, and as their lithe shape suggests, they are exceedingly fast.

The finest struggle I ever had with a Hammerhead was one day on a glassy sea ten miles off the New Jersey Coast when we spied a high sharp dorsal, "gaff topsail" sailors call it, cutting the surface half a mile astern and following straight in our wake. Slowing down our engine, I let out three hundred yards of line baited with a fair-sized bluefish. As the bait skittered along on the surface the Hammerhead overtook it, circled it and came on. There was really no disappointment in this because it was exactly what a man, familiar with this wary fish, would expect. We opened throttle, dragged the bait past the fin, and this time the shark dashed at it, splashed around it, showed great interest, but was still too timid to strike so we slowed down and then—Bang! He had it! On he came straight for us while I wound frantically. Fifty yards astern he seemed to associate us with his toothache; increasing speed, he swung wide around us, and I wound hard to take up the great bellying sag in the line. With the fish a hundred yards to port, the line came straight. I threw off the free spindle lever, thumbed the pad, screwed down drags, struck hard to set the hook and then—what a performance!

Straight toward us dashed the fish, whirling and pitching on the surface, barely clearing our bow. Then away he went—two hundred yards to the other side while the boatman, leaving his wheel, clambered atop the deckhouse to clear the line. Like a flash he turned and was back again, just clearing the stern while John, the boatman, fended the looped line from the propeller with a boat hook and I struggled in vain to take in slack. Again and again this was repeated and then the Hammerhead changed his tactics to short dashes back and forth on the surface, and dives and loops beneath it; once, in spite of our backing and turning, he went under the boat.

He had not been allowed to put much strain on the line but he was entirely too lively to fight at close range; so as soon as we could, we worked away on a long line where we could keep him under tension with the boat.

John had had a lot of practice with his engine and rudder, my wrist ached from winding and my thumb burned from the hot pad when we finally got the fish to circling. After an hour of that, the big gaff hook drove into his gills and the fight was over. It had been like a tarpon-fight except that this demon was bigger and stronger than any tarpon, and he looped in the water instead of going into the air. Hammerheads are wary, fast, and game but I have never seen any fish put up a finer fight than this one did, from hook to gaff. I forgot to measure and weigh this shark so I can give only my estimate—9 feet, 250 pounds.

TACTICS OF DIFFERENT SPECIES

I wish I could include here accounts of the fighting of the Mako (*Isuropsis make*) of the South Seas which is admittedly the sportfish par excellence of all selachians but I have caught but two or three of them and am not qualified to discuss them. I believe, however, that even that experience justifies me in concurring with Zane Grey that the Mako is "a premier sporting fish, as game as beautiful, as ferocious as enduring."

Dr. Grey published in *Natural History*, June, 1934, an account of his fishing for Mako in New Zealand, where he tells of the characteristic fight of this great fish which combines the tactics of tarpon, swordfish, and shark.

From the accounts of my struggles with sharks on the line, I have omitted those with the less sporty varieties and have told of but one fight typical of each species. Characteristic as I believe these tactics to be, they are not to be taken as illustrating fixed methods by which the various sharks fight, for, while each species seems to have a characteristic method, it is not averse to using the tricks of others.

The White and the Mackerel, of which I told, used speed and power out on a long line, sometimes at the surface, sometimes down, and they resorted to sounding. The Blue, a little slower than these, used about the same tactics though he did not sound. The Dusky did little rushing, stayed closer to the boat, and, from the beginning, sulked mulishly at the bottom. The Hammerhead, on the other hand, made neither long rushes nor soundings, but dashed frantically back and forth on the surface or dived and looped beneath it. Yet, I have seen Duskies run, Mackerels sulk, and Hammerheads sound. All of them are vital, powerful, and enduring, so if the fight were to be a test of mere brute strength, the man would be licked before he got well started.

Unfortunately for the fish, however, the man has more brains, and even an angler is expected to show more intelligence than a shark who, furthermore, is at a disadvantage. Reversing conditions, suppose the man in the cockpit to have a 14/0 Grinnell in his mouth while the shark, comfortably harnessed, tugs at the line to pull him overboard. How many hours would the contest last? Before the shark could call to the ray—"Give him the spear!" Then, hanging the man's jaws on a coral branch, they could discuss the fighting qualities of the human species—"Which is the gamest, Jew or Gentile, Ethiopian or Indian?"

RIVERS AND STREAMS

SIX

Summer Steelhead

Roderick L. Haig-Brown

The summer runs of steelhead to Pacific Coast streams offer fishing comparable in quality to that of the best of Atlantic salmon rivers, even though the fish are generally of smaller average and far smaller maximum size. Unfortunately, really good summer steelhead streams are few and far between. For some reason, the streams of the east coast of Vancouver Island, with the exception of the Nimpkish and to a lesser degree the Campbell, have no important summer runs. Some of the lower mainland rivers have fairly good runs. The rivers of the west coast of Vancouver Island are likely to have good runs; one or two streams in the Queen Charlotte Islands have runs, and there are runs in some of the rivers and streams that feed the great inlets of the northern coast. But with the exception of the lower mainland rivers and the Stamp River, which flows out to the west coast of Vancouver Island near Alberni, these streams are accessible by boat only and have not yet been much fished. Largely because good summer steelhead rivers are hard to find and reach, the interest of the average angler in this type of fishing is not nearly so great as the quality of the sport would suggest, and very little research work has been done. I think it is fair to say that neither the life history of the summer steelhead nor the relation of summer fish to winter fish is even nearly understood.

One factor which makes valueless any casual study of the fish is the difficulty of distinguishing, by any method short of scale reading, between migratory and non-migratory rainbows. Size is an indication, though in a stream with an accessible lake somewhere along its length a big fish—a five- or ten-pounder—may always be one that has made his growth in the lake and has dropped down to the stream from there. But in case of a coast stream with no accessible lake, it is fairly safe to assume that any trout, cutthroat or rainbow, of over two pounds has had some salt-water feeding—in fact, I doubt that the majority of coast streams have sufficient feed in them to produce even one-pound trout.

It is known that there is no structural difference between, say, a ten-inch land-locked rainbow trout of Buttle Lake and a ten-pound winter steelhead of the Campbell or any other stream open to salt water. It is known also that rainbows of land-locked lakes are likely to be migratory in that they ascend to tributary streams to spawn and drop down from those same streams, as fry or yearlings, to feed in the lake; and, more fundamentally, that any trout, even the brown trout which may appear season after season at the same feeding post, or the cutthroat locked in a lake with no accessible tributary or draining stream, will tend to move at spawning time from a feeding area to one more suitable for spawning and to return when spawning has been completed. So it is necessary to define what is meant by "migratory." When speaking of the winter steelhead the word means, as it does in the case of the Pacific salmon or the Atlantic salmon, a fish that spends the first period of life in fresh water, then descends to the sea and makes by far the greater proportion of his growth in salt water, usually feeding at some considerable distance from the parent stream and returning to it only at full maturity, to run up and spawn.

Such a fish is in the full sense not only migratory but anadromous—having made nearly all his growth in the sea he runs up the river to spawn. A cutthroat trout in an open stream is also fairly certain to be migratory; that is to say, he will move down to the estuary or out into the salt water near his river to find food that he cannot find in the fresh-water pools. And he is anadromous in that he will certainly return to fresh water to spawn. But he differs from the strongly migratory fish such as winter steelhead and Atlantic and Pacific salmon in that he probably does not move out into the sea very far beyond the influence of his river, and he is likely to return to the estuary daily at certain stages of the tide. And he differs from the strictly anadromous fish in that he returns to fresh water not only to spawn but quite often to find food; he will move up into fresh water to pick up humpback alevins in the spring, caddis in July and humpback eggs in the fall.

Fish are individuals, and the individuals of some species differ more widely in habit from one another than do the individuals of others species. It is possible to set an outline of what the general life history, feeding habits and structural characteristics of a certain species will be, but only with the mental reservation that a larger or smaller number of individuals will depart at some point or other from this programme. The quantity and degree of departure varies with the species; it is possible, for instance, to set harder and faster rules of migration for the humpback salmon than for the spring salmon, narrower limits to the feeding habits of the sockeye than to those of most other fish. It seems fairly safe to conclude that evolution has drawn these species, of more predictable habits, into a greater degree of specialisation, and while it is not necessarily true that less specialised species are at a lower stage of evolution, it is altogether possible that they are at present more actively evolving—that is to say, their imperceptible tendency, through a rather wide degree of individualism, is towards greater specialisation.

Most ichthyologists agree that all trout, all char, all Pacific salmon and the Atlantic salmon have been evolved from a common ancestor within what is, geologically speaking, a comparatively short period of time. It is not known exactly whether this common ancestor was originally a freshwater fish or a salt-water fish. Many scientists believe that it was a salt-water fish and that the habit of migrating to shallow water to spawn and of working along the shore to get as far in as possible, led the fish to the heads of inlets and bays and so inevitably up into the streams. Another opinion is that freshwater fish, driven by the search for food, gradually worked farther and farther out to the sea. Though the former opinion is probably more generally held I am inclined to believe that the second theory has a good deal to support it; the search for food certainly has an important influence in modifying the habits of fish at the present time. If we accept, for the sake of this present argument, that the common ancestor was strictly a fresh-water fish then the alteration of the humpback, which spends almost ninety per cent of its two-year life in salt water, is the most complete; and that of the non-migratory trout is the least complete. The alteration of the other species touches nearly every degree between these extremes.

While the degree of alteration varies with the species, it also varies within the species so that a sockeye may descend to salt water in its fry year, as a yearling, a two-year-old, or even five-year-old and a spring salmon may return to spawn after a year in salt water or after as long as seven or eight years. The factors influencing such variations are not easy to measure, but since the major part of the run of any species to a given river is likely to fall into one, or at the most two age-groups, it is not unreasonable to suppose that the habits of the species are still in evolution and that eventually all members of the species will more nearly conform to the general habit.

Somewhere in the line of descent from their common ancestor with the Pacific salmon and Western trout the European species—Atlantic salmon, brown trout and sea trout—must have had an ancestor common to themselves alone from which they evolved to their present state. At the present time the brown trout and the European sea trout, though each has a different life history and both are separated structurally from the Atlantic salmon, are themselves structurally identical. Perhaps it is not too much to assume that their species is the common ancestor of two fish that will one day be structurally different from each other.

Of all the native fish of the North American continent, the closest, structurally, to the Atlantic salmon is *Salmo gairdneri gairdneri,* which is the coast rainbow, the summer steelhead and the winter steelhead—structurally and scientifically one and the same fish, yet in practice sufficiently different from each other to require separate consideration. Drawing a dangerous parallel, match the non-migratory rainbow to the brown trout, the winter steelhead to the Atlantic salmon, the summer steelhead to the European sea trout. The inference then is that *Salmo gairdneri gairdneri* is the common ancestor of three future separate subspecies and perhaps eventually of three separate species.

The controlling factor in this evolutionary process is food. In New Zealand, where the rivers hold plenty of food for him, the rainbow trout has little inclination to move down to salt water; more remarkable still, in those waters the Pacific spring salmon, a strictly anadromous fish in his native waters, has shown a strong inclination to live out his life in the rivers. British Columbia's coastal lakes and streams are generally so poor in feed that they have almost exactly the opposite effect; brown trout of non-migratory stock show an immediate tendency to adopt migratory habits. The steelhead or coast rainbow, then, is adapting himself to this scarcity, and the adaption is so plainly a current process that one reasonably expects to find, between the full migratory habit of the winter steelhead and the non-migratory habit of some rainbows in streams open to the sea, a full range of variation.

It seems certain that this range does exist and that many of its degrees are evident in the fish of the summer runs. There can be no doubt that the bulk of the winter run is composed of fish which have spent two or three full years in the sea and have travelled long distances from the mouths of their rivers in this feeding migration; whether or no they are the progeny of truly migratory fish, these fish are themselves truly migratory, and the extreme rarity of immature fish in the winter runs suggests that they need the stimulus of maturity to guide them back to the parent streams. The same is probably true of the larger fish of the summer runs, though it is possible that even these make a less definite migration than most winter fish. But the smaller mature fish and the considerable proportion of immature fish to be found with the runs in some streams may well have grown to their size without travelling more than a few miles from the parent stream or perhaps without leaving the estuary; if estuarial feeding will produce a four-pound cutthroat one may expect it to do the same for steelhead.

I am well aware that this is an outrageous piece of theorising and that I am drawing inferences from experience on a stream that has a patchy rather than a good summer run of steelhead, but nothing could show more clearly how complicated the problem is. And it is not altogether unreasonable to assume that a stream with a varied and patchy run may have shown things that would have been harder to learn from a more orthodox water. The Campbell has a run of summer—or rather, spring—steelhead that is certainly not typical, but which seems to me strongly indicative of what I have suggested.

Though one has a very fair chance of picking up a fresh-run summer steelhead in the Campbell at any time between March and early October, the main run is generally to be found in the Canyon Pool and the Islands Pool between April 10th and June 1st.* The fish that make up this run vary a great deal in size and in degree of maturity, so much so that an account of averages and percentages does not present a very clear picture, and the figures certainly should not be applied to rivers which have a more orthodox summer run. The point of difference, I believe, is that the proportion of truly migratory fish—that is to say, fish which travel well beyond the influence of the river in sea feeding and return only to spawn—is much smaller than in the case of more typical rivers. The average size of a hundred fish from this run was 2½ lbs., with a maximum of 8 lbs. and a minimum of 13 ounces. In spite of this variation in size, the scales of every fish showed very clearly the change from river to sea feeding; ninety-five had left fresh water at two years of age and the remaining five at three years.

Sixty of the fish were returning to the river for the first time at four years of age, after two full years in salt water, but twenty of the others were veterans, between five and seven years old, which had also made their first return at four years. The remainder were back in the river after a very short migration and were all below the average weight. These and ten of the four-year-olds were quite obviously immature, and their return to the river was in no sense a spawning migration. Thus, the composition of the run differs sharply on several points from that of the winter run. It is composed chiefly of maiden fish returning for the first time at four, instead of five years. The proportion of immature fish is very much higher, and includes at least some fish as large as the smaller spawners. And, finally, 20% of the run is composed of fish returning to the river for the second or third time, while only about 10% of the winter run are

---

*It should be emphasized that this is in strong contrast to more orthodox summer steelhead streams. In these the summer run usually starts in the last half of May and makes good fishing in June, July and September. In August the rivers are generally too low, but the greased line method opens up new possibilities in this month.

veterans. Incidentally, this figure of 20% compares with a figure of 3.4% given by Long and Griffin for veteran spawners in the summer run of the Columbia.

Of the mature fish in the run, typical specimens were between 3½ and 4½ lbs., clean, bright, well-conditioned fish with firm scales and some spawning colouration. Of the immature fish, a majority weighed between two and three pounds and were very bright, with loose, silvery scales. Milt sacs or ovaries almost invariably showed some development, and it seems likely that these fish, running as true grilse, would have gone back to salt water almost at once and returned as mature fish in the following winter; in other words, this part of the run is probably not sharply separate from the winter run.

A broad theory would suggest that the run is composed of a nucleus of mature and truly migratory fish, accompanied by a certain number of slightly smaller immature fish, and drawing after them in their migration a certain number of mature and immature fish of a less strongly migratory type—fish feeding near the river or in the estuary. These last may account for the high percentage of previously spawned fish, since their shorter migration would give them a better chance for survival. Of the few kelts taken, it is notable that those under five pounds were in fairly good condition and had firm, red flesh instead of the white, flabby flesh of winter kelts.

Another peculiarity of this run is the high proportion of feeding fish. Over sixty per cent had food of some sort in them, and about twenty per cent had evidently been feeding fairly freely. This is probably due in some measure to the greater availability of feed during the warm months, and perhaps helps to account for the high survival; but I feel that it is also another indication of partial rather than complete migration.

The Campbell run suggests that a certain proportion of summer steelhead are not much more definitely migratory than sea-run cutthroat, and therefore that their progeny will not necessarily be migratory at all, though scarcity of feed will probably make them so. It also suggests that there may be an extremely close connection with the winter-run fish—that an immature fish running up with the summer spawners may be going to spawn with the winter run, and so, by rather remote inference, that summer-run fish do not necessarily produce summer-run fish. From the cultural point of view this is of vital importance. It may well be that examination of a more typical run—that of the Stamp, for instance, or the July and September runs of the Nimpkish—would show a sharp and clear separation—or the inferences I have drawn might very well fail to stand up under a proper examination of even the Campbell runs. But before anything of value can be done, the exact truth must be known. The present runs, even in good streams, are not large enough to stand the drain of heavy fishing and occur in only a small proportion of the streams that seem to be suitable; nor are they sufficiently good to be a really strong attraction to the anglers of other countries. But a complete understanding of the life history of the fish might very well show ways of building up the runs in those streams which already have them, and perhaps of establishing them in streams which at present have only winter runs.

The summer steelhead, like the winter steelhead, is probably an easier fish to catch than the Atlantic salmon, though one may well go about trying to catch him with almost exactly the methods that are used for Atlantic salmon. The larger mature fish of the orthodox runs are not likely to be feeding seriously, if at all, and in the low water of late summer and early fall the steelhead can be quite dour; but they are always, at any time of the season and any stage of water, essentially fish that deserve to be caught by the fly only, and fishermen are better advised to turn, in the difficult times, to low-water fly-fishing methods than to spinning and bait-fishing.

One of the most important items of equipment for summer steelhead fishing is a pair of felt-soled or well-nailed waist waders, and with them a belt or shoulder-strap to which a good wading staff may be attached. There is plenty of wading to be done, sometimes in heavy water and nearly always over round and slippery rocks.

As to the rod—well, the streams are of a fair size, particularly early in the year, and spey or roll-casting is the only way of getting out line in many places; so a double-handed thirteen- or fourteen-foot split-cane is not out of place for fishing an honest wet fly. I belong to a young and cocksure generation, and prefer for myself a single-handed eleven- or twelve-foot rod of the Wye or Wood type; dry-fly habit and early training have taught me to prefer keeping my left hand free for the line, and if the fish seem to suggest at any time that I change over to the dry fly or to greased-line fishing, my rod is right for the work. It is perfectly possible to use effectively a lighter and shorter single-handed rod than these; for several years I used a 10-foot Crown Houghton which weighed eight ounces, and before that a six-ounce rod; but with such small rods one is often reaching, and it is not nearly so easy to keep full control of the line on the water. A six- or eight-ounce rod will handle the fish, though an eight pounder in heavy water is a strain on everything and is likely to have fairly full charge of the proceedings for several minutes. I do not think it is possible to match the fishing more exactly than with an eleven- or twelve-foot single-handed rod, and if the angler finds this too tiring he will be well advised to turn to a double-handed rod unless he is fishing a small stream or in very low water.

Hardy's No. 2 St. John is a reel that matches almost any of the powerful

11–12-foot single-handed rods; it will carry 35 yards of IBI fly line with 100 yards of backing, or 42 yards of No. 5 line with 60 or 70 yards of backing. The makers generally recommend the IBI line for these rods, but I believe this line more nearly fits a 10-foot trout rod, and though it is good enough for low-water conditions it does not develop the full possibilities of a powerful 11-foot rod. The less amount of backing may seem too little, but it should be enough for summer steelhead, though they are strong fish and far more active than the larger winter fish. The strongest summer-run fish I have ever hooked was a $4^1/_2$-pounder, lying in a pool so tiny that it is almost lost in the rapid below the Lower Island in the Campbell. This pool, which extends out into the rapid only ten or fifteen yards from the left bank of the river and is not more than twice as long as its width, lies a little way upstream of a similar but rather larger pool under the right bank of the river, just above the mouth of the Quinsam. The fish took a No. 8 Lady Caroline and started to run almost as he touched the fly. The pool was too small to interest him and in a moment he was out of it and half way across the rapids. I held him hard, trying to turn him with the current and bring him in a semi-circle back to my own bank. The pressure made him jump several times, right in the white water but always downstream and across towards the Quinsam Pool; each jump took out line and I felt that 0X gut, for once, was not enough. He reached the pool and I found that I had 40 yards of fly line and a little over 50 yards of backing out, with the width of the river of fast, broken water between me and the fish. As he held in the pool I released the pressure a little and he began to swim upstream. I moved down along my own bank until I was below him, then tightened again, and he ran at once upstream and out of the pool. I turned him when he had travelled a little way and brought him diagonally down and across the rapid to the beach.

Before and since that time I have had to give as much as 30 or 40 yards of backing to a summer steelhead, but it happens rarely and nearly always in heavy water. No fish I have ever hooked has shown the confidence and watermanship in manoeuvring across a really strong rapid that this good four-pounder showed me. He went free, with a tag in his tail, but I have not met him since.

Good wet flies for summer steelhead are, as are good wet flies for Atlantic salmon, dependent upon the fancy of the angler rather than upon the preferences of the fish. One could fish satisfactorily through a season with a range of full-dressed Jock Scotts, on hook sizes from 1 or slightly larger up to 12. Most of the trout flies in the boxes of the average British Columbian fisherman, especially the Kamloops flies, will catch fish. Most of the flies tied for Atlantic salmon will catch fish. European sea-trout flies and lures, such as terrors and demons, will take fish well. And to add to this wide choice there is a great variety of flies tied especially for the purpose—most of them rather bright flies and a good proportion of them winged with bucktail or bear-hair.

Generally speaking, I believe the fairly bright flies are likely to catch more fish. Over several seasons on the Nimpkish I fished two flies on a cast, one of them a dark fly such as Greenwell's Glory, the other a bright, full-dressed salmon fly, Torrish, Silver Doctor or Durham Ranger. I found that the bright fly took the steelhead and the dark fly the cutthroats, with surprising regularity. What I have seen since has persuaded me that I should probably have caught just as many fish had I not offered them a choice, but the division of the catch was quite definite enough to suggest that there is likely to be some degree of preference.

Like most fishermen, I generally carry with me a tremendous diversity of flies; but if some unkind realist ordered me to confine myself to three wet flies only I should choose without hesitation the Silver Lady, Jock Scott, and the low-water Lady Caroline. In these I should have a sufficient variety to please myself, and more than enough to please the fish. I should regret most the loss of one or two favourite bear-hair patterns that have often done well for me.

For greased-line fishing, I think only two flies are necessary, the Blue Charm and the Lady Caroline; even the Blue Charm is probably superfluous, but on a really dark day it is possibly a little more effective than the Lady Caroline. Steelhead like the Lady Caroline surprisingly well, whether she is fished as a simple wet fly or by the greased-line method.

Of all dry flies I have tried I prefer the bi-visibles, though La Branche's Pink Lady and the regular Palmers are good at times. Generally, dry flies should be large, tied on 8 or 10 hooks, and frequently sedges will do well on these sizes. There is rather an important advantage in using sedges if, as many people believe, the hackles of flies tied palmerwise tend to shield the point of the hook and so make striking difficult.

No other fish chooses a better meeting ground for himself and the angler than does the summer steelhead. The young streams of Vancouver Island and the mainland coast are incomparably, heroically beautiful, in the mould of the wet-fly man's ideal. Clear water between tall trees, lost from sight at a little distance, yet world filling when one is by its side. White rapids with resting places lodged and hidden here and there about them; deep pools and shallow pools, smooth, slow pools and wide, broken pools; current to pull at a man's legs and test his footing, to carry his fly and give it life; the breath of a breeze and sunlight in the time of the run; the problems of high water in the first months of the run, calling for the long cast and strong searching; the more intricate problems of low water later, summoning the delicate and subtle method, the difficult thing faithfully accomplished.

The beauties are those of the rough mountain streams, magnified a hundred times, lost in the magnification yet drawn to a full and broader perfection of their own, with room for the doing and a setting for the deed. But such water, fast and clear over clean rocks and gravel, is not of a type to produce fish to scale. The still waters of a lake, the trailing weeds and quiet reaches of older streams, are the places where trout grow large and difficult. Only a migratory run, grown bright and strong in the plenty of salt water, could put proportionate fish into the setting.

It is unquestionably a fly fisherman's setting, and the fly fisherman is free to enjoy it; when the summer steelhead are in, the fly will take them. Everything else, spinners and devons and lures, phantoms and plugs and worms, can be laid aside and forgotten. There need be no anxious wondering about the light spinning rod or the advisability of taking along one or two small spinners, just in case they make all the difference between a few fish and a blank day. If the fly fisherman is versatile and knows the variations of his method, he can depend upon the fish to respond to it—if they will respond to anything at all on that particular day. Real summer steelhead fishing—that is to say, fishing for mature, truly migratory steelhead—is essentially Atlantic salmon fishing, though the fish be a thousand times a trout. As in fishing for winter steelhead, the slow, thorough searching of all the holding water, and a good knowledge of favourite lies and the currents over them, will catch fish. Match the size of fly to the height of the water and the brightness of the day; in high water and cloudy weather a big fly between No. 2/0 and No. 4. On a bright day, unless it is a great, wide water you are searching and you feel you need confidence, do not be afraid to go down to No. 6. In low water and sunny weather, small flies—No. 10 is often not too small.

It is straightforward, satisfying fishing when the river is still holding from the stored-up snow in the high hills. A good holding pool in July, with a strong rapid at the head but an even flow of water over a wide part of the pool's surface; some big rocks in deep water near the tail of the pool. The river has fallen a lot, but is not yet down to summer level; the day is sunny, but somehow not too bright on the water. Starting at the head with a No. 4 Jock Scott. A few short casts to cover the water immediately below the rapid, then across the current and around, slowly and easily, to the side. Another cast, delaying the fly for a moment in the slack water of the far side with an upstream "mend," as in greased-line fishing. Following round with the rod point, holding a little at the edge of the strongest current. A fish shows well behind the fly. Fish out the cast. Rest him. Change to a No. 6. Cover again, hanging it where he took; this time he has it and is into a run without waiting for the strike. An upstream run and across towards the far side, unwisely checked a little too soon. The second run is downstream, with two clean jumps. He comes back from that unwillingly against the current, but there is no point in following him down all that new water so early in the day. He runs straight across and the strain of the rod lifts him very near the surface in the fast water. Time to get out, on to the gravel bar. It is easier from there—the rod is suddenly longer and one is suddenly taller; but the fish works in short runs, trying for the current each time, rolling and twisting jerkily as the pressure draws him up and stops him. He is quiet at last, and slides easily on to the gravel.

The rest of the pool fishes blank, but it is a good holding pool and there are more fish in it. A short rest and start back with the same fly, casting across and a few degrees upstream, covering the best spots with short casts as well as long ones, to vary the angle. A fish comes from behind the rocks to a short cast, but the fly is suddenly free as he turns at the end of his first run. But the day is very young, and there are other fish and other pools.

Those are the good wet-fly days, when a run is fresh from the sea and conditions are right. There are others. And later in the season, with fewer and staler fish, the wise angler will not be content with the wet fly, unless it happens to do well for him. There is always the dry fly, which may take fish, and there is greased-line fishing, probably the most delicate and worthwhile method of taking dour non-feeders under difficult conditions that man has yet thought out. The essential principle of greased-line fishing is a small, lightly dressed fly fished right up in the surface film and without drag. The normal cast, in straightforward water, is across and slightly downstream, with a slack line. As the current pulls the slack into a belly that threatens to draw the fly, the fisherman makes an upstream "mend"—lifts the belly of the line without moving the fly and places it upstream—and the fly continues to fish down and slightly across at the speed of the current, instead of being drawn against it by the pull of the line. But it is not necessary to go into the details of the method here; that has been well and fully done in "Jock Scott's" book, *Greased-Line Fishing for Salmon.* It is enough to say that summer steelhead will respond to the method and that the streams of the country lend themselves to it almost perfectly.

The feel of fishing a run of less strongly migratory fish, such as the spring run in the Campbell, is altogether different. The non-feeding fish are there, five- and six-pounders generally, and one searches for them diligently and carefully, tempts them from every angle and with every trick of the trade. But because many of the fish are feeding, one works over the water more easily and confidently once they are found. It is trout fishing again, and very good trout fishing. On the best days—there are not more than one or two a year, and they are generally between April 11th and May 24th—one finds the fish in the Islands Pool, most of them towards the tail and to one side of the main run of current, in about four or five feet of rippled, flowing water. Sometimes they are rising and will come to a dry fly, but the wet fly is usually better; the Silver Lady always does well, particularly with the larger fish, but I think Lady Caroline is better; the feeding fish like her well, and unless the run is very freshly in from salt water, they are the better fish. On these days it would not be difficult to pick up fifteen fish of two to five pounds, if one chose to and felt prepared to argue with a game warden that the fish were rainbow trout, not steelhead. But it is easy to break the barb of the hook so that it is nothing more than a little hump and, standing there in the water, let the fish shake the hook from him, after the rise and strike and a few moments of running and jumping. It is not too difficult, even with a barbless hook, to net the two or three especially fat and silver ones that deserve a place on the table.

Other days are less easy. When the fish get up into the Canyon Pool it is difficult to wade deep enough to reach them properly with the fly, and they take less freely. Often the Islands Pool seems empty of fish, or rain in the hills and melting snow have brought the water too high for one to wade out to the bar. But the few great days come every year, and there are many times in the season when two or three fish, hardly found and tempted only by stern persistence or wild ingenuity, seem worth all the great days of a dozen seasons.

SEVEN

On the Water & in the Mail

Roderick L. Haig-Brown

It is not altogether difficult to make a list of certain essential things that help to make good fishing, but such a list would not be inevitably a description of good fishing, or even of fishing at all. The pleasures of angling are many, and they have many sources; both pleasures and sources are intermingled and interdependent, working together upon each other to produce the mood, the day, the ultimate satisfaction. Good fish, attractive water, the right tackle working smoothly, fair weather—one can have all these and the combination may produce a good bag of fish, yet the day may be forgotten while a day yielding fewer and smaller fish is remembered.

One remembers not merely the actual fishing, but all that led up to it and followed upon it—the journey, the country, the people, food, lodging, conversation, ideas and thoughts. Nothing wears better, for instance, than the journey up the Fraser valley to the interior; pulling out from Seattle or Vancouver and heading north, with all the dirt roads of British Columbia ahead, and Kamloops trout in a thousand lakes. I put rods and reels and flies in the car and started from Seattle that way in May of 1936. After crossing the border and getting over the last of the paved roads, hurry seemed to fall away from me. I drove lazily and stopped to eat sandwiches somewhere between Rosedale and Hope, where a little stream runs under the road and on through an alder thicket to the Fraser. Down along the stream a ruffed grouse drummed, and through the alders I could make out the end of the old rotten log on which he was standing. I walked down until I could see him and then, moving too clumsily, I flushed him. For a moment of time he was brown movement against the pale-green leaves.

Through the rest of that day I was with the Fraser, brown, turbulent, streaked always with the strength of its current, broken sometimes to white, a mighty river. The hard mountains were its banks, and down their steep sides running water sought the river—water in rushing streams, in tiny creeks, in mare's tail falls that made long lines of white against green and brown and grey

or against the reds and yellows of mineral-stained rock. At dusk, a cold wind
down the canyon and the beginning of the dry belt; and always that wonderful
road, narrow, writhing its way through the hard country, having nothing to
guard the sharp outer edge, nothing to hold back the slides that threaten it
from above; not a scenic highway, but a road through a difficult place because
people have to get through; by virtue of its function, its gravelled surface and
its spareness, truly a part of the country it serves.

When it was quite dark I stopped at an inn that was perched on the outer
edge of the road, where there seemed nothing but a straight five-hundred-foot
drop to the river. There was a good bed there and good food, and the people
talked untidily of Aberhart and Buchman and Marx; it was not yet fishing
country, and the year was 1936.

Before noon the next day I was at my first lake. I stopped the car where the
road crosses the outlet, and walked up until I could see the lake. It was a warm,
pleasant day, full of spring; light clouds passed now and then across the face of
the sun, and a little breeze scarcely moved the surface of the water. It was easy
to stand there at the edge of the lake and look along the wooded hills; water
that one is shortly to fish for the first time always seems abundantly full of
promise, and I could see points and bays and could guess where the shoals ran
out. A few small fish were rising near me, just above the outlet, and as I watched
there was the quiet rise of a big fish just beyond them. It was a cruiser's rise,
slow and smooth, showing a great part of the shoulder. He was a long cast out
from the shore, and for a moment I hesitated. Put up the rod and try for him?
No, I thought, I'm too old for that; he'd be gone before I was ready, or I would
find the cast just too long, with the scrub alders and little cottonwoods so close
behind me. I went back to the car and drove on to the lodge.

But I knew as I drove that I should go back down to the outlet to look for
the cruiser; he was not so very large and he certainly would not be there, but
he was my fish—or I was his fisherman. I felt bound to him in some way, not
free to try for other fish until I had at least looked for him. So I put up my rod,
took one of the lodge boats and drifted back towards the outlet on the light
breeze. Before I had time to get out the oars to hold the boat from drifting too
far, the breeze had died away; the clouds were all gone and the sun shone hot
and bright on the still surface of the lake; a few fish were rising, probably feeding on chironomid nymphs. I looked over a box of wet flies, but there was
nothing that seemed to fit the big cruiser and his slow, easy rise. I remembered
other Kamloops trout, feeding on chironomids, which had come to the brown
and white bi-visible.

I tied a bi-visible to 3X gut and saw a small fish rise within easy reach. I hesitated, still waiting for my cruiser to show. The small fish rose again, and I set the bi-visible near him; he came to it sloppily and missed it by two or three inches, so widely that I was not even tempted to strike. A second later he had turned and taken the fly quietly and gently. He made one fast run and a noble jump, but he weighed barely a pound and I netted him quickly. As I freed the hook and slipped the fish into the box, my cruiser showed, almost exactly where I had seen him before, and well within reach.

I dried my fly quickly, arguing with myself that it could not be the same fish, though I knew it was. He rose again. I dropped the fly ahead of him and waited, resolved not to strike to his first rise unless I actually saw him take the fly under, in his jaws. He came suddenly, right out of the water and down on to the fly. In spite of my resolve the tip of my rod jerked up a little, but the fly did not move. It lay there very flat on the water, and he came back and took it with one of his great, quiet, bulging rises. I struck, and he ran a little from the pull, then turned sharply and came straight towards the boat. I kept pace with him, hand-lining until he turned again and ran out and down. I felt him start upwards at the end of his run, and felt the line quivering as it was drawn suddenly against the water instead of through it. A moment later he was high in the air, shining in the sun, the broken water falling back all around him. He jumped again and again, five times going away from me, then I was able to work him back and draw him over the net. He weighed an ounce less than two pounds—but he was something I have learned not to expect too often in British Columbia, a good fish, marked down, re-found and hooked strictly according to plan.

On that same trip there was another day—a whole day, this time—that I remember clearly. It was a day of mountain weather on Paul Lake; there were strong winds, now from due east, now from due west, scattering squalls of heavy rain; and, once or twice, the sun shone through broken, racing clouds. Jack Marsh and I were fishing together in one boat, the Doctor and Bill Nation were in another. In the morning there were at least a dozen boats out, scattered all over the lake, searching for fish. By lunch time our two boats had worked along the south shore of the lake to the Beaver House Shoal; Marsh and I had only one fish between us; the Doctor had about five.

We went ashore and began to collect wood to make a fire and boil coffee. Soon Bill Nation said: "No more wood; make a little fire and get up close."

We talked about mosquitoes and fish and the wind, and why the wind seemed to have discouraged the fish but not the mosquitoes. Bill said, "They'll come on early this afternoon."

"They ought to be on sometime on a lively day like this," I said.

"Hope so," said Marsh. "It was certainly pretty slow this morning."

The boats were still scattered when we got out on the water again. Marsh was fishing, and wanted to change his fly; he had been using Nation's Green Sedge all the morning. One nearly always did fish Bill's flies at Paul Lake in those days, and the Green Sedge had been doing well for several days, but Marsh wanted a change anyhow.

"To hell with Bill," he said; "what shall we try?"

I had some good Grizzly Kings, tied with olive seal's fur bodies, badger hackles and well-marked wings. They seemed not too far from the Green Sedge.

"What about these?" I asked him.

"Fine," Marsh said. "I like a Grizzly King."

Marsh is a good fisherman. He casts accurately and cleanly, with a strong arm and wrist. When he wants to, he can put out a long line, and he handles his fish quickly and smoothly. There was a sunken log, just visible through the shoal water, jutting out from the shore. He pointed to it. "Looks good to me," he said.

I held the boat so that his fly would cover the end of the log. He hooked a good fish at once, and I netted it for him, holding the boat in position against the wind. Still casting to the log, he hooked several more fish and landed three of them, all good, bright fish in perfect condition. By that time the boats were no longer scattered. They all closed in, the party of Scotsmen in two or three boats, trolling red and white plugs, the man from China who hadn't been doing so well, and the others. I held the boat where it was, and Marsh kept hooking fish all along his sunken log, losing some and landing others. The other boats were getting only an occasional fish.

"We'd better move out and let someone else in," I said.

"To hell with that. We don't crowd them when they're catching fish. I'm enjoying this."

So I held the boat where it was, and Marsh went on hooking fish. He was fishing beautifully and was very happy, laughing a lot. He urged me to fish while they were still taking, but I didn't want to, it was enough to be watching him and holding the boat, seeing the whole water and where the fish came from and how they came. When he had eight or ten fish in the boat I let the wind carry us away from the log and started slowly for home, following the shore line. Marsh soon picked up a couple more fish and wanted to keep the last few of his limit for the evening fishing, so I gave him the oars and began to fish myself, using the Green Sedge. Fish came easily and I had about a half dozen more in the boat by the time we were past Gibraltar Rock and within sight of the lodge. Then the wind shifted and began to blow really hard from the foot of the lake, dead against us. My fly dropped pleasantly on the waves and worked down into them in a lively way. One or two more fish took in the rough water, and I offered to spell Marsh with the oars.

"No," he said, "go on. I need the exercise and you're doing all right with that little rod."

Off Killkare Shoal the wind was very strong, and there were big whitecaps.

"Lord," I said, "I'd give a lot to hook a four-pounder now."

"You might," Marsh said.

The shoal was good, and I netted three nice fish as we worked along it. Almost at the end of it a big fish rose well and began to take out line very fast; he jumped once, well clear of the water.

"It's him," I said; "a three-pounder, anyway."

The fish turned in his first run and came back fast towards the boat. I recovered line easily enough and kept in touch with him until he turned again and began to run out. He was a strong fish and ran deep against heavy pressure with thirty yards of fly line and some backing. I felt the angle of his run turn upwards a little, then the line was suddenly slack. The fly came back to me; and for the first time in several seasons I felt really sorry to have lost a fish. He had looked splendid in that first jump, and I wanted to see him again and again, silver and steel-grey, with the spray blowing from his jumps against the whitecaps. And there would have been difficult, anxious moments when he was ready for the net. In lake fishing one too seldom has the luck to hook a big fish when the conditions are all in his favour. As Marsh rowed the last two or three hundred yards to the float I counted the fish. There were twenty-two of them, all bright and in perfect condition, the largest just two and three-quarters pounds.

The Doctor stayed in after dinner, and Marsh and I went out with Bill Nation to try the water at the foot of the lake. The wind had gone down with the sun, and the lake was very calm. I was still fishing the Green Sedge, and hooked the first fish before we had gone very far. Marsh was after something really big to finish off the day, and had put on a tremendous Big Bertha; it was so big that it seemed likely to defeat its own purpose, but he had not used one before and wanted to see what it would do. Bill worked the boat gently across the still water, and big fish rose all around us. Marsh hooked a good fish and killed him. I was listening to Bill and enjoying the stillness of the evening after the windy day, fishing lazily. Marsh hooked another good fish and killed him. Most of the daylight was gone, and Bill told me to change to Nation's Special; I began to fish hard, knowing that he wanted one of his own flies to do as well as Big Bertha. But Bertha hooked and lost three fish while I was losing one on the Special. She hooked yet another and killed it. It was too dark to see the rises and we both hooked and lost fish. Nation's Special killed the last fish of the evening on the way back to the float, which pleased Bill.

I don't think we realised how good that evening had been until we really looked at the fish the next morning. Each of the five was perfect, silver and clean as a salt-water steelhead, without the faintest trace of mature colouring. The largest just shaded two pounds; the smallest weighed a bare three ounces less than that. They might have been hatched from the eggs of the same spawning pair and spent their whole lives within casting distance of one another, though we had taken them one by one all the way across the lake from the lodge to the north shore.

It is some years now since Bill Nation died. I am quite sure he brought to Kamloops trout fishing the most original mind it has yet known. In a very real way he made the Kamloops trout his own special fish and his active mind seemed never to rest from thinking about them. Bill was a small, slender, soft-voiced Englishman who talked almost incessantly from behind a pair of big spectacles, yet listened well enough to seem almost silent. He was a really good fly fisherman himself and as fine a guide as a man could want—excellent company on the water and tireless in searching for fish even on the worst days.

Bill was well read in the world's fishing literature and he was a keen observer. But his mind had a happy, poetic slant that must, I think, have developed through some Celtic strain in him. He loved to theorise well up into the realms of fantasy but always managed to come back down again with something that had solid worth even though it still retained the incandescence of fantasy. The frequent visits of good scientists like Rawson and Mottley to Paul Lake helped Nation a lot both in his ascents and descents—their sound and detailed natural history made fuel for his fantasy and guided the ideas he put into practice.

Nation will always be remembered for the series of wet flies he developed. In 1938 he sent me a list of the patterns he considered set, naming the natural prototypes as follows:

Nation's Blue	Coupled bluets *(Enallagma)*
Nation's Red	Coupled dragonflies *(Sympetrum)*
Green Sedge	Sedge nymph *(Glyphopsyche)*
Silvertip Sedge	Sedge nymph
Green Nymph	Dragonfly nymph ⎫ Species according to size
Grey Nymph	Dragonfly nymph ⎭

Nation's Black   Chironomid nymph
Nation's Special ⎤
Nation's Fancy   ⎬ General patterns
Nation's Silvertip ⎦

Few men who fish Kamloops trout waters do not carry at least one or two of these patterns and I imagine that Nation's Special alone has accounted for more Kamloops trout than any other half dozen flies together, if one leaves out the immensely popular Col. Kerry's Special. I often used to argue with Nation that most of his flies—except the two dragon nymphs and the chironomid nymphs—were fancy flies rather than true attempts at imitation, but he would never concede me anything at all on this and brought up beautifully involved arguments to support his views. For instance, he wrote me of Nation's Red: "One rather new fly I released the fall before last is an imitation of the coupled red dragon flies. You will see that the red front part of the body, with the red stripe on the wing, represents the strongly coloured red female in the lead, while the silver end of the body, with the light mallard tail, represents the lighter coloured male in tow."

Even allowing for the life that a wetfly fisherman can give his fly by artificial motion, I felt that this was a little far-fetched. So far as I know, the females of very few dragonflies descend below the surface to lay eggs, and even those that do so are rarely accompanied by males. I could find no record of any such activity for the two species of *Sympetrum* identified by Rawson from Paul Lake. Bill had a ready answer though. "The enormous gorge of dragons that the trout collect sometimes is composed practically entirely of adults taken on the wing. Therefore it is wrong to fish either the Red or the Blue as a floating still dry fly. For every natural floating red or blue there are 10,000 winged ones flying an inch or two above the water, therefore fish the Red or Blue artificial with a greased line and a vertical rod, work it fast enough to keep it no farther below the surface than the natural fly is above, say one inch. If you fish the fly slow and deep you will interest no trout."

I have quoted this discussion at some length to show Nation's bold and keen thinking and to give some idea of how closely he observed. His Red fly does take fish when the *Sympetrum* hatch is on and whether this is because of its appearance or because of the method of fishing it doesn't matter very much. The point is that he has departed a very long way from the flyfisherman's usual business of imitating mayflies and sedges, and has made something of it. He set great store by the motion of the wet fly at all times, and I am sure he was quite right. "Underwater life movements," he once wrote me, "might be classified into those that flick like a prawn, the large dragon nymphs; those that crawl like a snake on a boardwalk, in one plane, as the *Enallagma* nymphs; those that walk like a sheep, as many of the sedge nymphs. And the working of the fly that imitates these forms should also imitate the action of the particular nymph. Note that the nymph of the Green Sedge moves in a series of tiny jerks; these seem to be of great intensity, but each fierce, convulsive jerk only manages to move the nymph forward less than an eighth of an inch. This nymph moves on the shoals each evening from 10 o'clock on for a few days before hatching and are in the chara weed, and the dyed seal's fur body of the sedge fly imitates the case more nearly than it does the actual body of the nymph. The fly is fished quite slowly under these conditions, and a very short, fierce jerk of one inch is sent through the line every ten seconds. This style of fishing works best during the four days preceding the full moon, so does not apply generally. For the Green Sedge it is advisable to carry peroxide of hydrogen to bleach the body to the desired shade of that of the sedge or nymph the fish are feeding on. I enclose some dyed seal's fur in various stages of sun bleach, and I pick the shade I want for my own tying."

Other men may solve more Kamloops trout problems than Bill did, make more ingenious imitations and develop more perfect ways of fishing them. But for me and for many another Bill will always be the true pioneer of the fishing, the man whose life was closer to those particular fish than any other man's had been or is likely to be. There is not space to write of the many things he did or attempted for his beloved Paul Lake fish—of how he tried repeatedly to bring the Traveller Sedge down from Knouff Lake, how he persuaded the government to introduce crayfish, of his suggestion that a proportion of Kamloops trout should be caponized by X-ray to ensure their continued growth without the interference of spawning. But nothing written of Kamloops trout could be reasonably complete without some account of him, and I hope there is enough of him in this chapter to show why that is so.

EIGHT

Why Fly Fishing?

Eugene V. Connett

There is a tendency on the part of a good many sturdy citizens of these United States to look upon fly fishing for trout as either high-hat or too difficult, in comparison with fishing with bait. Not so many years ago I used to meet a lot of men who didn't take many pains to hide the fact that they looked upon me—a fly fisherman—as a cross between a darn fool and a city sissy. Wading along a stream in late April I'd come to a brother of the angle either perched on a rock along the edge of the water or trying to preserve his precarious balance in a pair of slippery rubber boots, facing downstream as he worked a worm through a necessarily limited area of water below him.

I think of one such who hadn't shaved lately, and who seemed to glory in the fact that he was a real he-man, a tough and stringy son of the outdoors.

"How are you making out?" I asked, as I came up to him.

"O.K." he growled, shooting a load of tobacco juice with deadly accuracy at a leaf that was floating by. "Guess you haven't done much with your flies, have you?"

"Nothing to brag about," I admitted.

By that time I was standing beside him, as he drew his worm against the current for a few feet and then let it drift back. Silently, but in a manner pregnant with superiority, he unlatched the cover of his creel, and let me look at its contents. Four trout, all under nine inches in length.

"Pht!" That fellow could say more with one squirt of tobacco juice than most men could in three paragraphs. "You got anything?"

By that time I was getting a bit fed up with his attitude, and I indulged in what turned out to be a pretty poor imitation of his superb expectoratory prowess. I swung my basket around and lifted the lid.

"I only kept these three out of the seven I've caught. I chuck back everything under ten inches." I'll admit that this, while the truth, was not exactly a praiseworthy manner in which to answer; but he had it coming to him. And let it be said that this was just the treatment he needed, for it wasn't ten minutes before he was trying to learn to cast a fly, and before the afternoon was out, we *had* become "brothers of the angle." Today we are fast friends, and he is as enthusiastic a fly fisherman as I am. Not long ago I came upon him giving the treatment to some bait fisherman he had met on the stream. In fact, he is a regular missionary now and many a former wormer owes his conversion to the pleasures of fly fishing— to say nothing of the ability to catch more and bigger trout— to his streamside crusading.

Aside from any increase in the fun of fishing, there is a real and practical reason today why the use of the artificial fly is desirable. Excepting privately controlled waters, there isn't a stream in the country that can't be reached with comparative ease, and that isn't heavily fished. The problem is how to give everyone who wants to fish and who buys the necessary license, a place to fish and some trout to catch. The modern fish hatchery has been geared up to a point where it can turn out enough trout, roughly speaking, to put a reasonable number of fish in the water for each angler. But so far we have discovered no way in which to stretch the length of our streams so that they will accommodate every fisherman with plenty of water to fish in, because the number of trout fishermen has increased so tremendously in the past few years. It is therefore necessary for an angler to develop some system whereby he can extract the greatest amount of recreation from a very limited expanse of water.

I don't care how expert a bait fisherman may be, he cannot cover as much water with his bait as a fly fisherman can with his fly. You can't whip a worm out in the air behind you and then send it forward through the air to a spot fifty or sixty feet from you; worms aren't made that way. But you can place your fly anywhere you want to, depending upon your ability. Therefore, the skillful fly fisher can squeeze the last drop of fun out of a limited piece of water—to say nothing of the last trout; while the worm fisherman can cover only such parts of the water as he can reach with a short cast, and if the water is too deep to wade all over, his fishing is limited indeed. Consequently, in order to equal the basket of the fly fisherman, he has to have a lot of stream to cover, and, what is very tough on his fellow fisherman, he has to wade all over it.

A trout is very likely not to enter into the spirit of the game, if he has had the lights and liver scared out of him by having someone wade into his parlor. I'd rather have one hundred yards of stream, with six fish in it, to myself, than have six hundred yards with sixty fish being hammered by six fishermen. The considerate fly fisherman can wade along quietly, keeping out of the parts of water in which trout will lie, and aside from putting down the fish temporarily by careless casting, will leave the water in good condition for the man who follows him. While he is fishing this piece of water, he will have a lot more to think about than the worm fisherman, whose one problem is how to get his worm—the same old worm—in front of a trout. If the fish won't rise to a Cahill, there are one hundred other patterns that can be tried. If they won't take a dry fly, perhaps they will come for a wet fly or nymph. What natural insect is on the water, and what artificial best imitates it? How can the fly be presented to the fish so that the leader won't scare it? How can the surface current be outwitted so that it won't set up a drag on the fly, which should float over or drift past the trout in just as natural a manner as the natural fly or nymph would do? Yes, the fly fisherman can spend a lot of time on his limited stretch of stream, and be contentedly occupied with scores of interesting problems which the trout, his feeding habits and the stream itself will provide.

The natural flies upon which trout feed are of course a matter of considerable interest to the fly fisherman, whose job it is to offer the fish an artificial representation of them. These insects are a fascinating study in themselves. The Mayflies, of which there are a number of varieties, lay their eggs on the surface of the stream. The eggs sink to the bottom and hatch out into tiny larvae. These live under the stones or in the silt on the bottom, and as they grow, shed their skins a number of times. In this form, which lasts from one to three years, they are known as nymphs, and are of great interest to the angler because three-quarters of the trout's food is composed of these submerged forms of the trout stream insects. Comes a day in the spring when some mysterious urge starts these nymphs to the surface to hatch out into winged flies. As they reach the surface their nymphal skin splits, and their wings are freed. They float along for a few minutes until they are dry enough to fly, and then take off. In this stage of their development they are known as duns, and how the trout relish them! The dry-fisherman is imitating these duns when he floats his fly on the surface, over a fish. The wet-fly fisherman, drifting his feathered artificial beneath the surface is imitating the nymph. The duns soon come to rest on a leaf or a stone, and their skins start to split. I have watched a dun slowly pull itself out of its skin in about fifteen minutes. When it emerges, it is a beautiful, transparent, gauzy creature known as a spinner. Toward evening the males and females take wing over the stream, and mating takes place. The spinner lives only about twenty-four hours, and when it has procreated it falls exhausted to the surface of the stream and dies. To tie artificial imitations of the various species of nymphs, duns and spinners is an absorbing occupation for the fly fisherman during the winter months.

During the past quarter of a century I have spent as much time on trout streams as most men, and it has been my observation that a skilfully handled fly, fished by an experienced and intelligent man, will account for more trout throughout the season than a worm fished by an equally good bait fisherman. I have seen the day in the Catskills, when the hills were still covered with snow in early April, and the water was so cold that the trout lay on the bottom in a semi-dormant condition, when the man who chucked a gob of nightwalkers on the bottom of a deep pool, would catch more and bigger fish than the fly fisherman. But I've seen it only a very few times. Some years ago at DeBruce, I saw a large tray of trout running from ten to eighteen inches—a magnificent catch—which were taken on nightwalkers from the bottom of a deep pool. This pool was usually the best on the Willowemoc above Livingston Manor. I fished there many times during that spring, and never saw another decent trout taken from the pool that season. If the water had been restricted to fly fishing only—as it now is in that particular place—there would have been reasonably good fishing in that pool for a number of men all through the season.

I have no objection to any man's catching all the fish the law allows, if he is able to—that's his business. But I believe it is a fact that the fly fisherman finds so many absorbing problems in his form of sport, that he inclines to place less and less emphasis on the number of trout he kills, and more and more importance on his ability to catch the trout. I see scores of fish under ten inches put back in the stream each spring by men who had their fun in catching them, and who are interested in taking home only the big ones. This isn't merely a snobbish pose on the part of a group of high-hatters; it is a genuine attitude brought about in part by the knowledge that the man can catch fish and doesn't have to prove it by lugging home a basketful to show his friends; and also by the realization that every smaller fish restored to the water unhurt is there still to be caught, or perhaps to grow up into a big 'un really worth catching and taking home.

Why can't the bait fisherman adopt the same attitude? He can, but it won't bear the same fruitful results, because so many of the smaller fish he catches can't be returned to water unharmed. When a trout takes an artificial fly in his mouth, it only requires an instant for him to realize his mistake and spit it out. But when he takes a worm, his one idea is to see how fast he can swallow it; and the hook may be anywhere from his lip to his stomach by the time he is in the landing net.

Now don't mistake me about this matter. I have no moral or ethical objections to bait fishing—none whatever. I don't say that the man who fishes with bait is no sportsman—not a bit of it. I don't say that there is no skill involved in successful bait fishing—far from it. I do point out, however, that with the ever-increasing crowding of our trout streams, that the best way to get the most fun out of the game is to fish with a fly. And I also call attention to the fact that

it has been my observation during the past twenty-five years that the more skilful a fly fisherman becomes, the more apt he is to kill fewer of the trout he
lands. It is my earnest hope that in time many of our trout streams, or parts of
them, will be restricted to fly fishing only—not because I have any desire to see
the bait fisherman done out of his sport, but because I know that at the rate
fishermen are increasing it is only a matter of time before the only trout fishing
worth the trouble will be on privately controlled waters. And these are increasing rapidly each year.

In Europe there isn't a foot of public trout fishing. The streams and the
fish in them are all privately owned. I've had better trout fishing within twenty-
five miles of the center of London than I ever had here in the wildest, most
secluded mountain stream. If we want to continue our system of open fishing
for everyone, we have simply got to devise every possible means of getting our
fun out of very limited stretches of water, which we leave in good condition for
the man who follows us. We have got to develop a real sense of stream courtesy,
and practice it—a willingness to let the other fellow enjoy his fishing, too. If we
don't, he will gather together a few of his friends and rent or buy the stream
right out from under our noses, and in time we will do our fishing in canals,
lakes and the ocean—none of which is ideal trout water.

In the East we have seen the last of trout fishing for large, wild fish—except
in certain waters in Maine where there are still very large squaretail natives to
be found. Maine, by the way, has been more foresighted in regard to the preser-
vation of fish and game than any other state in the Union. At Kennebago
Stream, for instance, which is one of the places where trout of four pounds and
up can still be caught, one is allowed to kill but one fish a day; all others must
be returned, unharmed, to the water. This, of course, means no bait fishing.

Such famous rivers as the Battenkill, the Beaverkill and the Ausable, to
mention but three, used to contain a real supply of big brown trout, fish that
would go two and three and even four pounds. But each year fewer of these are
caught, because they just aren't present in any considerable numbers. These
streams are all stocked annually, but the catch of fish is so great these days that
very few of the stocked fish live long enough to become "big 'uns." Under very
favourable conditions trout will grow about four inches their first year. The
following spring they would be about seven inches long. A four-year-old would
measure from ten to sixteen inches, depending on the available food and other
conditions. A fourteen-inch brown trout should weigh about a pound. So you
can see that if a stream is stocked with fish from six to ten inches—which would
be a pretty generous size for general stocking—and is then fished to death by a

horde of anglers, there is very good reason for the absence of two- and three-pounders.

To give some idea of the magnitude of the stocking operations carried on by some of the states, let me quote the figures of New Jersey for the year 1935. A total of 653,000 trout were liberated in the streams, of which 20,200 were over twelve inches in length. In 1934 Connecticut liberated 165,238 adult trout, weighing 45,115 pounds. In 1933 the same state liberated 214,637 adult trout weighing 45,750 pounds. In the case of New Jersey, in 1935, 546,000 of the trout liberated were over the legal limit in size. From my experience and observations when fishing some of the New Jersey waters late in the season, I should say that about 90 percent of the fish liberated had been caught during the open season. In view of the fact that the catch for 1934 reported by sportsmen when taking out new licenses the following year was 440,504 trout, my guess is probably a pretty good one. It is obvious from these figures that wild trout in a state like New Jersey are a thing of the past.

All the varieties of trout found in the United States can be artificially raised in hatcheries—thank fortune! In the East the native trout is the Squaretail Brook Trout (*Salvelinus fontinalis*). The Brown Trout (*Salmo fario*) has been introduced from Europe, and to my mind is about the best of the lot, as it is a very free surface feeder. The Rainbow Trout (*Salmo irideus*) has been brought from the Pacific Coast and is thriving in a number of Eastern streams today. It is a wonderful fighter and jumps continually when on the line. These three varieties are now found in varying numbers right across the country. In the Rockies the native trout are the Cutthroat (*Salmo clarkii*) and the Rainbow; while in the Sierra Nevadas in California is found the Golden Trout (*Salmo roosevelti*). There are a number of variations of these species, such as the Steelhead (*Salmo rivularis*), the Tahoe Trout (*Salmo henshawi*), and the Dolly Varden Trout (*Salvelinus parkei*) which isn't a trout at all, but a char, like its cousin the Eastern Brook Trout or Squaretail.

There is no doubt in my mind that stocked fish are easier to catch the first season they are released than are wild trout of similar size. Fishing a stretch of Brodhead's Creek in Pennsylvania in the spring of 1936, a friend and I after a very leisurely day's fishing kept eight trout that weighed something over eleven pounds—all fish that had been put out early in the season. The biggest wild trout either of us caught went about ten inches. That there are some large wild trout in that water I know to be a fact, because on a later date I caught some of them, and saw others which I didn't catch. But on the day I speak of, the only big fish which rose were the stocked fish. In that section they are known as "mullet," which indicates how the local anglers look upon them in comparison to wild fish.

I believe that stocked fish are about the equal of wild fish after they have been in the stream for a year. The problem is how to protect these hatchery-raised trout for at least a year, so that they will become "acclimatized" to the stream and as difficult to catch as their brethren. I suggest that if all fish of nine inches or more were tagged with the year of their release, and it were made illegal to kill any fish caught with the date of the current year on their tag, it would not be long before a fair stock of large fish could be built up. But as long as people fish primarily for meat rather than sport, this would be a difficult law to enforce.

Another possible solution, but one of considerable difficulty in practical accomplishment, would be to stock certain waters heavily and not permit any fishing in them until the following year. Perhaps a certain percentage of trout water in each state could be set aside each year for this purpose. The result, of course, would be to put an even heavier drain on the open waters; but if fly fishing only could at the same time be enforced, there is little doubt in my mind that a real improvement in fishing would result. Connecticut closes a series of small brooks to all fishing, using these as nurseries for small stocked fish, and also as natural spawning grounds for wild fish. In other places certain waters have been set aside for fly fishing only, to the great benefit of such waters. While the suggested methods of protecting stocked fish seem difficult, the problem of having open fishing of any quality for some eight million citizens throughout the country is so great that there can be no easy solution.

Each year finds more—many more—men, women and youngsters on the streams fishing for trout; and, frankly, I can't picture how reasonably good fishing for this ever-increasing army of people can be maintained under present conditions, let alone under greatly improved conditions. There are just so many miles of trout waters. They can support just so many trout—even if the money for stocking them to the maximum were available. With the constant increase in interest in trout fishing, fostered by outdoor publications, and manufacturers of fishing tackle, outdoor clothing, automobiles and what not, the limit is going to be reached some day quite soon. To date the answer has been, when certain sections of the country have no longer been able to afford reasonably good fishing, to travel to some other less heavily fished locality. This coming summer some of my friends will travel from New York to the Madison River in Wyoming, and some others are going clear across the continent to the Rogue in Oregon. I did it last summer. The latter will be surprised to find out how many other people will be fishing the Rogue, which is now lined with fishing camps.

No: the answer is no longer to go further afield. We must figure out how to maintain our own local fishing, wherever we may be; and believe me, it is going to take some tall figuring. Edward R. Hewitt has solved the question on his three miles of the Neversink River in New York, where he provides grand fishing for a limited number of rods—fish of three pounds up to six. BUT, he controls the number of people who can fish, and restricts them to fly fishing. So far no one has been able to provide really good fishing for unlimited numbers of fishermen.

Four years ago I resigned from a fishing club to which I had belonged for a number of years. Aside from having broken out in a bad rash of poverty, I rather welcomed the idea of relying on open water for my sport. I have rejoined the club; the open fishing in my part of the world was, according to my lights, a snare and a delusion. There are still some parts of the country where this is not the case, but it won't be long before it is the case everywhere, in my opinion, if the annual increase in fishermen continues at its present rate.

Do I sound too pessimistic? Well, I don't really think I am, because I have seen such a vast change take place in fishing conditions during the past twenty-five years. We have tried to meet this change with splendid hatcheries, stream improvement and reduced bag limits. I think there are actually more fish in the water on April 1st than there were twenty years ago. But I know that the even greater number of anglers on approximately the same miles of stream, do not get as good fishing. I say "approximately" the same miles of stream, because stream improvement *may* have kept up with and exceeded stream ruination through pollution and other causes.

It is my firm belief that one most important and practical step that can be taken *now,* to help conserve what we have, and to divide the pleasures of trout fishing among the greatest number of anglers, is to use the artificial fly instead of bait. This is not merely a theory. Wherever fly fishing only has been enforced, a marked improvement in fishing has resulted. It may be said that there are some small brooks which cannot be practically fished with a fly. My answer is that such small brooks would be better unfished, as the State of Connecticut has shown. Others will say that fly fishing is too difficult. My answer is that anyone who won't take the trouble to learn how to use a fly ought to take up some other sport. I taught my boy in one season to be a successful fly fisherman, and I can teach any grown man in less time—particularly if he has been a bait fisherman and knows something about trout. Casting can be learned in half an hour; not the polished casting of an expert, but casting that will catch fish. The outfit need not be expensive; my first rod, with which I fished for many years, cost $5.00. And if I know anything about fishermen, and I think I do, they are not ones to balk at spending money for their sport. But strangely enough, it is difficult to get many of them to spend any money for *improving* their sport. If it is suggested that by increasing the cost of a state fishing license by the price of four drinks, the fishing can be greatly improved, there is a loud roar from a vast multitude of highly indignant "sportsmen." When they have become hoarse with their roaring, they then spend the amount of the increase over a bar in thirty minutes, soothing their irritated throats—and complaining about the rotten fishing.

However, if all the bait fishermen in the country could have the same experience as my friend of whom I told at the beginning of this chapter, they wouldn't feel any sense of injustice in being asked to give up bait fishing for fly fishing. And once they had done this, they would—one and all—find out that when it comes to *fun,* let alone improved fishing, fly fishing is about the finest sport in the world.

NINE

And So It Goes

Eugene V. Connett

Some years ago I went fishing with a friend who had made an excellent reputation for himself as a successful fly fisherman, during the six years since he had taken up the sport. He was a man of unusual attainments, and I had always believed would become a really great fly fisher if he continued to apply himself to the fine points of the game.

On the day I speak of, conditions were not very propitious—in fact, the water was high, the air cold, and no hatch of fly present. We therefore used wet flies.

In something less than an hour my friend came downstream to where I was enjoying myself, and in marked disgust suggested we leave the stream and seek another with some fish in it. I was somewhat surprised, as I had seven trout in my basket, and I told my friend that this was as good a stream as I knew of within a reasonable distance of where we were.

His surprise at the fact I had seven fish was almost laughable. If he should ever see these lines, I know he will not object to my telling the story, for I had undergone an exactly similar experience some years previous with my friend George LaBranche—and it was one of the most valuable lessons I ever learned about fishing. Briefly, in those days I thought I knew as much as LaBranche, he having fished for more than twice as many years as I! And so my friend was convinced that although I had fished for more than twice as long as he had, nevertheless his skill was such that it must make up for his lack of stream experience.

Having seen my seven fish, looked at the stretch of water from which they had been taken, and examined the fly which took them, my friend did just what I had done some years earlier. He intimated that I knew a lot more than he did about catching trout and asked me to take him in hand. I had been waiting for this opportunity and accepted the rôle of tutor in a most willing and friendly spirit.

Rather than step into the stream myself and deliver a lecture on how to catch trout, I suggested that we walk down to an undisturbed pool below us, and that he fish it in his most skilful manner, while I watched for mistakes. The first one was not long in coming!

Fishing wet, he started in the run at the head of the pool, and did so by stepping into the stream about nine feet above the most likely lie for a good trout. Before he had even made his first cast, I requested him to leave the water and sit down beside me—much to his annoyance. However, he was a sportsman and took his medicine like a man. When he sat beside me I asked him:

"Where is the best spot in that run for a good fish to lie?"

After looking the water over with care, he pointed to a certain rock.

"If you wanted to frighten the fish lying in front of that rock, where would you enter the stream?" I inquired.

"Just where I went in," he replied, in some surprise.

Then I asked him to fish the lower part of the run, down to where it spread out into the pool. With commendable forethought, he took stock of the water before wading into the stream and when he did enter it, he was close to the bank, well above where his fly would be fished, and instead of standing up straight, was kneeling on a rock and using a side cast to keep his rod down. He cast his fly nicely to the far side of the run and let it sweep down across the current, lengthening his line until his fly had covered almost all the water. Each of his casts had been clean looking, with a tight straight line. When he was through I suggested that he back out from the water carefully and let me have a try.

On the far side of the stream was a rock, about two feet from the bank, with a branch hanging out over the water which ran along the bank, and I felt that a fish would be lying on the inshore side of the rock, enjoying the protection afforded by the situation. In order to interest this fish, it was necessary to drift the wet fly down between the rock and the shore, under the overhanging branch—not a very difficult thing to do, if one employed a curve cast to the left, with plenty of slack line on the water. The second cast rose the fish, and my friend was a trifle annoyed, as he could not see why his fly had not taken this fish as it swung past that rock on the offshore side. From where he was sitting he could not see my fly, and therefore did not realize exactly what had happened. When I joined him on the bank, I explained it, telling him why I thought the fish would be on the inshore side of the rock, pointing out the excellent protection from winged enemies afforded by the branch, and the satisfactory feeding possibilities of the current. I also showed him a piece of old leader tangled in the branch, where some other fisherman had got himself into trouble.

My friend agreed it was a perfect lie for a fish. I asked him why he hadn't thought of that before he started to fish the easy open water which every other angler who had fished the run before him had carefully covered.

This little lesson resulted in a half-hour of learning the curve casts—and any reasonably efficient caster can learn them in half an hour, although he will have to practice a lot longer than that to achieve real accuracy.

My friend was then asked to fish the pool itself, a large quiet expanse of water, fairly deep along the far bank, with patches of rhododendron hanging out over the water here and there. It was a long cast across to that inviting bank, which was the only place a fish would lie during the day.

He stepped gingerly into the calm water and began working out his fly toward the first patch of rhododendron, under which a fish was undoubtedly lying—probably a good fish, too. When the fly was ten feet from its mark, it fouled some branches behind my friend on the next backcast. This elicited several highly justified cuss words, and when I had freed the fly, he waded out several feet further into the pool, sending a series of waves rippling across its surface to the far bank—thus notifying the trout that someone was in the pool, and arousing their instinct of self-preservation to a point where their instinct to feed was entirely submerged.

After ten minutes of futile casting, I remarked that while patience might be a great virtue in the art of catching trout, it should be applied at the proper part of the proceedings, and suggested that my friend take a rest with me on the bank. I explained to him that the longer he continued to drop his fly near the fish, the more convinced the fish would probably become that this particular fly was one to eschew. Assuming that the fish had not been sufficiently frightened to leave its position, there was but one thing to do: rest it thoroughly, and while doing so, plan some method of attack which would put the fly— preferably a different size or pattern—within taking distance of the fish without any accompanying ripples or waves to warn it of danger.

My friend agreed to the logic of this, but did not see any way of avoiding at least a few ripples when wading into the stream, unless he stood on our bank to cast—which was obviously out of the question, due not only to the distance, but to lack of space for a backcast. I must confess that the outlook was not encouraging. The only chance I could see, was to walk to the bottom of the pool, cross the stream in the fast water below it, and then quietly walk up the far bank to a group of rocks lying near the shore, forming a small peninsula out from the bank. With care it should be possible to wade out below these rocks without sending any ripples upstream along the bank to where the fish was supposed to be lying. Then a curve cast to the left might place the fly near enough the fish, with leader and line away from him, to induce a rise.

An awful lot of trouble, you say. So did my friend. But that is what had put the seven fish in my basket that morning, and is what will put them in yours on any heavily fished trout stream.

It was decided that I should be the goat, and I made my way across the stream, and got into position according to the plan, without sending any warning waves to the fish. Now, there was one thing in my favour which I had not noticed until I was ready to begin casting: at intervals a faint breeze wafted across the pool toward my bank where the fish lay—or was supposed to lie. Thought I to myself, if I put on a long light leader, one of those little puffs will gently blow my fly as much as six feet, especially if I use a light, fluffy fly. Somewhat to the disgust of my expectant audience of one, I began changing my leader and fly. When I explained why, my friend settled back in a better humour.

At last—and it takes an awfully long time to make a change at such a juncture—I was ready for the first all-important cast, with some twelve feet of leader, carrying at least five feet of 4X gut at the bottom, with a spider pattern knotted on.

Next I made a high cast well short of the fish, to see just how the wind would act on the fly. The next puff carried it about four feet toward the bank, without any necessity for a curve cast, so I lengthened my line enough to reach the vital spot, and continued false casting until a puff of breeze started across the pool. It caught the fly in the air at the end of the forward cast and—gracefully blew it into the overhanging bushes!

"Haw! haw! haw!" from my friend. "All that trouble for nothing!"

I didn't feel so very happy, myself. But I remembered that the long hackles and the small hook on my spider fly provided a chance that it might not stick in the rhododendrons, and I carefully twitched the line a bit. It started to come, and the fly bounced from one rubber-like leaf to another until it finally drifted clear of them and fluttered to the water.

Simultaneously there was a big swirl and a yell from my friend. Just like any other human being I struck much too hard and left the spider with that trout, to say nothing of three links of beautiful 4X gut. And so it goes!

TEN

The Selection of Salmon Guides

Charles Phair

The guide not only must be a good boatman or canoeman, but he must be congenial, if your fishing is to be enjoyable. Remember, he is going to be your companion every day for the entire trip; therefore you want someone who not only knows the duties of a guide but is good company.

Most guides on the different salmon rivers of Canada are good fishermen and fly casters, but there is a great difference in them. Some are extremely anxious that you catch fish and will work hard and give you every opportunity, while others are not quite so painstaking. Perhaps the most important thing is their knowledge of the pools to be fished, such as knowing where fish lie at different stages of the water, and where the "sore spots" are. Good guides want no noise or racket going on in their boat, such as kicking the paddles, knocking the ashes out of your pipe on the side of the boat, or any disturbance that will create a vibration in the water.

The experienced guide is extremely careful in approaching the pool to be fished. In going up river to the head of the pool to commence the fishing, he will keep well in to the shore, so as not to disturb any fish that may be lying there. He usually first drops the killick, which is a lead weighing from twenty to thirty pounds, and which holds the boat in position, well at the head of the pool, a good long cast from where he would expect the fly to go over a fish, and from then on every drop he makes through the pool—i.e., every time he takes up the killick and drops it again to hold the boat in a new position—he does very carefully and with as little disturbance as possible. Then, provided he does it for you, he ties on the fly which you are to use, with the figure-eight knot; and you will notice he leaves about one-eighth of an inch of the end of the leader showing after the knot is tied. This is to prevent any danger of the end pulling through and untying when it tightens on a fish. This extra eighth of an inch of gut lies dead straight with the fly and is tucked in between the wings out of sight.

His eye will never leave the fly from then on. He is watching your backcast, both on his own account and yours, and the position of the fly on the water while it is being fished. If the fish raises and is not hooked, he can pretty nearly tell you whether he missed the fly or whether you took it away from him. The chances are he has been on this pool for years and knows every rock in it, and is full of stories of happenings there, all of which keep you interested. When you hook a fish, if you struck instead of tightened, he will remind you of it, and probably add that it is a mighty good leader you have on to stand the jerk you gave it. With the fish on, he pulls up the killick and eases the canoe off to one shore or the other, opposite and a little below your fish, so you can make him fight you and the current both. When you bring the fish in to the gaff, there will be no mistakes, such as cutting your leader with the gaff when he makes the stroke. After hitting your salmon a couple of clips on the head with the priest, he puts him in the canoe with plenty of grass under and over him to keep the hot sun off and hurries to set you out in the pool, just where you hooked this one, and is all ready for you to take another.

I had a funny experience in gaffing one season with a guide, Jack Mack, whom I had taken to the camp on the Restigouche. Jack was born on a salmon river, the Miramichi, but as a young man had come over into Maine, where I lived, and had taken up the guiding business. He was one of the most conscientious and willing men I have ever known, and it was said of him that he could carry a heavier pack on his back than any man in that country, and could stand more grief. He had fished and hunted with me in Maine for a great many years, but had never done any guiding for salmon fishermen.

The first salmon he gaffed for me he took across the beach, which was quite wide at that particular place, disappearing in the bushes, and, when I went to get my fly out of the fish's mouth, I found him some fifty yards into the woods. I asked him why he went way off in the woods with the fish, and he said he was afraid the fish would flop off and get back into the river again. I told him that was all right, but not to go so far the next time. But every fish after that, Jack would keep on going until he got into the woods. One day some fishermen stopped at my camp for lunch and I was telling them how Jack, when he gaffed a fish for me, always took him into the woods and up on the second ridge, for fear he would flop back in the river. Jack happened to be standing on the piazza and overheard me, and at four o'clock that afternoon when I went down to the boat to go out for the evening fishing, he walked over to me and said, "Charlie, any time you don't like the way I gaff fish for you, you can get somebody else, but by God, no fish I gaff ain't going to flop back in no river!"

Most all guides are good with the gaff; some are exceptionally so. A number of times I have had them gaff grilse which would take a quick run up river past the stern of their canoe. That is quick work as the grilse is small and very fast.

One season when fishing was especially poor on the Tobique, and club members were taking very few fish in their water, one of my pools was yielding fish every day and I was having great sport all to myself. This, of course, in time became known all up and down the river. Colonel Robert Emmett, president of the club at that time, a fine fisherman and most delightful gentleman, one day invited me to Wainright Lodge for the day's fishing. "You fish Wainright Pool today," he said after breakfast, "and I'll go on down river." Now, Wainright Pool was and is the poorest excuse for a salmon pool on the whole river, and only infrequently is a fish taken there. Jimmy Waters, a well-known Tobique guide, one of the best in my acquaintance, and a grand fellow in every way, was guiding me; and if there is one guide for whom I'll fish hardest and the best I know how, Jimmy is the one. We gave that pool a real overhauling, from top to bottom, and managed to kill two fish. That night the Colonel came back late and reported that he had not seen a fish all day, and when I asked him what water he had fished, he replied, "Yours, at Hayden's." I'll never forget the expression on Jimmy's face when he heard that; he was very well pleased.

If a fish weighs twenty pounds you should be about twenty minutes killing him; for the old saying, "a minute to the pound," is about right, provided, of course, he is not one of those sulky fish that wants to put his nose up behind a rock out in the heavy current and stay there. That being the case, the guide will drop the canoe well down below him to one side and show you how to put a good side strain on and hand line him. This soon pulls his nose around and the current washes him out of there. However, the guide sometimes has to go out with the canoe and frighten some of these fish away from the rock with a pole. After the day's fishing, he sees that your rod is hung up on the pegs, and all the line that is wet is stripped off and crisscrossed back and forth between a couple of these same pegs which your rod rests on, to dry it. These are only a few of the many things your guide will do for you.

If you have your own lodge get a good woods cook, that is, a man who cooks in the lumber camps winters. He not only knows how to cook well, but can do many other things. If you want to smoke some salmon during the summer to take back home, he knows just where to build the little smokehouse on the bank. He will have his fire down below on the shore, so that when the smoke gets to the fish it will be cool. While they are being smoked he takes them out two or three times, and with a brush gives them a good coat of olive oil. This not only helps preserve them but makes them turn a beautiful color. Then they are packed away between sheets of birchbark and put away in a cool place. You can take them home and have smoked salmon all winter. If you want to take some home which will keep fresh indefinitely, he knows how to preserve them and puts them up in glass sealers.

Your guide's knowledge of the pool you fish, very often makes the difference of whether you get fish or not. He knows where to anchor his canoe in the pool so that your fly will fish to the best advantage, because he has probably tried fishing this pool anchored from several different places, and knows from which one it fishes best. He will not be able to give you any scientific reasons or use any technical terms for doing this or that, but he knows the right way from experience.

It is well not to wear any conspicuous clothes, such as a white shirt, for instance. Some color such as green or gray is much better, especially when you are bringing a fish in to the gaff. Once I brought a fish in to the gaff on the shore near a small village, and a great part of the population was standing on the bank watching the proceedings. Just as I had the fish up within about ten feet of the guide, a woman in a white dress rushed down to where he was standing, with the result that the fish made a wild rush across the river, jumped, and got away. The guide used some pretty strong language to her, and I never saw her near the river afterwards.

The most particular man about the position of a boat in a pool was Mike Broderick, and it seemed as though the killick had to go down within an inch of where he wanted it, or the stern man got a growl. Mike certainly knew his salmon water.

If you are outfitting your own lodge, whether you should purchase a Gaspé or canoes would depend entirely on whether you were on a big river with heavy water, or a small river which was more quiet. In the first instance you would want a Gaspé boat, as it is not altogether safe to fish big heavy water from canoes. A good Gaspé, twenty-two feet long, costs about $100. On a small river canoes are much better. You can get around easily and quickly with them, and without any danger. A good one, such as a White or Chestnut, built eighteen feet long, would cost about $90.

The killicks which any tinsmith will run for you, should weigh about thirty to forty pounds for a Gaspé. For a canoe, under ordinary circumstances, twenty to twenty-five pounds is heavy enough. The guides will make these for you themselves if they can find some lead, and will use an old tin coffee pot for a mold, setting a swivel in the top when they run it. To this swivel a coil of window cord makes a good line. A killick for a canoe costs about $3; one for a Gaspé, $5.

The Indian guide, until you understand him, is more or less of a puzzle.

He has ideas of his own about fishing and no one can change them, but if you treat him well, there is nothing he will not do for you. Three of the Melicete Tribe in Canada, Nick Lola, Newel Francis and Tom Moulton have been with me most of the time for ten years, and are not only good fishermen but faithful men.

The Melicete Tribe reservation is at the mouth of the Tobique salmon river in New Brunswick, and their land fronts on about five miles of the river, and what fishing there is on that water belongs to them. So if you want to fish any of it, you can do so by employing one of them as guide.

Some of them are good fishermen; Newel Francis and Tom Moulton are the best. They anchor the canoe in what they consider the best spot in a pool and fish there all day, always casting the same length of line. Their idea is that the fish must come up past them at some time or other, and will be sure to see their fly; whereas if they dropped, they might go past one. Upon hooking a fish, they lay down the rod, take up the killick, and pole ashore. If the fish is still on, all right; if not, it is all right just the same, and they go back for another. They do not fight their fish very hard, with the result that they have them on a long while and eventually lose a great many. The hook wears a hole and drops out. They fish for days in the same spot, casting the same length of line, and to show that this is not such a bad idea, I will say that in 1934 Tom Moulton, fishing alone, from the bank at one particular place, killed seventy-two salmon. This was especially good fishing considering the tackle he used. They make their own rods, using ash for the butt and generally hornbeam for the second joint and tip; some of these rods cast well. It is quite usual for one of them to fish one fly until it is worn out, that is, if he thinks it is the right one. These men all handle canoes well.

When I was eight or ten years old and wanted to go fishing, which I did most of the time, if I could get an old Indian, known as Newel Bear, to go with me, it was all right with my father, for he had great confidence in him. Newel was in those days Chief of the Melicetes and I had my first experience at salmon fishing with him.

The Aroostook River in northern Maine then had quite a few salmon in, but there was practically no fly fishing done for them. If a man wanted a fish, he went out in a boat at night with a flambeau in the bow and speared himself one. About this time a dam was built across the river at a town called Caribou, and no fishway was put in. It was what was called a roll dam and had an apron. The fish would jump up on the apron and swim up over, provided there was water enough. If not, they would be washed back in the pool below. The first few years this dam was in there, it was a great sight to watch the fish jumping all over it, and some of them were caught by local anglers on a fly. One summer Newel built a bark canoe and he and I, taking a tent, supplies and what trout fishing tackle I had, started down river for this dam twelve miles away. I caught no fish with my trout outfit, but they were jumping all around us and all over the apron. After three or four days and no fish, Newel said he was going to the village and told me to watch the tent. He came back in about two hours with an iron about eight inches long, flat and sharp at one end. He then whittled out a pair of jaws, and lashing the iron on the end of a pole with the jaws on each side of it, was ready for action. That night after dark we went down to the dam and he waded out, as there were only about six inches of water running over the apron, and having caulked shoes on, such as a river driver wears, had no trouble. He only had to wait a little while before a fish jumped up near him, and, driving the spear into him, he brought him ashore. After that we had all the salmon we wanted. The iron of this spear went down through the salmon's back and cut the backbone, the jaws at the same time closing around the fish, springing out as the man strikes, and springing back around the fish and holding him on.

One day a man caught one in a net below us and I bought it to take home. I did not notice that the net marks showed plainly and Newel did not tell me. When I got home I showed the fish to my father, who asked me how I had got it. I told him I caught it at the Caribou Dam, and he turned around and walked off with the remark, "God, how I hate a liar!" He had seen the net marks.

My father was the first conservationist I had ever known, although I did not realize it at the time and did not think very much of his way of fishing. He would not catch enough fish to suit me. He would catch enough for a meal, and then take me home. I wanted him to stay and catch them all. Some nights after supper he would take me up river to where a cold spring brook came in, and one night he caught two trout there that weighed four pounds each. I coaxed him to stay and catch some more, as there were a lot in there, but he said we had enough, so that ended it. The next day I took Newel and we went back there and caught about fifty—all there were. I remember I had to stay in bed all the next day for that, but it did not stop me from wanting to catch all the fish there were, everywhere I went.

When I was twelve I was taken to the Skiff Lake Club in Canada. This club was composed of twenty-five men who controlled the fishing and owned the twenty-seven islands on the lake, which was four miles long and one and a half miles wide. This was landlocked salmon fishing, and the water was protected by wardens. Joe Jefferson, the actor, fished there during those summers, and I remember seeing him being rowed around by Andy, who was considered the best guide there. This was my first really great fishing—the late John Stewart, who was Superintendent of the Canadian Pacific Railroad and also president of the club, used to take me with him. He was considered a grand fly caster in those days, and, as I remember him, he would not look bad in anybody's company today. Lord Northcore of England had been coming over each year for this fishing, and had built a fine lodge, which he presented to Mr. Stewart. Major Howe of New York, another great fly fisherman in his day, also fished there. His wife was shot by some Indians while coming down the Tobique River in a canoe. The guides at this lake were all Irishmen, as this was an Irish settlement, and I remember they were great storytellers. The fishing was all done from rowboats, and when I took an Indian with a canoe there the first time, a lot of the men and women gathered on the shore and coaxed me not to go on the lake in it. They had never seen one before and thought it too frail. I always used a canoe there after that.

When Joe Jefferson came to Skiff Lake he stayed in tents which he pitched on what is now Club Island, which was covered with white birch trees and was a very lovely spot. Each year just before he left he gave a farewell party on the island to all the natives who lived nearby. At one of his parties, after mingling with all of them for a while, he managed to get away in the woods unnoticed, and about the time the party was at its height, a very old man with long white hair and whiskers came hobbling out of the birches on a stick. As he drew near, the natives all became panic-stricken and when one old Irishman hollered, "Holy Jasus!" they rushed to the boats. Then Jefferson took off his Rip Van Winkle outfit.*

It is well to let a cook make out a list of food supplies for the lodge himself, as he has probably been doing this sort of thing for a great many years and knows exactly what salmon fishermen like to eat.

If you are running a real up-to-date lodge on a big river where things are done right, the cook will have a helper who gets up the wood and assists him in his work. This man or boy will act as waiter also. Guides, when they come in at lunch time or after dark at night, do not like to have to go out and cut wood and do things like that. Their job is guiding you at salmon fishing and nothing more.

---

*Joe Jefferson was a nineteenth-century actor famous for his portrayal of Rip Van Winkle.—Ed.

ELEVEN

The Spark Is Kindled

Howard T. Walden, II

The exact date of my first trout fishing escapes me, but I would say that the year was 1910 or thereabouts, placing the experience within that magic time of life when all of one's perceptions have a heightened beauty, a freshness of form and color so exquisite and fragile that they cannot endure into later years.

The fishing itself was far from spectacular. It was worm fishing, in a small brook that meandered through woodland and meadow not more than two miles from home. The trout were not large: seven or eight inches was average; a fish of ten inches was considered a prize. Yet my first trout fishing on this stream will always remain with me as the most thrilling I have ever had.

The brook was typical of dozens of others in that part of New Jersey, yet to me, in that remote time, it was the most distinctively individual, the most promising and alluring of all water. I came to know it as I knew my own back yard. I could go on a straight line through dense woods, leaving a path that ran parallel to the stream a quarter of a mile away, and arrive directly upon any one of the brook's ten or twelve likelier pools. I knew where each spring rill fed the main stream, and where each slough of slack water backed away from it into the damp woods. Many fallen trees crossed it, the wreckage of some long-past cyclone. These made natural bridges to facilitate an angler's passage upstream or down; some of them partially dammed the current or diverted the channel, and many ideal trout holes were formed thereby. Most of these pools were difficult indeed to fish, and threatened the almost certain loss of a hook among the roots in their deep dusks; but they were the abiding places of *Fontinalis*, and a worm dropped carefully by a hidden angler would often evoke that incomparable, smashing strike of the native trout.

The stream took its source five miles north of our town, flowed south four miles and east two more, emptying into a broad tidal river. In the course of its journey it wandered through open meadow and deep woods, through a large farmyard and two ice ponds, and, in its lower reaches, skirted the back yards of another town. In our pre-trout era the stretch between the two ice ponds was our favorite water for sunnies, roach and an occasional catfish. We did not fish the part opposite and below the town, for the water there had a perceptible murk of pollution and an environment decidedly unappealing by comparison with the sylvan surroundings upstream. Nor, though I have never quite known the reason, did we fish that part above the upper ice pond. It was farther from home, of course, but that scarcely would have deterred us. Perhaps, being smaller than the middle reaches, it seemed not worth our while. But I rather incline to the opinion that our long-postponed exploration of these parts was the natural result of boy nature. Boys are, I think, more eminently creatures of habit, more consistently the true conformers than grown men. Our activities were devoted to a certain area. We grew to know every foot of it, and its potentialities of fish and game, and it sufficed us. As if we were an Indian tribe, we marked for ourselves—subconsciously and without ever speaking of it—the established boundaries of our domain. To stray beyond these was a matter of such consequence that, when it occurred to one of us at last, it was not casually acted upon, alone, but placed before the entire clan as a project requiring a collective judgment.

The plan to fish the stream below the town was conceived in a mood of reluctant experimentation, induced by the failure of that usually reliable part of the brook which was "ours." We ventured down the strange lower waters to the "Railroad Pool," an abnormal widening of the stream below a railway trestle, where we made a catch of fifty or sixty roach and sunfish, taken on bits of dough mixed with cotton.

That exceptionally profitable enterprise had, for a while, a somewhat unedifying influence upon us and our fishing. We went back to the Railroad Pool again and again, fishing this unlovely lower stream to the neglect of the crystal water and virgin glades of the upper brook. We were a little ashamed of ourselves for this; our repeated sallies to the Railroad Pool seemed indicative of some preference in our natures for the grosser aspects of angling. At the Railroad Pool we could count on a mess of fish with a minimum of effort, but in the woodland and meadow stream above we had to proceed with some caution from hole to hole; and not only was the fishing harder work but the spoils were at best not nearly so rich as those yielded by the big water below the town. But this avidity for fish rather than fishing should not be characteristic, we were sure, of decent anglers. A reaction was inevitable.

There came a day when I knew I was surfeited with the Railroad Pool and its easily taken denizens. I would leave that place for good and all and head north for my fishing—not immediately north, in the water we knew so well, but far, far up, above the second ice pond where none of us ever had gone. This daring plan, broached as usual to the partners, was received with mingled expressions of amazement, skepticism and sympathy . . . I would get nothing up there. The brook was too small; no one ever fished it in those parts . . . In effect, no one ever bothered with that undersized rill, whose dark water came quietly out of the deep woods above the second ice pond, as if colored by the somber shade and mystery of the uncharted region through which it flowed.

That water's reputation of not being "bothered with" might have made it all the more alluring to me. But as a matter of fact I had heard—some time before and in so remote and vague a fashion that I had scarcely given the tale credence—that it *had* been bothered with. A boy I knew (he was not a fisherman) advised me that a boy he knew (also not a fisherman) had seen a man emerge late one afternoon from that wilderness above the upper ice pond. The man had carried a very slender rod in his hand and over his shoulder a willow creel in which three extraordinarily beautiful fish reposed on damp moss. These fish, it seemed, were larger than the average run of roach and sunnies, were without scales but were decorated with brilliant markings—bronze-green, mottled backs, brightly-spotted sides and yellow-orange underparts.

Although, up to that time, I had never seen a trout, I had seen pictures of them; and the description of these three fish, disjointed as it was as I received it, tallied with the pictures. Yet it was not conceivable that trout could inhabit our brook. One had to go to the storied fastnesses of Canada or Maine to catch trout. They were not a boy's fish, but a fish for mature anglers. One graduated to trout, eventually, from the sunfish and roach school. It was a man's business, like driving a car; there was something preposterous even in my serious consideration of it.

Thoughts like these almost battered down the small persistent hope that kept me on my way upstream after leaving my companions at the Railroad Pool. It was a long walk, and it led by all of that lower water I knew so well. The temptation to pause at some of these deep holes was strong, for fishing water never looks so inviting or so surely potential as when you are, from some necessity, passing it by unchallenged. The day was gusty and cool, past the first week of June, a day of alternate brilliance and shadow as the rent fabric of clouds hurried east across the sun. The water of my stream was by times sparkling and dark: in the lee of an old stump it was quiet as a summer dusk, but a long meadow stretch of the brook built up a respectable sea in the wind and was traversed incessantly by the hurrying dark tracks of the gusts.

I kept on like some crusader, armed against temptation. I crossed the brook above the lower ice pond, negotiated the boggy low length of a pasture, passed the swimming hole—deserted in this blustery chill—and headed north through a grove of hardwoods until I reached the upper ice pond.

An east-west road, little used in that remote year, crossed the upper end of the pond. Immediately north of the road the brook was rather aimless in a small area of lush meadow; and then, abruptly at the limits of this little lea was the wall of the woods. It confronted me like a challenge: for all we knew in those days that lofty timber marched uninterrupted to the shores of the Arctic.

I stood for a moment on the little bridge where the road crossed, looking north, looking hard at that looming barrier; it looked back at me with no expression, or perhaps with all expression, threatening and beckoning. It was the whole of Nature and in its countenance was all that Nature ever had offered man.

After a moment I went ahead, north. Beyond our accustomed reservation at last, I was glad of the narrow path that went in my direction. I followed it across the little field north of the road and with it entered at last the deep woods. The path went its way, the big trees stood aside in deference to its narrow progress; it had courage and persistence and seemed to know what it was about, and I drew some measure of confidence from its manifest reliability.

The crown of this forest seemed enormously high and remote, as if it were a veil of dark clouds over the world. It moved ceaselessly aloft, as the wind tangled in its infinite patterns, giving a play of sifted inconstant light to the path and lower trunks and ferns and all that grows in dampness and deep shade. The continuous sighing of the lofty wind seemed to insulate these lower strata in a stillness. There were close low dogwoods, witch hazel, aspen and beech; and in this green gloom they lived in a breathless taut suspension of all motion. Skunk cabbage and ferns, and last year's leaves, and the sodden rotted litter of a century's fallen trees and branches gave off a smell that seemed almost a perceptible vapor, the very odor of life, an emanation from the striving of a myriad minute organisms and the infinitesimal stretching of countless roots, and the yielding of the earth to this microscopic push of growth.

As I went along I felt the strangeness of my presence on that path, as if I were invading some profound privacy of the woods. But the woods were persistent in keeping their secrets intact. One cannot get at the essential inner quick of Nature. I traveled the path in a stillness but I began to realize, after awhile, that the stillness was traveling with me. It was as if all that small swarming activity of growth was suspended as I passed, to be resumed when I had got safely by. The woods quieted as I approached, like April peepers in a pond. The strained and ever-present hush was like the still shyness of children before a passing stranger. A murmuring would start up again behind me—I felt rather than heard it—and I was sure that the same murmuring lay ahead.

I forgot, almost, that I had come to fish. The path had slanted gradually west in its deep northward boring—gradually west and down. There was a rift in the ground-growth at my feet and a whisper barely audible in that profound quiet of suspended germination. The brook was there, black below some overhanging ferns, talking to the roots of an oak as it went by.

I had to look twice to make sure I hadn't had an illusion. And, being a student of brooks, I lay down on my stomach and peered in through the dusky rifts in that complicated lower jungle . . . Doing so I was surprised at the volume of water immediately before and under my eyes. A wandering beam of sunlight vaguely illuminated the extreme secret bottom of this pool, two feet down in the interlacing convolutions of black roots. The light hovered there a moment, showing me a patch of sand, a sparkle of iron pyrites (that "gold" of the northeastern rills) and then the light was gone with the ceaseless motion of the forest crown. I waited for its return, peering into the liquid twilight, and gradually my eyes became accustomed to this deeper, subaqueous gloom. Close under the bank was the imponderable dusk of the roots, like a nest of snakes; out beyond that the vague bottom of sand and pebbles. For all I could see this microcosm contained no life. Such shapes as were in it were still, as if they had been there forever: waterlogged sticks, a stone or two, blurred as shadows. I looked until the intensity of the unaccustomed focus hurt my eyes. But, as I was about to turn away, the faintest imaginable movement arrested my gaze, directed it again to the dark floor of the stream. I couldn't be sure—it might have been some caprice of a strained vision—yet I could have sworn that one of those longish blurred shapes had moved. "Moved" is scarcely the word: the change was barely perceptible and was not a movement of the whole object but only of its downstream end.

Peering down through the gloaming of that little pool I saw again that gentlest shadow of a motion. There was no doubt of it now: the lower end of that object stirred from side to side in the current like a flag in a zephyr.

The wandering sunbeam returned, miraculously, as I watched, suffusing the pool with its rays, giving the dark water a misty luminosity. But it was enough. In the soft amber glow I saw all of that iridescent beauty of the trout. Then once more the pool grew dark.

My eyes had not wavered in their focus during the alternate lightening and darkening of the pool, but now I perceived that my trout was gone. I had not seen him move away and I shall never know how he accomplished this bit of magic. That fish de-materialized, merely. He might have been a figment of the sunbeam which had revealed him, coming and going with it, some solar pre-cipitation visible, as the iron pyrites were, only in the full sun.

It was about then, I think, that my respect for *Salvelinus* was born; and probably the same moment saw the end of that part of my fishing career which was concerned with sunnies, perch, catfish and roach, all those typical boyhood prizes of our fresh-water estuaries. That sunbeam had presented me a sort of diploma.

In my fishing that afternoon I was successful beyond my most extravagant hopes; more successful, in fact, than I have been many times over the same water in recent years. Whatever Red Gods presided over that windy forest crown rewarded me, perhaps, for my humility, for my sense of reverence and awe in their temple and my extreme quietness along its dusky aisles. I was rather glad there was no one about but the Red Gods to see my hands tremble as I assembled my three-piece, hardware-store bamboo.

I went downstream to begin fishing: it would have been a sacrilege to fish in the spot which had shown me the secret essence of this upper stream . . . The brook followed an amazingly devious course, as if deliberately lingering in this woodland. I crossed and recrossed it, clambered over windfalls, and occasionally, at some bend where the water was dark and deep, paused to drop a worm into the slow-curling current. Nothing occurred for some time, beyond the fascination of the fishing itself: the promise, the challenge of each bend of the stream, the ever-new aspect of the water and the endless variety of problems it offered.

When long continued, fishing that is unproductive of fish—or even of strikes—immerses the angler in the routine rhythms incidental to his progress along the stream and his manipulation of the rod. The expectation of a trout becomes almost nonexistent, so deeply is it sunk beneath the immediacy of the mere fishing.

It was in this state of lapsed alertness that I had my first strike from a brook trout. I retain a singularly clear impression of that little run of water. The brook there effected a straight cleavage of the banks for perhaps twenty feet, a preco-cious riffle, swift and sun-flecked and achieving something of a miniature roar over its pebbly bottom and building four-inch waves in midcurrent toward the downstream end. A child riffle, true in all respects to riffle type. I have seen grown ones—in the Esopus and the Neversink in early season—where the peb-bles were boulders and the four-inch waves were nearer four feet, and they were exactly the same except in degree. And this one came at length to a pool, as do most riffles, great or small. This pool was a deepish cavity of still water beneath the overhanging branches of a big oak. The worm coursed down the little rapid, entered the green-shaded stillness. As I have said, I was not keen: all my faculties were not concentrated, as they should have been, on the worm. A gleam of silvery light, deep in that shadowed amber, brought me alive. My rod, too, had a simultaneous reaction: it bent its over-stout tip a full six inches toward the water. The line between reel and first guide went taut in my left hand. The whole ensemble of rod and tackle was convulsed with the living resistance at the far end.

Nothing like this had ever happened to me. No sunfish, roach or catfish had ever charged my bait with such unexampled ferocity or felt half as strong as this fighting fish felt now. I knew it was a trout, and I knew above all else that I must land him. There must be no bungling here; if everything else in my life was destined to failure, the act of this particular moment must succeed.

I can remember a distinctly conscious effort to be as calm as I led that fish up the little rapid, trying to strip in line fast enough to keep it taut but not so fast as to free the hook. He came closer and closer—I could see now his exquisite color and markings. The war of hope and apprehension was too bitter to support . . . Hope won; in seconds more the trout was on the bank, safe at last. I killed him in the quick humane way—the backward bend of the head—laid him carefully on a bed of moss and sat down on the bank to look at him and to think about my success. It was a full moment, flooding warm with victory. And there was something else: a good leaven of remorse to prevent any smugness in that moment of triumph. I hadn't foreseen this development, in my desperate hope for a trout. But it was there. (It has followed me down every stream I have fished since and caught up with me each time I have stopped to take a trout.) I could not be completely glad at having removed that gem-like creature from the water which was his element. Though I could not express it he seemed then—and he seems still—a crystallization in the flesh of all the changing character of a running stream: the suavity of deep water, the dusky immobility of a still pool, the gay abandon of a rapid and the incalculable play of light and shadow over them all. It is as if he were born of these patterns of nature rather than by the biological processes of eggs and fertilization, as if some unapprehended chemistry of beauty had precipitated this life-form from a rare combination of elements: shadow and white sun, clean sand and mossy stone, roots and the derelict leaves, the ease of the tideless backwater and the high strife of the central current. All of the endless diversity of the stream is there, before he begins to fade in death, in that amazing color and in the clean fair lines of the fish, the immaculate continuity of head and body, body and tail.

I went on downstream in the aging afternoon, keener now, as one is always keener after his first fish. The stream widened gradually, a tributary came in from the west and piled up a sand bar at the confluence, a long, sun-illumined shallow where six inches of water hurried over the white bottom. It was the most glaringly exposed water of that brook's entire length, but in the center of it a trout lay over the bright sand. I saw him from afar, saw that he was bigger than my first. Approaching on hands and knees, I put the worm gently fifteen feet upstream and let it go down while I watched, trembling, for the anticipated strike. It came at once, violent in that shallow water. I hit back but there was a little slack line—it had been a delicate manoeuvre to get the worm to him at all—and my line came back to me and beyond, weightless, entangling itself in the streamside foliage. The water continued calmly over the white empty sand. It was as if nothing had happened. I might have imagined a trout had been there.

But farther down, in a pool almost large enough to swim in, I took a ten-incher from an infinite maze of roots. My line was perfectly taut here and I drew him out the way the worm had gone in, with never an inch of slack. His struggling weight amazed me as he came up; he was much the biggest fish I had ever caught. But my day was not yet at the crest.

After that second trout I felt a little guilty even in trying for any more. But I kept on; I was not particularly hopeful of another, anyway, in that part of the brook which remained still to be fished. Though the stream was completely strange to me, I knew I had come a good distance from the starting point. Light ahead through the trees confirmed me. The clearing was there, perhaps a hundred yards below, then the short stretch of meadow brook, and below that the ice pond whence I had started into this wilderness.

Every bend of this little stream was a surprise, so dense was the June foliage that shielded its secrets. The edge of the woods was closer now but the trees marched up to that edge in mass formation and hence the forest gloom was not attenuated. It was thus that I came all at once upon a wood road, a bridge across the brook, and below the bridge a pool of much greater dimensions than any I had fished this afternoon. The wood road had not been used in years; the bridge was far gone in decay, sagging to the eternal stream. A big spider moved out of sight into the black underparts of the tumbled structure. The water here was dark and fast, finding its way through the soft wreckage, complaining at the obstruction. One of the old boards, pivoting on a single remaining nail, swung back and forth in the current in a slow changeless routine. On the downstream side the brook freed itself from the tangled ruin and spread deeply and wide. The black water of the central current was effervescent with bubbles that rose and floated away under the towering forest.

Perhaps by now my confidence was inflated, or perhaps the brooding mystery of the place gave me the certain conviction that a trout was there—at any rate I have never put a worm or a fly into any water with less doubt of success. The strong current below the bridge had its way with the worm; I took line from the reel and let the stream have it through the guides. The stream would have taken all of it, I suppose, had not a trout been equally greedy and intolerant of the slow patient ways of streams. The worm had gone perhaps half the length of the pool when I perceived that although I was still paying out line the far end had not only ceased its down-current drift but was actually coming back upstream, toward me! That was in keeping with the dark mood of the place: something of the sort was rather to be expected in this ancient glen which had been so long apart from the world that it had forgotten about physics and the rational ways of life. But I did not quite succumb to this witchery of perverted principles. I remembered that the way to land a trout is to take in line and keep it taut, and this I proceeded to do, gathering the yards of curving slack until I came up short against that vibrant, deep-boring body of *Salvelinus*. He turned downstream, presenting his full strength, now, to my startled calculation, and I knew that he was by far the heaviest fish my rod had ever known. I suppose my tactics were indelicate and too avidly swift, but they sufficed. That trout would have required a landing net had I been using a fly rod, but this instrument was a stout coarse yokel of a bait rod with all the blunt plebeian action of a derrick. I loved it then, but I have rather hated it since, remembering how it brought in that trout as if leering at his magnificent courage. He was well hooked (by some chance, for he did not deserve to be) and the matter of landing him was a simple brutal affair.

I laid him out on one of the old boards of the bridge with the two others, dwarfed, beside him. He would go well over a foot, I decided. A thick, wide fish, he mounded up on the board, an extravagant pile of beauty. (I do not think that this beauty is magnified when I try to see it now through the fogs of twenty-five years. The trout in that stream were all startlingly beautiful in both form and color, superior to most of the native trout I have caught since in other waters.) Just then I had a feeling of guilt at contemplating that fish, a sense of the destruction of some rare and precious thing. I wish I could report here that I took him off the hook with a wet hand and returned him to the water. But I cannot.

I sat there on the bridge for some minutes looking at that trout and his lesser brothers of the upper stream. Then I wrapped them carefully in some big leaves and bore them back to civilization, to the Railroad Pool where my comrades were still taking sunnies and roach from the dull water. This, perhaps, was the supreme sin of that day. Those fellows looked at me and my trout in a still wonder, as if I and my fish were new arrivals from Mars. They took down their rods in silence; I think they left their strings of roach and sunnies on the bank. But they were not long in defeat. There were many questions, and before we reached home their own trout were as good as caught.

We did have sense enough to restrain ourselves. We seemed to realize, even then, that this little stream was not inexhaustible and that only the miracle of its seclusion had kept trout in it. We took a solemn oath of secrecy and established certain private regulations for ourselves, based upon principles of conservation. We set bag limits which, in the light of experience, seem to have been dictated by an unwarranted optimism for there were very few occasions when any one of us took more than two trout from those upper waters.

In time we acquired better tackle and possibly more skill, but there were many days when we returned empty handed; and I remember no single day to compare with that first afternoon, and only one subsequent trout to match my leviathan of the deep pool below the ruined bridge.

The stream became known, as was inevitable. Strangers found it in the deep woods; cars were parked at the upper ice pond. The State became interested in it and made yearly plantings of brown trout and rainbows. The fishing improved, from a quantitative standpoint, but it was apparent that the wild native trout were decreasing. Worst of all, that dusky privacy which had been the little brook's ineffable charm had been ravished.

For many years we fished it—those two or three of our original clan who remained in that part of the world—once a season in deference to the old tradition. But a certain melancholy pervaded this annual ritual. The stream was losing character—our civilization being still too immature to be concerned overmuch with the guarding of a trout stream's virginity—and we gave it up at last. The memory, at least, could be inviolate.

A new bridge has replaced the ancient ruin at the lower pool; and the road that passes over, cleared and tidy, has the flinty look of ambition, as if it hopes to be a suburban street before long. The ranks of the forest have been thinned and harsh sunlight has flooded in upon the secret cool dells. Water that used to be black under the dripping fern banks is now exposed all the way to the bottom, bright with sun and with emptiness. The brook is doomed. Life there has reached its peak and passed over. Possibly the water and the old trees know it: there is a wistful note in their gossip, nowadays, when the June wind is in the tattered old forest crown and the brook ruffles up and talks to the old roots and the rocks. Perhaps this is just my imagining—but I have seen it when it hummed with the joy of its abundant life and I think now that it is dying, that it knows the feel of the cancer of progress.

III

STORIES

Sam Fario

Howard T. Walden, II

"It's a strange thing," I was saying to the Professor, "how women who fish for trout seem to have the killer instinct to a much greater degree than men."

The oak chunks, still a little green, had caught on at last. My waders and heavy socks were drying slowly, draped over the fire screen. The Professor had arrived in camp late that afternoon, too tired, after a day's drive, to essay the evening rise. I had been out there until dark, throwing a dry fly over the long Club Pool and a shallow riffle downstream. But chiefly I had been watching something else—probably the fastest and most violent piece of trout-fishing action I've ever seen. Thinking about it afterward, it seemed to confirm certain old ideas of mine about women who fish.

"I haven't noticed it particularly," the Professor said.

"Have you fished with women much—or watched them fish?"

"With one, a good deal. With others rarely. The one I fish with has so little of the killer instinct that I wonder, sometimes, why she fishes at all."

The Professor is not old but he is older than I, much wiser and, as I've intimated, a much better fisherman. Sometimes, when talking to him, I feel like a small boy talking a little over his head on an exciting subject newly and imperfectly learned. He wouldn't want me to feel that way, but I do. But what I had seen on the stream tonight was a cold irrefutable fact to plank down in front of the Professor's erudition.

"Maybe it's the way Nature evens up against maternal tenderness," I suggested. "Some women who don't fish for trout have it, too. Business women and women who go in for competitive sports. Just watch a woman tennis champ polish off a third-rate opponent, sometime. They do it differently from men. They're merciless."

"How does this thing manifest itself in trout fishing?"

"Get him to the net and get him there quickly. Did you ever see a woman give a nine-inch trout his head for three minutes? Or a nineteen-inch trout, for that matter, any longer than she had to? Or put a good fish back after she has caught him?"

"They're rhetorical questions and I'm supposed to say 'no.' But the answer is 'yes'—for the one I've fished with."

"She must be the exception to prove the rule. The woman I watched tonight was typical of the rule. She could cast and wade like a man and she used imagination and brains in her fishing. But she was a killer. She was ruthless, like all of 'em."

The Professor looked at me curiously for a moment, as if about to ask a pointed question. But that sharp interrogation in his face lost itself in a faint meditative expression of amusement, a kind of inward smile. He got up to poke the charcoal off the oak chunks and was rewarded at once with a nice purring blaze. "Tell me about her," he said.

I took advantage of the Professor's renewed fire to turn my waders inside out and drape them again over the end of the screen.

"I passed her upstream early this evening, on my way down to try the Club Pool. She was not fishing then, just sitting on a big rock alongside a fast run, smoking a cigarette. I stopped and asked her what luck and she unwound an eighteen-inch brown trout from her creel and showed him to me. She must have had some fun with that fish. I noticed her rod and gear in the minute or two I was with her. The rod was a fairly big one but she had a long tapered leader and a small fly. A number twelve Quill Gordon took him, she said, up in the Poacher's Pocket. She seemed to know her place names along this stream but I've never seen her up here before.

"I went down. I dabbled over the Club Pool awhile, picked up a couple of pan fish and went below to try the shallows above the Elbow. I found a fourteen-incher there after some time. It was getting a little dark by then and I decided to go back.

"As I got up to the Club Pool again she was in the broad reach just above its lip, working slowly upstream with a dry fly. I stopped, well below her, to watch. I sat down and lit my pipe because I didn't want to appear to be snooping at her if she should turn around and see me. I felt a little sneaky—but I couldn't help looking at her casting.

"It had a quality of smoothness beyond any words that come to me offhand. It had grace and accuracy, but they looked ancient—if you know what I mean. They had always been there—she seemed so used to them that she could take care of them subconsciously, like breathing. There was no apparent effort to achieve any effect or any result. It was all easy, and rhythmic, and a little drowsy, maybe, like the wind blowing in the trees. No great length of line, except at one place—which I'll tell you about later—where she suddenly amazed me by shooting out a good eighty feet. The rest were thirty, thirty-five, forty. The floats were short but lifelike; the drag never bothered her though it would have played hob with a long inexpert cast and a long float, in some of the places she worked over. The retrieve was mostly with the rod, and the false casts were few and slow, seeming to carry the rhythm. It was about the least fussy casting I've ever looked at.

"Where she shot the long one—and the way she did it—showed her killer instinct. And what happened directly afterward proved it beyond doubt. . . ."

. . . The water of the Big Stony charges narrow and deep into the head of the Club Pool, then widens and slows a little, downstream. The main current hugs the far bank but some special character of the bottom creates a secondary drift there, a flow at right angles to the real channel, and that secondary current sweeps in toward shore on the Club side. It's shallow there, only up to your knees for perhaps fifteen feet out from shore where it drops off sharply. It's a spot I've seen passed up again and again by fishermen—supposedly good ones—who were too intent on the main channel along the far shore. It should be fished before the channel gets any attention at all, and fished from as far downstream as possible because a trout in that shallow water can see a mile in all directions. . . .

I didn't say all that to the Professor. He needed no description of the Club Pool, knowing that water—and how to fish it—better than any man in the world. I told him merely that this woman was getting up toward that stretch as I watched her.

". . . casting easily with her short throws and short floats. There was a little hatch of the blue dun on the water but nothing was coming up. In a few minutes she was in range of that shallow water off the head of the pool. I was curious to see how she'd fish it—whether she'd wade through it while fishing the main channel or start casting over it from where she stood.

"At this point she reeled in to change flies. And just then a fish rose, far up, where that right-angle drift breaks away from the head of the pool. It was a good rise, not snappy and splashy but one of those up-curving lifts of the surface that a good trout makes. You know the kind.

"She seemed terribly deliberate in getting her fly changed. Her back being toward me, I couldn't see whether she was taking all this time to decide on her fly or perhaps having trouble with her leader. Maybe it wasn't a long time but just seemed so to me because I had seen the rise and was keyed up to it. The thought occurred to me that she hadn't seen it. If she gave no sign of having seen it I was going to tell her.

"Or maybe she was studying the layout, trying to decide on a tactic. That thought occurred to me too, for there were more ways than one to fish that rise.

"But I don't think so, now. I think she had her mind made up all the time—the way she went after that fish when at last she got her fly changed. No reconnoitering, but an immediate frontal attack. Up to that moment not a cast had been over forty feet. But now, with that rise a good eighty feet upstream, she aimed at it. In about four false casts, still easy, she had it all out in the air but eight or ten feet, and on the next she shot that much and let it all come down. If a handkerchief had been floating over the precise point of the rise her fly would have settled on its dead center.

"He had it the instant it touched, as if he'd been waiting for it. The same lazy upsurge, no splash, just a swelling of the surface and the wave rings, and he was down with it. She stripped in a few feet easily as he came toward her, then held him against pressure with her rod high while she reeled in the slack below her first guide. Very pretty, so far. But I perceived in a minute that the line she had gained by stripping she considered velvet or net profit or something, and, by all the Red Gods, she was going to keep it. It looked as if no one had ever told her that you have to give back what you gain, with a big fish, again and again before you win it for keeps. When I saw that trout's size—the first time he came clear—I knew she'd lose him. She was giving him hell. No light tippet was going to stand that sort of stuff. If he wasn't two feet long the difference wasn't worth arguing.

"He came downstream and went by her. She turned to face him as he went below and gave him the butt as if she had a surf rod in her hands. I couldn't stand it any more. I shook myself loose from that spot and went up to her, feeling guilty about my snooping even in all the excitement. But I knew she needed me—or anyone who had had a big trout on before in his life and knew what it could do to light tackle. For the moment I forgot that she had another big fish in her creel. If I had remembered it I'd have concluded that somebody had given it to her.

"I said something to her, excusing myself for offering advice, about the necessity of giving him line. She looked at me, then—and listen, she is beautiful—with a kind of disdain. Her mouth was closed tight—she was gritting her teeth on that battle—and it didn't open a millimeter to smile or to answer me. In fact, as if by way of reply, she started stripping in again. . . . Well, I knew he was gone, and I was going to be kind of glad of it. But he wasn't. She brought him in, so help me, over her net—as lively then as when he'd taken her fly. By all the laws of everything she should have lost him there. But she scooped him out, thrashing like a shark, and took him ashore. The whole thing had taken less than five minutes and she hadn't moved a yard. With me it would have taken half an hour and I'd have gone down the whole length of the Club Pool, babying that fish and praying every step of the way."

The Professor got up to nurse his fire again. "Too bad she had to put back that one," he said. "I don't know but what we ought to waive our rule of only one big fish a day—where women are concerned. Yet it's hard to break with a tradition that old."

"Well, you've come to my point yourself," I said. "She didn't put it back." "She didn't?"

"No. When I saw her last she was heading toward the kitchen with both fish. . . . I tell you they're emotionally incapable of putting back a big one, rule or no rule—and all your Club traditions can go to hell."

The Professor turned from his business with the fire and looked at me sharply, intent as a pointer rounding up to a bunch of quail.

"Did you see her kill the second fish?" he asked, quietly.

"No, come to think of it, I didn't. She carried him away in the net without even stopping to take down her gear. But remember, it was almost dark. She could have killed him in the kitchen, or had the cook kill him, where there was some light on the subject."

The Professor knocked his pipe out against the side of the fireplace, refilled it carefully and slowly, lit it and blew a couple of great puffs that curled over the top of the fire screen, caught the draft and rushed up the chimney. "Your waders are dry and too warm," he said. "Better move 'em." He settled back in his chair and was silent for a moment. I knew he was about to talk, about to launch upon some narrative, probably in rebuttal to mine. That's the way the Professor begins a story: regiments his words in his brain, gets them organized into platoons and squads, some sort of practical marching order, before giving the command.

In this little space of silence I looked across the smoke and the lamplight at him and thought about him, thought of how really empty and pointless a sport trout fishing could be without him after you'd known it with him.

In the past four or five seasons his attendance upon that delectable water had been infrequent and uncertain. This present occasion, in fact, was my first sight of the Professor in years. There had been two tragedies in his recent past, and the second one had profoundly affected his fishing. I don't mean that it had touched his fishing skill: that had always been in a class by itself so far as our Club membership was concerned. But something had happened to his enthusiasm for fishing. It hadn't been killed, perhaps not even blighted. Maybe it was only mellowed, like an apple after a couple of frosts. But it was different.

The stark facts were that his wife had died in childbirth eleven years ago;

and the child, a boy, had been struck and killed by an automobile six years later. Since the death of his son the Professor had made only a few brief trips to the Club water and had missed several of our winter meetings. I had heard that he had married again but I didn't know the details. Up to this evening I had not seen him in two years. He and I lived far apart at the time and neither of us was much given to written correspondence.

"I'd have given you this sooner or later, anyway," he began, at length. "But your account of your experience tonight makes it highly appropriate that I tell you, now, of something that happened to me when I was last on this water, two seasons ago.

"There are *two* women in this thing. The elder was the Aunt, important to what I'm going to tell you only because her actions helped to reveal to me the character of the younger who was, of course, the Niece. The Aunt could be your Exhibit A, beautifully illustrating, not only on the stream but in the confines of this Club, the womanly fishing characteristic you have just now exposed. The Niece would not have conformed.

"The Aunt was a large and formidable and freckled fisherwoman, militantly physical, emanating a kind of hearty outdoor robustness all over the place. She was up very early in the mornings, stamping about, wallowing in her cold bath like a walrus—her room adjoined mine and you know these partitions are not strictly soundproof—and devouring great platters of ham and eggs for breakfast. Then to the stream which she would flail unmercifully with a stout ten-foot rod and with wet flies three sizes too large.

"All of this might have been mildly amusing had the decent qualities which usually go along with so resounding a character as hers, been evident. Strangely, they were not. She tried to bully the Niece with her mere seniority. She would post the Niece upon a stretch of water and announce her imperious decrees for the day, as to lures and procedure. From what I learned of her precepts and from the amount of air in her creel each evening I judged of the Aunt's talents as angler and as teacher, and mentally I conceded her a mark of about C-minus in each. She did, however, take a few fish, most of them horsed out in the dusk on bucktails and her large wet flies. The Niece had taken none up to the end of the third day, much to the Aunt's articulate disgust—and, I think, unspoken delight. The Niece bore her defeat like a sportsman, though, which was praiseworthy in the face of the Aunt's frequent innuendoes, pointed at her own superiority to her pupil, which she let drop at strategic moments and spots about the Club.

"The bully, however, had picked the wrong kind of prey. The Niece—I judged her to be in her early or middle twenties—was a girl of spirit. The signs of it were unmistakable despite the nicely tailored cloak of her reserve. The tradition of respect to her elders, which the Aunt had tried to capitalize, was strong in her but the integrity of her own character was stronger, and her fine pride was going to be served. I could see a rebellion smoldering and I determined to apply the bellows. I would teach her to fish: if for no other reason than that she must, before I left camp, trim the Aunt as the Aunt deserved to be trimmed.

"On the fourth day I asked her to fish with me and she accepted.

"She proved to be an apt pupil. Her gear was mostly good—a really fine rod and the right weight of line for it—and that gave me a head start in teaching her to cast. Her leaders were wrong for the dry fly and she never had heard of tippets. I rigged her up, there, with my own stuff. Plainly she had been reading about trout fishing: she had a typical book education in the subject, without the practice. A skeleton knowledge, as all such lore is: the bones of theory without the good meat of experience. But she was otherwise equipped in a good way. She had an easy athletic grace, the sort of reflexes which are rare in a woman and which were totally lacking in her Aunt. It was a good basis to work on. We took it easy, and by evening she was laying out forty feet with some accuracy and handling her false casts and her retrieves well.

"By that time I had six fair fish. She had had that many rises and had missed all but one, a ten-inch brown which she had brought to net at the Pasture Pool very nicely indeed. I could see that she was disappointed—she had wanted something more to show to the old vixen. I was a little uneasy myself, the six-to-one ratio seeming a bit top-heavy. There was a fair hatch that evening and trout were coming up to it, and I knew I could take the limit if I kept on. So I declared myself through.

"It was a little awkward. I didn't want her to quit and she didn't want to, either. Though she had accepted like a dutiful student all I had tried to teach her, she had a fine aloofness, an independence, a way of keeping to her own water, well away from mine. I respected that in her, yet I didn't quite know how to show it. Letting her go on alone was suddenly a displeasing prospect, yet I felt that to tag along, just watching her, would be embarrassing to both of us. So I told her to carry on while I sat down on a rock and had a smoke. That was at the Monolith Glide. I had heard that a tremendous fish had been seen there but I hadn't given it much credence.

"She started upstream to fish the riffle above the Glide. But at that moment there was a perfect brute of a rise almost directly opposite us.

"'See what you can do with *that*,' I said.

"'I'll toss you for him.'

" 'You'll do nothing of the sort. I'm down and I'm staying down. Now go ahead, and I'll keep out of it.'

"She looked at me then with an expression I had never seen on anyone's face before. It was a compound of emotions, packed tight and close. It had a trace of everything: nervousness, a little fear, a shy and terrific will to get that fish, gratitude for the chance, and over it all, like a kind of veil, a soft wash of surrender to me. . . . Did I imagine all that, then, or do I only now see it that way? The answer is perhaps yes to both questions, for I knew something, in that moment, which gives conviction to any crazy tangent of one's imagination. I knew I was in love with her.

"What happened in the next two or three minutes was so swift and so furious that it got beyond my full comprehension. I am still trying to take it all in in retrospect—still wondering how big a fish he really was. Her cast was one she could be proud of in the tension of the moment. The fly settled lightly down, two or three feet above the point of that first boil. He rose with a great deliberate dignity. He may have hooked himself—I don't know—anyway he was on and immediately going away from there, upstream, like a train of cars. Her reel gave out a sound she had never heard it make. I remember her saying quietly: 'No advice, please. You gave me this—now let me handle it.'

"He didn't stop. He didn't even slow down. Probably no advice in the world would have been the least bit of use. He took out the line left on her reel as straight as if he were measuring the length of the Glide. I don't know what she did to brake him, and she couldn't remember afterward. Likely there was nothing she could have done. Fortunately she lowered her rod in time, for he was still going when the last foot of her line was straightened out taut. And then, of course, he was gone. The whole business was suddenly and quietly slack. It was a strange effect—that let-down. It was like silence after some great racket that has been banging in your ears for a long while.

"She looked around at me, shook her head a little and reeled in. That was all. No word from her. I don't know what I said—if anything, it was futile and banal. Her fly and tippet were gone. I had to go to her, then, to tie on another tippet because she didn't know how to tie a barrel knot. I realized, without asking, that she wasn't through yet. When I stood next to her she was shaking a little, and by God, I had difficulties with that barrel knot and I knew she saw it.

"She went ahead, upstream, while I sat down on my rock and resumed my smoke. She drew away from me, casting and wading easily, and the dusk was getting a little thicker. Trout were coming up, here and there—not many, but those that rose looked as if they meant it.

"I took my eyes away from her for a few minutes to watch the nearby water. If another good rise occurred there I was going to call her back. When I looked at her again she was into something and in a moment I saw that he was big. He didn't go straight up in the air but he rolled, once, on the surface. I saw his flanks, and his tail followed the flanks down. I judged him to be about a nineteen-inch fish and heavy for his length.

"I went up toward her, but not close. She waved me back. 'Let me, let me,' she said. He came downstream and she came with him, and I backed away, thanking God that she was showing some respect for a big brown trout. He swerved and bored over to the far side, toward a nasty mess of roots. But she turned him and he was still on, heading upstream now like all possessed. He came up again and showed himself. I started to yell something but held it in. She was doing pretty well—and I saw, after awhile, that her fish was well hooked. He won slack a couple of times, coming in toward her, but he stayed on, and as he went away she'd give him what must have been the right amount of pressure. All of this was on her own, mark you. There had been no chance for a lesson in the handling of big fish. But she had sense if not finesse, and nerve enough to use it in a crisis.

"I knew she had him, after fifteen minutes or so. She knew it, too, I think. Her whole lovely figure was expressive of victory, and only God and herself and maybe I knew how dear that victory was.

"I didn't go near her but I called out to her to give him five minutes more. I couldn't help that bit of advice. I've seen too many fish lost that way—some of my own included—and I was damned if I'd see this one. Aside from that piece of instruction—perhaps superfluous—she did it all herself, devising her own technique as she went along. I had my watch on her and I called to her again when the five minutes were up. She brought him in, put the net under him and scooped him out. . . ."

The Professor's pipe had gone out. He lit it again, walked over to the fireplace to toss the match over the screen and returned to his chair.

"I was imagining a lot of things again, perhaps, but I tell you I saw then an abstract quality personified in the flesh. I saw the emotion of triumph—which cannot, supposedly, be rendered without shouts or gestures—manifest itself in that girl who was still silent and who still made no sign. An inexpressible elation and relief, as she took her fish ashore. And she was considerably upstream from me, a hundred feet or so. As I walked up toward her I saw her light a match and bend over the fish for a moment. Then I saw her go back into the water with the fish still in the net and her rod still under her arm. I saw her dip both hands in the stream, take the fly out of that trout's mouth and let him go. I saw the big, slow bow-wave he made as he swam away."

"But why—?"

The Professor looked across the lamplight at my astonishment. "Wait a minute," he said. "There's something else you must know in order that the foregoing may make sense to you.

"The summer before my son died—that was five years ago—he was up here with me. He was just six that summer, a little young for fly fishing. But I had bought a seven-foot, three-ounce rod for him—not an absurd extravagance because I used it myself, at times—and I coached him along. He was putting out twenty feet of line and leader with that little wand within a week. Occasionally he would have a strike but several days went by before he landed a fish. Of course I did the actual landing, but the boy kept him hooked and brought him in to my net. It was a brown trout of just twelve inches and it must have felt like a tuna to that little kid. Then something funny happened. He had been tremendously keen about fishing up to that point, full of questions and full of ideas of his own. He thought about fishing all day, dreamed about it at night, talked in his sleep about currents and backcasts and the drag. Then, when at last he had brought a trout safely in, some odd revulsion of feeling got hold of him. I was about to bend back that beauty's head when he stopped me. There was to be no killing here. 'No, no. I want him for a pet, Dad.'

"Well, I carried that fish up to the hatchery rearing ponds. Luckily there was an unoccupied pool at that time, and I prevailed upon old Bill Sykes to give it over to my son's fish. Bill, of course, is a wizard at trout culture. Bill and my boy took over the feeding of the new pet. 'We don't want to make him too fat, Bill,' my boy said. 'We want to keep him hard, like a wild trout.' The boy didn't fish again, once, after that, but he would spend hours every day watching his trout in the hatchery pool. 'He likes it there,' he would tell me. 'He swims around fast some of the time and takes flies on the surface. It's good he's happy there—if he wasn't, Bill and I would have to put him back in the stream. And he'd be caught.' . . . 'We've named him, Dad,' he said, one evening. 'Guess what.' I made a couple of tries, missing completely the answer that seemed so right when he told me. 'Sam Fario,' he said. 'I told Bill today that we ought to name him. Bill said, "The Latin name for a brown trout is Salmo Fario—how'd that do?" Well, the Fario was all right but I never heard of Salmo for a first name. I tried to call him that for awhile but I don't know about Latin and it was hard to say, if you said it fast, and once when I tried to say it I said "Sam Fario" instead. But Bill said he liked "Sam Fario" all right so we decided to call him that.'

"We went home when our time was up, the boy leaving instructions with Bill to keep us posted on the growth and state of health of Sam Fario. That was late July. In September the accident happened, one morning on his way to school.

"The next year I didn't get up here but I heard from Bill that Sam Fario was a much bigger fish. The year after that, after the season closed, I came up for two days. Sam was still in the pool but getting too big for it. Bill was concerned about him. 'It's all right to keep him here forever,' he said to me, 'if you want him to get fat and slow. But your boy wanted him kept like a wild trout, remember?'

"There was only one thing to do, of course—put him back in the stream. And that meant the risk, almost the certainty, of his being caught. So I decided to appeal to something—the charity, I suppose, of men. I had a round flat tag made, with a sort of rivet device, suggested by Bill Sykes, to attach to his dorsal fin. That fin was by now nearly three inches broad. I had the tag made one inch in diameter. On one side it read: 'I am Sam Fario, a boy's pet.' On the other: 'Please put me back.' It was a special printing job, guaranteed to be legible after a long while in the water—three or four years, I was told. . . . I didn't say a word to anyone and I swore Bill to secrecy. I was by no means certain of my ground—I mean in the moral sense. It was, in a definite way, selfish. It was my private sentiment against the sporting rights of everyone on this water. Sam Fario was over sixteen inches long when we tagged him and put him back in the stream, and he had nearly a year to grow a couple of inches more before the next season opened. Someone, I knew, would land him after a long fight and then see that tag. Eh? You know how *you'd* feel. . . ."

"I see," I said. "At this point I can put two and two together and make four. When the Niece caught him the following year he must have been, as you say, close to nineteen inches."

The Professor got up and put more oak chunks on the fire. "To my knowledge Sam was never taken until that night," he said. "And when *she* took him she had no cue to put two and two together to make four or any other sum. And when I saw her put him back it never dawned on me at all.

"After I got up to her she told me about reading the tag on his fin. Her words came with a little catch in them—not entirely from disappointment. She was smiling a little, and laughter was just under the surface of her voice—as if somewhere, implicit in that tragic mess, she had recognized the neat little joke on herself. It didn't fool me. No one ever wanted a good fish more than she had wanted one then,—with that damned Aunt back at the Club waiting to gloat over her when she came in.

"But when she got him at last she could put him back—as soon as she saw who and what he was. She might have asked me to come and see the tag and if she should take it seriously. Equivocation is easy in a spot like that. And remember, my little sentiment was as foreign to her as the finer shadings of a Buddhist prayer. . . .

"I proposed to her that night, right there on the stream. I married her a month later."

With this announcement I gathered that the Professor's story should dovetail, somehow, with what I had witnessed on the stream an hour or two ago. But just how, I could not see. Things wouldn't fit, the way it seemed they should. The girl who had finished off a big trout as a tigress would a gazelle and who had kept him despite the presence in her creel of another big one, in defiance of an ancient and honorable Club rule—that girl was going to turn out to be the Professor's wife. But the apparent contradictions annoyed me, probably because I was too tired and comfortable, just then, to be enthusiastic about solving any mystery. And idly I was speculating on how big Sam Fario was by now, if he still lived. Two years ago he was nearly nineteen inches—

Footsteps on the porch outside chased the vague ghost of an idea that was shaping in my mind. The girl herself entered the room. She had changed from her fishing clothes but I recognized her at once in the lamplight. When she had looked at me tonight on the stream I had known certainly that I should never forget her.

"A stage entrance," said the Professor, greeting her and introducing me. "We were discussing you—and your sex—while you were in the wings."

"I waited for my cue to enter," she said, "without trying to eavesdrop. Among other things I caught something about these partitions being not strictly soundproof."

The Professor and I looked at each other.

She stood erect and tall before the fireplace, smiling at us like a child who has some mischievous secret.

"I didn't hear all," she said. "Part of the time I was wallowing in my cold bath like a walrus."

We all sat down, she on the arm of the Professor's chair. "Any luck this evening?" he asked, innocently enough.

"Two big ones. One was Sam Fario." She announced it quietly, her voice charming with a kind of mock casualness. But I could detect the tense eagerness which underlay it, as if she knew her words had lit a fuse to an explosive charge deep in her husband.

He looked at her blankly without speaking. Then his face relaxed a little in an understanding that was not quite complete, and a half smile twisted the corners of his mouth.

"The second one was Sam, eh?" he said.

"Right." She looked at me: "You know who Sam is, of course?"

I nodded. "I do, now. When I saw you take him, I didn't."

"I know what you thought of me for the kind of tactics I used on Sam," she said. "But please don't think it's my usual method. The *first* fish—the one I showed you upstream—really was taken on a 3X tip and a number twelve Quill Gordon, as I told you, and he gave me plenty of trouble. . . . But I *had* to get Sam, you see. It was not a sporting matter. I had terminal tackle, when Sam was on, that I shall not have to use again, thank heaven,—a leader that would hold a horse. I carried it with me in case I should see him. Poor Sam."

The Professor was still puzzled about one or two things, and so was I.

"He felt as if he was well hooked," she added. "But that part was just luck. If he hadn't been I'd have torn the fly out."

"What made you change in time to the heavy leader?" the Professor wanted to know.

"I saw Sam rise, my sweet. I saw the tag on his fin when he came up. It's about all that showed of him."

I sat there, with things coming clear to me all at once, dumbly admiring that girl and dully despising myself, recalling how I had wondered, as I had watched her, whether she had seen that trout rise or not. She had seen not only the rise but the tag on Sam's fin as he rolled up. At eighty feet! And she had seemed to take a long time changing flies because she was changing her leader, too. She had *had* to get Sam. . . . And that was another question.

"Why did you have to get Sam?"—I voiced it—"just to continue this inquisition."

"Because I was sure he needed a new tag—to protect him in his old age. And he did. No one could possibly read the old one. It's two years since the first time I caught him, and he'd been in the stream with his tag for a year, then. . . . That's why I had to get him—why I put the heavy leader on when I saw him rise—why I gave him no more quarter than the rod could stand. Poor Sam. . . . Am I clearing myself of all the incriminating evidence which seems to surround me?"

The Professor and I looked at each other again.

"He's much bigger," she said. "And he's lean and hard. You can see him tomorrow. Bill Sykes has him back in his old rearing pool behind the kitchen—where the cook will throw things into his pool and make him fat and soft. . . . But Bill will order Sam's new tag tomorrow."

THIRTEEN

Lost: Two Reputations

Edmund Ware Smith

The Canadian press, like Canadian rivers, is exceedingly cordial to visiting fishermen—and their wives. My first trip to the Nepisiquit River in northern New Brunswick was deemed worthy an item in the *Northwoods Axeman,* weekly. Mr. and Mrs. Oliver H. P. Rodman were my companions in the adventure, and even a casual reading of the news item establishes the fact that Mrs. Rodman, hereinafter known as Doro, attracted the spotlight to us.

Gloomily I quote from the *Northwoods Axeman,* issue of July 22, 1933: "Mr. and Mrs. Oliver H. P. Rodman, and Mr. Edmund Ware Smith, all of Massachusetts, U.S.A., have been fishing the Nepisiquit River this week. Mrs. Rodman, an attractive brunette, caught a brook trout of four and one-half pounds, as well as several of about four pounds. Mr. Rodman and Mr. Smith also fished."

How we "also fished" is described with fidelity, detail, and minimum acrimony in the following narrative which, like all true confessions, begins with a quotation from a diary, thus:

JULY 14TH: OLLIE, DORO, AND I BOARD BOAT FOR ST. JOHN, N.B. MY FIRST FISHING TRIP IN COMPANY WITH LADY. APPREHENSIVE!

We leaned on the after rail of the six-thousand-ton coast liner, *S.S. St. John,* and sighed with that curiously exalted relief which comes of work done, play begun—and the destination a strange river six hundred miles to the north. I felt a sudden affection for this little steamer. Outward bound, she was our transport to freedom, our ferry to some of the finest squaretail trout fishing in North America. And homeward bound, she seemed to respect the melancholy of journey's end.

Sundown: No land in sight, and we quartered into a heavy swell. The sky, the sea, the following gulls—all were abruptly swallowed in a Bay of Fundy fog. We could hear the monotonous *"o-o-o-o-o-m"* of the fog horn at forty-second intervals; and away to starboard the answering "[o-o-o-o-o-m]" of a ghost-ship asking to pass in the night.

From a dance-floor on A-deck a good orchestra had begun to play "Stormy Weather". It was cold outside, and we went into the Beverage Room, contrasting its luxury with tomorrow's imagined wilderness. Traditionally, a place where drinks are served is called a bar. But the people who sponsored the *S.S. St. John* must have revolted under the shackles of custom. They called it Beverage Room, and there we sat in red leather chairs sipping Scotch and water, and discussing rivers, trout, and probable weather. There was a particular scrap of dialogue which bears like the stern of a hornet on subsequent events. Ollie and I were speculating as to whether it was more fun to fish with one fly or two on a leader, when Doro interrupted our weighty discourse by saying, dreamily: "I wonder who'll catch the largest trout."

From such a speculation comes only misery. It is the sort of thing that ladies should not be allowed to wonder about. And I hold that even men should wonder about it only in the dead of night when they are alone in bed. Courteously I assured Doro that she herself would catch this superlative fish, adding that the important thing was not size or numbers, but *how*. Her husband also awarded Doro the likelihood that she would take the biggest—but both he and I felt secretly that we were lying.

Under date of July 15th, my diary says:

GOT CAR OFF BOAT AND DROVE TO BATHURST, N.B.

That threadbare entry is a howling injustice to a tireless spruce forest; to fifty rivers, big and little; to glimpsed bits of blue sea, such as Shediac Bay where Balbo's Italian invincibles wet their pontoons on their six-thousand-mile flight from Rome to Chicago; to the forty-mile road hewn through the forest from Chatham to Bathurst, on which you are likely to meet no more than one car, one wagon, one bicycle, one cow, one goat; to the neat signs which, spelled perpendicularly, announce the names of tiny wood-burning towns; to the inspired absence of bill boards; to conversation with natives in rusty French; and, lastly, to the town of Bathurst, where a man may still see sparks flying in a blacksmith's shop and English sparrows feasting happily in the street. Diaries are too succinct. The next entry:

WENT UP RIVER THAT NIGHT

The Bathurst Hunting & Fishing Lodges are four picturesque peeled spruce cabins twelve miles apart on the Nepisiquit River. Number One cabin is thirty miles up, above Grand Falls. To get there, you drive from Bathurst five miles in a car to what is known as the "Y." The "Y" is the point where the Canadian National Ry. separates from and abandons for all time a railroad which is its exact opposite. The C.N. Ry. has called itself the longest railroad in the world. But the Bathurst & Lower Nepisiquit Seaboard Airline Ltd. is the shortest, and is otherwise unique in matters of cross-country navigation. It has sixteen and one-half miles of rails which were laid by a crew having independent ideas of direction. Here no dull, scientific precision, but instead a fine carefree road with a sort of here-a-rail, there-a-rail spirit prevailing.

The rolling stock consists of a pint-size flatcar with a tent pitched on it, a one-lunged gasoline engine, Mr. Link LeBritton at the throttle, and practically no brakes at all. We all climbed aboard of her and took firm hold. Link ignited his corncob pipe, opened the throttle wide, and leaned back for peace and contemplation. Concerning the railroad experience, the diary has just a word. The word is:

RABBITS

I am more than ever convinced that my diary is a paragon of understatement; for, from the "Y" to the abandoned iron mine above Grand Falls, is virtually an unending vista of rabbits. They haunt the road-bed in quest of salt. Of course there are a few jack pines and mountains en route, but the rabbits dominate in the end. Using the ties of the Bathurst & Lower Nepisiquit Seaboard Airline Ltd. to sit down on, they regard the onrushing flatcar with sedate unconcern, waiting until it is within three feet before deftly side-hopping into the bush.

Darkness dropped a black wing over the wilderness as we reached the deserted mine. We said good-bye to Link LeBritton and nosed our three canoes into the sleepy current. In the stern of each canoe was a guide whose name we had heard, whose hand we had shook, but whose face we had not seen. A mile of meandering water, and old man Nepisiquit burst into song.

To start up an almost legendary river at night is a strange and beautiful experience. A night hawk who-o-omed in pursuit of some hapless insect. An owl hooted from the depths of the black forest. The river hissed in the unseen grasses of the shores. The sky burned with brilliant northern stars; and, as we crossed a quiet eddy, a heavy trout—oh, it *must* have been a trout!—broke the surface, swirled, and went down. My eyes bulged in the dark, and I felt near to whatever it is that makes the universe move.

Lloyd Black, my guide, shipped his paddle and pulled a shod canoe pole from under the thwarts. I heard the steel shoe click on the rocks of the river bottom, felt the canoe lunge forward as Lloyd leaned on the pole. I squirmed with that itching discomfort which comes when one man is doing alone the work which two may share.

"Got another pole?" I said.

"Sure," said Lloyd, and presently we were working together, and the sweat came on my forehead and trickled down my nose, and Lloyd and I were calling each other by our first names.

At ten o'clock we reached the Narrows cabin. It is situated on an eighty-foot bluff, where at night you can hear the river. But you can't see it! Where, if for six months you have been dreaming about that river, you stand with your heart thumping, and try to wipe away the dark; where you picture in your mind just how the water will look, the shape of the rocks and trees, the color of the sky; where you tremble with excitement, with hope, and with hunger for the light of day.

I have never been capable of unpacking my fishing tackle within an area much less than half an acre. In two minutes, Ollie and I had made of the cabin floor a dismaying litter of rods, reels, lines, flies, flies, flies, leader boxes, packs, rain shirts, and bottles of fly dope. We jointed our rods, and put leaders to soak. Every now and then, as if it were carefully rehearsed, we glanced at one another and silently stepped outside to listen to the river, and smell it. It sounded to us like the laughter of angels, and it smelled clean and cool as a lawn after a rain. But the night was drenched with the scent of damp spruce which is solely a wilderness odor. Above us, almost low enough to touch, hung the magic northern stars.

Back in the cabin, Doro was examining the contents of a fly box by lamplight. She selected a Royal Coachman, held it to the light, and asked if it were a Wickham's Fancy. Ollie grinned wanly. Then she picked up a Dark Montreal, and said: "I know the name of this one."

"You do? What is it?" Ollie asked.

"It's a Black Gnat!"

Lastly she selected a red and white feathered fly with a silver body and jungle-cock shoulders. Ollie winced, and before Doro had a chance to guess again, he said: "No it isn't! It's a Doctor Breck!"

"I knew it all the time," Doro said. "Why did you tell me? It's the fly I'm going to use first tomorrow."

"Why?" her husband asked.

"Because I knew the name of it."

In the light of coming events, I am not here justified in going into an ancient theme—the logic of womankind. It's a great cause, but a lost one. It will get you in the end, like death, and taxes, and the lone mosquito in the tent. But I am fairly obliged to say that Doro had poled bow in a twenty-foot canoe four miles that night; that she did not shudder when owls hooted; that she helped her guide, Jim Black, tote the duffel up the eighty-foot bluff in the dark; that when June bugs banged against the screen door she did not make Ollie go out and see if it were robbers; that it was her first trip north of Boylston and Tremont Streets, Boston; that, hang it all, she very definitely belonged!

Morning came with a blazing orange sunrise, and I took my first look at the river—just stood there gulping it in. Directly below me, Douglas Goode, and Lloyd and Jim Black had started a tiny birch fire. In the still air, the smoke climbed slowly up to mingle with the fir tops. The boys had heated the ring of an old boom chain, and were patching the canoes with marine glue. They harmonized perfectly with their surroundings, and they satisfied my conception of good guides and companions. Otherwise, they proved to be the most skilful rivermen of my experience.

The Nepisiquit flows east by northeast, emptying into the Bay Chaleur at Bathurst. Its average width is about sixty yards. Its water is clear as glass, its depth, except for pools, about two feet in normal water. Its banks are crowded with spruce, fir, white birch, and popple.

When you cast a fly in the waters of the Nepisiquit you are never sure whether a seven-incher or a three-pounder will rise. To the fly fisherman, this kind of uncertainty is sheer perfection. It gives him that taut, tingling suspense which puts an edge on the finest sport in the world. There are more and larger trout in the Nepisiquit than in any river I have fished. To my certain knowledge there is at least one trout which weighs seven pounds. I have seen him, touched him, hefted him, felt the power of him. So has Ollie. But wait!

Trout water! What is the point of a mortal trying to describe something which is timeless, which in color, sound, and form is ever changing? A river which has both voice and silence?

Late on the first day up river, Lloyd held the canoe on the edge of an eddy: boulder, leaning cedar, birch and jack pine in the background. There I straightened out my first business cast on the Nepisiquit River. One of Joe Messinger's Pink Lady fanwings drifted for five seconds below the boulder. *"Whack!"*

Ollie and Douglas Goode saw the trout take, and they let out a brace of full-toned war whoops. I netted the fish—twelve and one-half inches, an even pound. That's a fat and beautifully formed trout. Outside he was the color of a Wyoming sunset. Inside he was salmon pink and tasted, along with half a dozen others, like something they design exclusively for the residents of Olympus.

"Nice little trout," said Douglas.

I traded a glance with Ollie, and his face elongated.

"You mean they come bigger?" he asked Douglas.

"Yes—three or four times as big."

Before we reached the mouth of Lazor's Brook, I learned that this was no idle affirmative invented for an occasion.

Ollie made a careful cast in the lower reaches of Lazor's Brook pool. Directly beneath his yellow bucktail, it appeared that a washtub, with attendant commotion, had sunk.

"Never touched him!" cried Ollie, his eyes protruding.

"Rest him," I said. "Change flies and try him again, later."

We held our canoe in the clear as Ollie began again to work on the trout. The late sun gleamed along the length of his backcast, and his Montreal dropped nicely. Nothing doing. He tried a Greenwell's Glory, a Leadwing Coachman, and three different bucktails.

"You try," he said, shrugging.

"No," I said.

"Yes."

"All right."

At this precise moment, Jim Black and Doro hove into view. They poled leisurely, nosing into the bank now and then to admire the fireweed or star flowers along shore. As they neared the pool, I remember Doro saying that she wanted to straighten out her line. Unaware that we had a big one located, she shot a very creditable cast over the velvet water and began to reel in. Well—she straightened her line, all right. At least something did! I have never seen a straighter line, nor a more surprised cluster of males in the aggregate.

"Give him line!" "Don't give him line!" "Keep the tip up!" "Get him onto the reel!"

The center of a group of four frenzied gentlemen, Doro alone remained calm. Quietly, peremptorily, and with perfect dignity, she caught the trout. This was the fish referred to by the *Northwoods Axeman*. It weighed exactly four pounds and eight ounces on the spring scales. Its length is emblazoned on Jim Black's paddle blade by a notch which he cut twenty inches from the tip.

After the trout was safely in the canoe, we gathered around and explained to Doro all the things she had done wrong. I told her some things. Ollie told her some things. Lloyd and Douglas added a few laconic suggestions. But Jim Black, who was her guide, said: "Me, personal, I figure she done all right."

Jim's philosophy, like that of Bliss Perry's immortal worm-fisherman, is one of results.

As she listened to our ranting, Doro's modestly downcast eyes regarded the fly which was attached to the end of her leader. It was the Doctor Breck!

How does a riverman recall his river? Why, by its rapids, its rocks, and its campsites, probably. There was Lazor's Brook cabin, where the great mosquito migration occurred; Indian Falls, where you sleep with the rapids' throaty thunder in your ears; and the Elbow, where the eating of the mysterious lost blend fish chowder took place; and Billy Gray's camp, where, carved on an old lumberman's tally stick, were these words: "Octubr 4, 1907, shot one carrybou today. All hans gut dronk. i gut dronk two time."

But the trout fisherman remembers his river by its pools: Gravelly Pool, where, on Joe Messinger's hallowed fanwings, I caught my two biggest trout of the trip; the Bear House Pool, where several trout rose and actually took tiny dry flies while they were still in the air. There was Indian Falls, where, in the lower pitch, Ollie took six beauties during a severe thunder storm, two weighing three pounds. And the Devil's Elbow Pool, where I fell in. And Doro Eddy, named for Mrs. Rodman when she caught a four pounder, and where, in his thirty-five years' experience on the Nepisiquit, Jim Black had never known of a trout being taken!

We had turned brown as Indians, and the black flies shunned us now, as being mere chunks of shoe leather or old scrap iron. Ollie and I fished industriously about six hours daily. Sheepishly we would nick a paddle blade for our largest fish each day—but along toward sundown, Doro would glide near a fishless pool, cast for half an hour, and come drifting into camp with another day's record.

I believe firmly that competition does not belong in fishing. But I was beginning to take it seriously, and so was Ollie. I can still hear Jim Black's delighted chortling. "You boys cast a very han'some fly," he'd say. "I ain't never seen han'somer. Heh-heh-heh."

And Doro would remonstrate with him: "Jim, you mustn't!"

The lady of the expedition catches the big trout one day, perhaps two, or even three days. Fine! You congratulate her with some show of honest feeling. But when she does it seven days hand-running, your words sound a little hollow, like someone muttering in an iron drum. You begin to lose confidence in your time-tried skill as a fly fisherman, and I submit that nothing is more doleful than a male fisherman with an inferiority complex attributable to this cause. Here, I am speaking for myself alone. But consider Ollie, poor wretch! Drastically trimmed by his wife, a thing under which few if any husbands can bear up.

For example, one day at Indian Falls, Ollie brought in one of the most superb trout I have ever laid eyes on. Three pounds and eleven ounces on the scales. Ollie's star appeared to be in the ascendancy, and we rallied around to admire the fish, when Jim Black sidled up and drawled: "Well, Miz' Rodman, she didn't fish none at all today."

During the last two hours of daylight, on the last day of the trip, the male sex almost came into its glory. After supper, I walked with Lloyd to the upper pitch of Indian Falls, one of the finest pools on this fantastically beautiful river. The sky was gold with the forerunners of a summer sunset, and the smoky haze of late afternoon hung in the air. I cast indolently for a time, standing on the ledge just below the falls, moved more by the spectacle of the river than by the desire to fish.

I was using two flies on a rather heavy leader. My dropper was a Yellow Montreal, and the point fly a white bucktail with a gold-ribbed body. Trailing at the edge of the pool in shallow water, the Montreal attracted a seven-inch trout, and the little fellow hooked himself, and made for the depths beneath the edge of the whitewater, quite unaware that he would have been released. It was his last mistake.

The sun slanted its bronze rays full upon him as he darted; and, while I watched, out from under the foam came the seven pounder! He nailed the little trout crosswise in his mouth, and vanished under the suds!

Lloyd Black, standing at my elbow, unloosed such an earsplitting cry that I nearly toppled off the ledge. Then all was still except the song of the rapids and the drumbeat in my heart. My line ran from the top guide-ring on a long slant straight to the center of the pool. I stood there, keeping a steady strain for about five minutes. Then the line came up, sluggishly.

The little trout still hung to the dropper fly, but he was quite dead, and showed plainly the lacerations of the big fellow's teeth. I had never witnessed such a cannibalistic performance, but I am told it is frequent on the Nepisiquit. They call the sacrifice-trout "slave fish."

I sat down on the ledge and drew a long breath. I was beginning to figure out a plan of campaign when Ollie showed up—and the light was borne upon me. He, and he alone, should catch that huge trout for the glory of mankind.

"Sit down," I said to him, solemnly.

He sat, and, after clearing my throat, I continued: "Ollie, you and I went to school together, didn't we?"

"Yes," he said, perplexed.

"For fifteen years we have hunted, fished, camped, and explored together, haven't we?"

"Yes."

"And once you pulled me out of the rapids when my canoe upset, didn't you?"

"Yes. What about it?"

"Then you went and got married, and I stood up with you at your wedding, didn't I?"

"Yes."

"All right," I concluded. "Then go down and fish that pool. Work your fly along the edge of the quick water. One of us—and it better be you!—has got to trim Doro."

"Why this pool?"

"Because under the edge of the foam," I said, pointing a shaky finger toward the whitewater, "there's a trout that will go seven pounds!"

"How do you know?"

"I had him on for five minutes."

Ollie gave an instinctive start toward the pool, hesitated, looked again, then decisively removed his hook from the keeper ring above the grip, and stepped onto the ledge. He shot his cast far out across the white feather that streaked below the falls through the center of the pool. Allowing the current to suck the fly under, he made his line loop slowly downstream and began a careful retrieve. He tried perhaps half a dozen times—then, just as his fly started upstream at the end of its loop, I saw his rod whip into a sudden curve. Ollie began to dance on the ledge. "Got him!"

He was using a five-and-three-quarter ounce Leonard Tournament, and he gave it all it would stand. Twenty minutes later, after an orgy of runs, sulks, and a pretty surface show, Ollie led the trout close to the ledge. Lying flat, I reached down and slid the net under him. But he stretched out over the rim on both sides, teetering and flopping. With one final twist, he slithered down the plane of the net, splashed back into the water, and moved off, taking his time. Dignified, austere, and, we thought, a little scornful, he swam down, down, down, until he disappeared.

There is little more to be said, this being a case where silence is particularly golden. But on the way back to camp I stopped and picked some blue gentians. They were of a delicacy and beauty worthy a champion—especially a lady champion. Rather thumb-handedly, I wove a sort of wreath and, with due ceremony, placed it that evening on Doro's head. It was very becoming, too.

"Any luck tonight in the upper pool?" she asked, looking at the garland in the cracked mirror by the lamp in Indian Falls cabin.

"None at all, dear," said her husband, thoughtfully. "We both had a strike, but we lost only one fish."

FOURTEEN

Old Medical Bill

Edmund Ware Smith

The doctor who delivered my daughter, pacified my phobias, and on Christmas during the prohibition years solemnly wrote me prescriptions for whiskey with which to treat a mythical bronchitis, has never sent me a bill. Whenever the matter of payment is mentioned, he becomes as evasive as a homing eel. My indebtedness to him struck a new high on the night my small son swallowed an unknown quantity of pills. I reached the doctor by telephone at the Young Married Men's Vice & Card Club, where he was enjoying a quiet game of poker—his first moment of relaxation in about four months.

"What kind of pills did he swallow?" asked the doctor, with the calm for which he is noted.

"We may be unduly alarmed," I said. "We hate to disturb you."

"What kind of pills did he swallow?" persisted the doctor, almost wearily.

"Alophen."

"I'll be right over."

He arrived in three minutes, and pumped out my son's stomach, remarking during the process, in a casual sort of way: "Alophen contains strychnine."

"Oh," I replied, limply, and my wife said: "Heavens!" and the doctor said: "Nothing to worry about, now. He'll be all right."

Thinking to turn the conversation to a subject less harrowing, I inquired about the poker game.

"Oh, yes—the poker game," the doctor said. "Let me see: I was sitting at the dealer's left, and had passed. John Freeze had opened for a dollar, and Alan Hodder raised. Bart Parker re-raised. Bull Roberts stayed, and I stayed. I had just drawn two cards, when your telephone call came."

"Sounds as if it came just in time to save you money," I said, optimistically.

The doctor acknowledged my remark with a tolerant look, and resumed: "Of course you know the club rule: if a man leaves the table during play, his hand is automatically dead."

"Yes—quite right."

The doctor smiled in a far-off way. "By the time I had put on my coat and picked up my instrument bag, the game was at the showdown. John had a straight, Alan a flush, and Bart won with a full house. I should say there were sixty or seventy dollars in the pot."

"Well, well, well," I laughed. "Lucky not to get caught in that, Doctor, eh?"

"As I went out the side door," said the doctor, unemotionally, "Alan Hodder turned up my cards, out of curiosity. He announced that I had four aces. Really, you know, you should keep alophen in a place where the children can't possibly reach it."

My wife, who is one of the few, truly great women who understand poker, said: "The least we can do is offer the doctor a highball."

The highball was but an item in a long list of frustrations. Life overtook the doctor again in the very act of reaching for his glass. A telephone call from the hospital informed him that a Mrs. Aggripponi was in active labor. I went out with him to his car, and said: "Then I'll take you to lunch tomorrow."

I did, too. But he insisted on lunching at the Harvard Club, where he could be on call. There happened to be a meningitis case he was watching closely. Since I am not a member of the Harvard Club, the doctor signed the check and subsequently paid. This was next to the last straw. The one that broke the camel's back was the fishing trip on which the doctor accompanied Henry Pegler and me.

Peg is the most expert dry-fly man I know. The idea of training a novice like the doctor, bringing him 'round to the right way of fishing, got Peg all excited. "Just let me at him," Peg said to me. "I'll show him—and show him *right!*"

At the time, neither of us doubted that the doctor would like fishing. Peg and I loved the sport, and were trapped in the common fallacy of thinking everyone else would. Introducing the doctor to our river, and sharing our art with him, was the greatest compliment we could pay him. Our motive was so pure, and our eagerness so intense, that we were not at all suspicious. I did notice that the doctor listened to Peg's preliminary discourse with what might be termed a wandering ear.

And there was another thing which, in our passion to enlist him, we ignored too thoroughly. We were showing him the Mopang River on the map. "See?" I said. "Here's the river, and the dam—fishing above and below. And here's the cabin. And here's where Les Morgan will meet us."

"Isn't it rather—uh—far away from things?" the doctor asked.

"Darn right it's far away!" said Peg, his eyes gleaming at the thought. "Why, hell, it's thirty-eight miles to the nearest railroad."

"Say!" I exclaimed, my hand on the doctor's arm. "Every night you go to sleep with the sound of water in your ears. Once in a while, from Musquash Lake, you can hear a loon calling, too."

"Oh," said the doctor.

"Wait till you see the place!" said Peg.

The doctor nodded.

On the train going up, I was disturbed just a little that a man like the doctor—well read, dignified, and a loyal friend—could, on the subject of fishing, be so abysmally ignorant. It appeared that he had not even enjoyed the bent-pin and grocery-twine experience common to all American youths. But it would be fun to teach him. Start a man from zero, and you really mold him.

Les Morgan met us at the end of the Mopang spur track. We drove to Privilege, and crossed the lake, and started upriver in two canoes. I remember how impressive the doctor looked in the bow of Les's canoe. He was wearing a trench coat with the collar turned up. He had removed his hat, and his greying hair gave him a look of distinction.

When we got to the cabin, the sun was low. We unloaded the canoes, and got the duffel up to the cabin; and Les cooked us a meal of beans, cornbread and browned salt pork. At the table Peg and I looked at each other, and grinned, and each knew what the other was thinking: that water out there, the pool above the dam, and maybe a good trout or two. But the doctor, as yet, had not savored this tingling expectancy. After supper, when we were on the porch setting up our rods, the doctor looked at the river, and said: "Well—"

"Not bad, hey doctor?" said Peg, unwinding a soaked leader with trembling fingers.

"Is—is this—everything?" inquired the doctor, including the cabin, the river, the forest and the sky, in his gesture.

"Sure," I said, happily.

"Bet you never dreamed it would be like this!" cried Peg.

"No," said the doctor. "No—I really didn't."

I rigged a four-ounce Leonard for the doctor, with an English reel and line, a seven-and-a-half-foot leader, and a small red and white bucktail for a fly. I thought it would be easier for him to handle a bucktail at first.

The three of us went down to the edge of the pool just above the dam. Here you can cast without danger of fouling your backcast, and your chances of picking up a trout are good. There are two gates in the dam, and Les Morgan had one of them full open—the one nearest. The strong current, sweeping down along the abutment logs on the far side, was perfect dry-fly water, and I thought it decent of Peg, right at this time, to give the doctor a practical demonstration of how things were done.

"Now, watch," Peg said, unhooking a Pale Evening Dun from the keeper ring, and lengthening line over the pool. "Over there," he went on, false-casting all the time, "you see where the current breaks over an underwater boulder. In such a place, just below the boulder, a trout can lie without working too hard. The idea is to get the fly above the boulder, so that it will drift down in a natural way. The trout is there, because *natural* flies drift over him there, and he doesn't have to move far to get them. There—now—there's the fly, lit just above the boulder. See? *Oh migod!*"

Peg's fly had drifted about six feet, when the water bulged beneath it. In the twilight I saw the rich, speckled bronze of a huge squaretail's side. He took the fly deliberately, as a big fish so often does, and went down. It was the width of his tail, visible as he turned, that accounted for Peg's exclamation. That tail was a strong five inches broad!

Peg's rod bent to its limit of safety, but it had no effect on the fish. I figured Peg was in for a forty-minute battle, and had started toward the cabin porch for a long-handled net, when the rod straightened, snatching the fly clear of the water.

Peg's eyes were as big as ten-cent glassies. "Did you see him?"

"Yes," I gulped.

"I mean—the width of his tail?"

"Yes."

"And his side, too?"

"Yes."

"Four pounds—easy."

"Yes."

Then Peg turned toward the doctor, who was kneeling on the river bank a little way above us at the edge of some slack water over a gravel bar. "Get a thrill out of that?" called Peg.

"Out of what?" asked the doctor.

"That big fellow that just took the fly."

"I didn't happen to notice him," the doctor said, apologetically. "I was watching these other fish, down here."

"What fish?" snapped Peg.

The doctor shaded his eyes with his hands, and peered intently beneath the surface of the water. "Lots of nice ones here," he said, proud in his discovery.

Peg glanced at me, and, under his breath, said: "Suckers!"

I nodded. "Sure, never mind, Peg. It's his first night in camp."

"Someone ought to tell him."

"I'll tell him, tomorrow," I answered, and went below the dam to the whitewater pool.

I took three beauties of about three-quarters of a pound each, two on a Leadwing Coachman, and one on a Light Cahill. They were just right for breakfast. It was almost dark, and as I started up to the cabin, I noticed that Peg had quit fishing the upper pool. I couldn't resist making a few casts there, and on about the third or fourth drift, the big fellow boiled under the Cahill. He was just playing, I guess. At least he never touched the fly. But the commotion on the surface was something to keep a man awake nights. The excitement must have shown on my face, because, as I entered the cabin, Peg said sharply:

"Well?"

"He showed again," I said. "Never touched the fly."

The doctor was walking thoughtfully up and down the cabin floor.

"If we get a warm, still evening, a humid one," said Peg, his eyes shining, "he'll take a Green Drake."

"You know," I said, "if you cast a left curve, so that it will float down within six or eight inches of the abutment logs—"

"Is there anything to read?" inquired the doctor, gently.

"Bet your life!" said Peg, and went to the wall cupboard and got La Branche's *The Dry Fly and Fast Water*. He tossed the volume into the doctor's hands, and said: "Best work on the subject I ever saw."

"Oh," said the doctor, turning the volume slowly.

The next morning I explained about suckers to the doctor. He listened patiently—but with wistful glances toward the gravel bar. For an hour that day, and on the next three days, Peg and I took turns giving him casting instructions. The doctor was a mild, attentive, and absolutely hopeless student. How a man whose fingers were skilled in the use of delicate surgical instruments could be so awkward with a fly rod is beyond me. How a man, whose putting on the greens of the home golf course was a byword, could start a fly in any but the predetermined direction is another mystery. Nor had the lesson on suckers really taken hold upon him. We begged him to stay away from them, to stay nearer the pool above the dam and try for the big trout.

"Once you get fast to a fish like that," Peg told him, earnestly, "you've learned about fishing."

But he would remain in the correct position only while Peg and I were on watch. The instant we became concentrated on our own fishing, he would creep four or five yards up to his gravel bar and kneel here, studying those dismal suckers. The rest of the time he was very quiet, and once asked us when we planned to go home. He had abandoned La Branche's great work on the dry fly for Fowler's *The King's English,* and a little book called *Backwoods Surgery.*

"My God," said Peg one afternoon, when the doctor was out of earshot, "you don't suppose he doesn't like fishing?"

"Impossible."

"Wouldn't be human," said Peg.

"Well," I said, "I owe that man a lot, and I'm going to find out tonight if he is having a good time, and if not, why not, and what we can do about it."

Peg blew out his breath in a puzzled sigh, and motioned toward the upper pool. There, by the gravel bar, kneeled the doctor, prodding about with the tip of that sweet Leonard rod, as if his sole purpose were to stir the water.

"What the hell do you make of that?" Peg hissed.

I couldn't think of anything to do but shrug, and change to a happier theme: "Tried the big one today, Peg?"

"Sure—couldn't start him. You?"

"Once, right after lunch. Nothing stirring."

"He'll come early morning, or in the evening, or not at all," said Peg.

"Just my theory."

"You take morning, and I'll take evening," Peg suggested.

"Right—fair enough."

That night after supper, when Peg had come in after a fruitless try for the big trout, I said to the doctor: "Will you answer a question truthfully?"

He looked up from Fowler's *King's English.* "Why, of course—that is, I'll try."

"Are you—are you enjoying yourself?"

"I find Fowler on 'airs and graces' rather amusing—yes."

"No. I don't mean that. I mean, are you having a good time, here, on this fishing trip?"

The doctor's fingers drummed uncomfortably on the cover of Fowler. "Well," he said, "it's a change."

"Change," muttered Peg, in a tragic voice. "Change!"

"But don't you really like it here?" I asked, searching for a crumb of satisfaction.

"Frankly," said the doctor, unhappily, "it has been rather difficult."

"Difficult?"

"Yes. You see, you and Peg have made it clear that to dislike fishing, or to show any originality in methods of catching fish, is a mark of mental delinquency. You invite me up here to fish, and when I fish, you impugn me. Still,

I have found those suckers interesting. I am glad to have made their acquaintance."

"And a four-pound squaretail within twenty feet of them!" breathed Peg, twisting his hat.

The doctor looked up without resentment, but with genteel curiosity in his eyes. "*Now*, what have I done?" he asked.

"Nothing," I said, quickly, "Really nothing—but you haven't yet realized the purpose of fishing."

"What *is* the purpose?"

"To have fun," muttered Peg, which was certainly taking the broad view.

"Just what I thought," said the doctor. "So if you—if you could just leave me alone with my suckers, I could have fun."

"But damn it to hell!" cried Peg. "Suckers aren't fish."

The doctor was quiet for a moment. Against the chill of evening, he drew his trench coat about his knees. Then he said: "In stolen moments, I have observed these suckers in the act of spawning. I notice further that they have gills, fins, and the ability to remain under water indefinitely. My conclusion is that they are fish."

"But not trout," I protested.

"A fish," said the doctor, in a mild but irrefutable way, "is a fish."

"You won't listen to reason," snorted Peg.

"I have not so far had the opportunity."

Peg, of course, was impatient. He is a man with set ideas on angling methods, and twenty years of experience in the study of stream entomology and the dry fly have made him intolerant. But there was absolutely no rancor in the doctor's voice or attitude. With any other man of my acquaintance, there would have been the misery of tension in camp. But the doctor's approach was gentle and scholarly at all times. It rather had us adrift. I tried a new tack.

"You wouldn't expect to perform a delicate operation, say an exploratory laparotomy, or a hysterectomy, with no previous training, would you?" I asked.

"Just the point I was coming to," nodded the doctor, approvingly. "You bring me fishing for the first time, and I do not wish to appear ungrateful. Quite the contrary. I am in your debt for a—for a—new experience. But you equip me with precisionless, awkward-seeming instruments—"

"Four-ounce Leonard!" blurted the indignant Peg. "Hardy Perfect reel! Transpar line, at sixteen dollars a copy—precisionless!"

"—and you expect me," the doctor went on, while Peg was taking breath, "to operate without further notice. When I fail, you snort. When I try to develop a technique of my own, you exchange glances. You click your tongues, and whisper together in a grieved way."

"Only because we like you," I said. "We do it for your own good. Think of what people would say if it got around about the suckers."

"No," said the doctor, courteously, "I think you tend rather to do it for *your* good. *You* care what people might say, not *I*. But tomorrow is another day. Tomorrow, by a technique I have been perfecting, I will endeavor to catch one or more of those suckers."

"What is this technique?" inquired Peg.

"Briefly, the noose."

"The what?"

"Noose."

"How?" said I.

In outlining the doctor's noose technique for suckers, it will be necessary to render it first in his words, and then substitute language. The noose technique, in his terms, follows: "I have noticed that the line, or cord, runs through little eyelets attached to the pole. It is my intention to pull the cord all the way back through these eyelets, suture included, until the hook catches in the top, or end eyelet. Do you follow me?"

Neither of us answered. The doctor took our silence as an indication that we were hanging on his words. We weren't, but Peg was choking.

"Now," the doctor went on, encouraged, "between the end eyelet and the one next, I propose to draw out a loop in the suture. By thrusting this end of the pole down into the water, and probing slowly and carefully, I believe the loop, or noose, can be slipped over a sucker's head. Then, by pulling smartly on the upper part of the line, near the reel, the noose will tighten, and—you see?—the sucker is lassoed."

If the fisherman-reader will take pains to go back over the doctor's exposition, substituting "guide" for "eyelet," "rod" for "pole," and "leader" for "suture," he will have a fair idea of what the doctor was driving at.

"Well?" said the doctor, hopefully.

"I'm going to bed," said Peg.

"Tired?" the doctor inquired.

"No," said Peg.

The next morning I spent an hour casting over the big trout, and got one rise. The light, however, was a bit too bright, and I think he must have seen me. He turned near the surface, and was gone again. I told Peg, who was fishing the whitewater below, that I thought he might take him in the evening. Peg grinned, and said: "Boy-oh-boy-oh-boy!" Then Peg looked a trifle conscience-stricken, and said: "Look, why don't *you* try him this evening?"

"No, Peg," I said. "He's really your fish. You raised him first."

"But—"

"No, we agreed. My turn in the morning, yours at night."

"Well, it's darn white of you. I want you to know that," said Peg.

"What fly you going to try on him first?"

"I was wondering about that," Peg said, pushing his hat back on his head. "How about a Drake?"

"I don't know, Peg. They've been coming to Quill Gordons pretty well."

"Maybe you're right. Maybe I better start off with a Quill Gordon—about a Number Ten."

We separated then, and I went downstream a hundred yards or so and started to work up carefully. It was a beautiful morning, sweet, windless, and if too bright for best fishing, it was a day to be out and enjoying. About noon I quit fishing and walked up to the dam, overtaking Peg on the way. Together we went to the upper pool to call the doctor to lunch. "Wonder how he made out lassoing suckers?" growled Peg, under his breath.

We found the doctor sitting disconsolately on the bank by the gravel bar, the tails of his trench coat tucked under him, his rod on the grass at his side.

"What's the matter?" inquired Peg, good-naturedly. "No luck? Didn't it work?"

"It might have," smiled the doctor, "but something got hooked. Something got tangled, and I can't shake it loose."

"How long you been fouled?" asked Peg.

"Oh, maybe half an hour."

"Guess you got bottom," Peg said. "Why didn't you give us a yell?"

"Well, I don't know. It seemed to move. I'd set the pole down for a while, and after a time the line would sort of go out—tighten up. Once the pole almost went into the water. But when I picked it up, I couldn't budge whatever's tangled on the hook."

Peg jerked his hatbrim over his eyes, stuck out a shaking right hand, and said between clenched teeth: "God Almighty, Doc! Give me that rod!"

"Certainly," The doctor graciously passed the rod to Peg.

Peg whipped up the tip, reeled in the slack, shot me a wild glance, and screeched: "It's him! He's got him!" Then he passed the rod back to the doctor, and admonished him in trembling voice: "Just keep your tip up and keep a steady pressure on him all the time—as much as the rod will stand. And take it easy, Doc—don't for *God's* sake get excited now. You'll be busy quite a while. I'll handle the net for you. Just keep as calm as you can."

"I am calm," said the doctor, reluctantly taking the rod.

"You won't be, long," Peg told him. Just then the trout gave a terrific surge, smashing open the surface of the water. The spray flew all over the pool, and we saw the full shape of the trout in the noonday sun.

"Yeo-o-o-w! Look out!" Peg shrieked, his fingers twitching. "Don't get excited, Doc!"

"I'm not," said the doctor, "he's done that two or three times before—only I couldn't see what it was."

"It's the trout—the big one—my big trout!"

At this moment, the big fellow ran forty feet of line straight off the reel. It's a wonder the end-plates didn't fly off or melt. What the doctor did was to point the tip straight at the fish, and shake it at him.

"Yeo-o-o-w! Don't do that! You'll lose him! Don't do that!"

"Lose him?" said the doctor, dropping the tip again to stare inquiringly at Peg. "I don't care. I was after a sucker—almost had him—when I guess this fish came nosing along and spoiled everything. The current had pulled the fly through the eyelets. It was trailing on bottom, and I guess the trout took hold of it."

Peg emitted a cracked howl.

"And the noose practically over the sucker," said the doctor. "It was the second biggest sucker of the lot, too."

I walked up to the doctor, got him by the shoulder, and begged: "Don't talk now. Talk later. *Fish* now."

I thrust the rod tip up where it belonged, and added: "That position, see? Don't let it wilt."

"Just as you say," he said, then sighed and went to work on the trout.

The big squaretail was circling the pool. He just went 'round and 'round. He hadn't showed a sign of tiring. Then, suddenly, he went into high gear, and Peg and I were almost insane trying to keep the doctor on the job.

The climax came when the trout charged in close and got a purchase on the fast water just above the open gate of the dam. Peg went grey to the teeth, and his forehead was wet and glistening. He jammed the net into the water downstream of the fish, and turned him just before he went through the dam.

I don't know how long the whole process took, but half an hour is a conservative estimate. Finally, Peg held the net low in the water, and I steered the doctor's wrist while he drew the trout over it. Peg came up slowly with the net, and it was all over. As the trout lay there on the grassy bank, Peg took off his hat, stared down at the fish, and said, with genuine reverence: *"Nomine—patri—spiritus—sanctus!"*

A few moments later Peg looked up at the doctor, who was plucking at his shoulder. "Well?" Peg panted.

"Unhook him, do you mind?" requested the doctor politely.

Mechanically Peg removed the bucktail from the bony structure of the trout's mouth. The doctor took up his rod, wound the line through the guides, leader and all, drew out his abominable noose, and went to his gravel bar. But he only stayed an instant. When he returned, he said sorrowfully:

"They've gone. All this commotion, I suppose. It must have scared them away. Please don't feel badly about it."

"But—" stammered Peg, his eyes bulging from his head, "you've caught the finest trout that ever came out of this river."

"I wasn't fishing for a trout," reminded the doctor, softly. "I was fishing for a sucker."

Peg sat down beside the trout, rolled over slowly on his back, clutched the grass on either side, closed his eyes, and asked, limply: "Is there any brandy left?"

FIFTEEN

The Fog Blew Over the Mountain

Ben Ames Williams

Ann was a bride, and this was her honeymoon, and the honeymoon was as Dave had planned it; but Ann was beginning to doubt whether Dave were as wise and as discerning as she had come during the year or so of their engagement to believe him to be.

For this was not Ann's idea of a honeymoon. The first two or three days, while they motored leisurely down the Maine coast and into New Brunswick, had been pleasant enough; the sun shone, and they were in no haste, and the month was June. But when they passed into Nova Scotia, Dave began to change; he drove faster day by day, and a haste seemed to brew in him, and a dreamy eagerness. There were long moments when he appeared to be lost in his own anticipations, to forget altogether the girl here by his side; and Ann, who in the first days had been willing enough to overlook the fact that her largest bag and her prettiest dresses had been left behind to make room in the car for fishing tackle, began to find this now a hardship and a handicap.

When they abandoned the car for the little steamer—a craft which to Ann's *Queen Mary* eyes seemed ridiculously small and inadequate—her misgivings grew; and the rising exhilaration in Dave's bearing, as he stowed in their stateroom the rod case and the tackle box and the pack sack and the camera and their two suitcases, increased her concern. He was like the war horse which scents the battle far off; but Ann was seasick before they were well outside the harbor.

She slept at last, miserably; but Dave woke her at dawn and made her look through the portholes into a swimming pot of fog, as white as soft wool. A nakedly rocky promontory leered at her through this veil. Dave's eyes were shining; but Ann's were half closed with sleep, and the fog and the rocky shore were fog and rocks to her, and nothing more.

Yet Dave was so anxious for her to get up that she did so—secretly promising herself that he should atone this outrage when they were come safely home again—and they shifted their baggage into the dining saloon, to be ready to disembark at the first minute possible. But before they could land they must wait forty long minutes, without even a cup of coffee to comfort them, because they were aliens entering a foreign land, and so subject to official scrutiny.

"It's outrageous!" Ann declared. This gray, foggy, hungry morning after a sleepless night had no place in her preconception of a honeymoon. She had known that Dave was a salmon fisherman; he used to tell her long tales about great fish, while she smiled in her adorable fashion and watched him with apparently attentive eyes and planned draperies for their living room. But even salmon fishermen, she would have supposed, had some self-respect. "It's outrageous," she insisted, "to treat us like immigrants! I'm not an immigrant; I'm an American!"

Dave chuckled. "That just makes us foreigners up here, though!" he pointed out.

"I suppose they'll test us for rabies and bubonic plague and things!" she predicted furiously; and Dave guffawed. She had suddenly a doubt of the essential sanity of a man who could guffaw with laughter before breakfast. Dave guffawed, but he reassured her.

"They'll treat you like visiting royalty," he promised. "I've known Mr. Bryce—he's the man in charge here—since I was eleven years old. That was my first trip, with Dad. Bryce is a fine man; always puts fishermen through with a minimum of trouble. You'll meet him when we go to get our licenses."

He was so persistently cheerful that she was amazed at her own blindness in that she had not perceived in him this cardinal vice before. It had gone all unsuspected, disguised beneath a good humor not in itself offensive. Her marriage, she decided, had been a hideous mistake; but it was a mistake that could not be remedied till they came home again. If she left Dave here and now, she would be utterly alone, a stranger in a strange land—an immigrant!

When at last they were allowed to land, she tottered down the gangplank, her eyes half closed. The fog bestowed a drop of water on her eyelashes, another on the tip of her nose. Then Dave grasped her arm and they rushed into the custom house—and came to a halt to stand and wait again till Mr. Bryce should be free to attend them.

Ann, hungry and sleepy and insensible to further torment, waited in a dull silence, but Dave talked steadily and cheerfully; and when he led her at last into Mr. Bryce's office, she followed him like a sheep. She heard his proud introductions; and Mr. Bryce offered her a warm, strong hand. She saw kindly eyes, ruddy cheeks, a grayish-brown beard; but he was a blessedly silent man, demanding of her no conversation, asking no questions nor offering remarks.

She felt toward him a swift gratitude; at least there were men in the world with the wit to be silent before breakfast. Dave was fairly babbling!

When the licenses were written, and their deposit on the rods was made, Mr. Bryce rose in dismissal. Dave grasped his hand. "And we'll see you when we come out," he promised the older man. "Two weeks from now—or three if we like it well enough!"

Mr. Bryce nodded; and he looked at Ann with—she thought—a speculative doubt in his eye. He seemed to hesitate, then said at last:

"Mr. Fearing went up last Monday!"

The remark was meaningless to Ann, but she felt Dave stiffen, and she looked at her husband in surprise, and saw the dawn in his eyes of a horrified dismay.

"He did?" Dave echoed, his tone incredulous.

Mr. Bryce nodded. "I thought it was early for him," he explained. "But he said your father wouldn't be there—and he didn't expect you would be coming this year."

Mr. Bryce's meaning was conveyed not so much by his words as by his glances. When he spoke of Dave's father it was with a dropping of the eyes, a sort of nod of sympathy; for the older man had died this winter past. And when he said that Mr. Fearing had not expected Dave to come, it was with a glance toward Ann, which explained Mr. Fearing's reason for this feeling. So much was clear.

But what was not clear to Ann was the reason why this intelligence should so distress Dave; she saw his stiff dismay; she could almost read his frantic thoughts. Here obviously was some emergency which he had not foreseen, which threatened the shipwreck of his plans.

And her quick compassion rose. A minute before, she had hated him for being so cheerful; but he was in trouble now! She linked her arm through his, loyally; she stood smiling by his side; and when they were in the corridor outside the office she made him kiss her! For if her man was in trouble, it was her joy and pride to comfort and shelter him!

When they were on the train and breakfasting, the world assumed for Ann a brighter hue. They left the rocky coastal lands behind. Bold mountain masses, with spots of snow in the ravines below their crests, like bits of lace against their reds and greens and browns, marched with the train for a while; then fell behind as others took their places like outriders for escort there. Flower patches, purple or blue or white, spotted the rocky meadows. The nearer thickets were like forests in miniature; massed groups of spruce trees and fir, perfectly proportioned, and no more than three or four feet high. Ann made Dave look and exclaim with her. She was amazed and interested by all she saw; by the curious cramped narrowness of the cars; by the perfect, kindly courtesy of the people who served them; by the stations, often no more than a name on a white board. The train seemed to stop anywhere; and Ann observed that when it stopped, everyone leaned out of the windows to see passengers alight or climb aboard. She saw men whose countenances belied the rough old clothes they wore; and the disjointed fishing rods which they carried in their hands proclaimed their preoccupation.

She and Dave rode for more than two hours on this train; and Ann was as charming as she knew how to be, and she won Dave back to at least a surface cheerfulness again. They had been married only nine days; but she had already the wit not to ask Dave why Mr. Bryce had warned him about Mr. Fearing— nor why Dave himself should have been dismayed by this intelligence.

They came at last to their alighting place. The premonitory bustle of prepa- ration on Dave's part warned her; he and the porter shifted their luggage to the vestibule. Ann looked out of the window and saw a quaggy upland dotted with boggy pools and studded with dwarf trees. A quarter-mile from the track this upland dipped sharply into a deep valley; and beyond, a mile or more away, a steep bluff thickly clad in spruce and birch and fir rose to a bold parapet against the sky. The engine puffed and panted; then its laboring eased and the train slowed, and Dave came back from the vestibule.

He was curiously white about the lips, and she read him easily. Worried, poor lamb, for fear she would not be happy in this wilderness. She vowed to appear to be happy for his sake, no matter what it cost her.

"Well, darling, here we are!" Dave said.

"It's beautiful!" she assured him, and rose and followed him down the aisle. The train had stopped, she saw, in the middle of a bog. She poised for a moment on the car steps—the ground was incredibly far below—and then dropped into Dave's waiting arms.

A tall man in very old clothes and rubber boots came toward them along the ditch beside the train. The porter was throwing their luggage off the car to Dave. Ann felt a trickle of water on her ankle and looked down and saw that she was standing on soft turf that slowly sank beneath her while black water seeped up through. Then Dave turned to meet the tall approaching man; he gripped the other's hand, shouting delightedly. The train slid away; and Ann was left alone, disregarded and forgotten, while these two old friends exchanged their greetings here.

She climbed up on the railroad track out of the bog, and Dave remembered her.

"And here she is, Mac!" he cried proudly. "The new recruit! We're going to make a fisherman out of her. Ann, Mac's the best fly-caster and the best cook in Newfoundland, and he knows the salmon by their first names."

When Mac took off his hat she saw that his hair was crisply black and curly, and his eyes were fine. He would not, she thought, have left his wife standing in a bog. She shook his hand, and felt how rough and hard it was.

Mac said, "There's a black fly on your cheek, ma'am!" She brushed it off, and he advised Dave: "You'll both need boots on. The trail down is pretty wet."

"How's fishing?" Dave demanded. He was already rummaging their boots out of the pack sack.

"Mr. Fearing got three yesterday. One of them sixteen pounds," Mac replied; and Ann saw their eyes meet, and Dave said quickly:

"Yes, Mr. Bryce told me he was here!"

"The water's low, now," Mac added; and he looked off to the southward. "They won't bite today," he said.

Dave followed his glance, and nodded; and Ann looked too. But she saw only a massed wall of mountains capped in a cloud, and she asked:

"Is the river over there? How can you tell the fish won't bite?"

"The fog," Dave told her, obscurely; but Mac explained:

"The old men used to say that when the fog blows over the mountain, the fishing's done till it clears away."

"Here, Ann," Dave bade her. "Put them on!" He had produced her rubber boots. "I never knew the sign to fail," he added. "When the fog blows over the mountain, you might just as well put away your rod!"

The men were shouldering their burdens for the walk down to camp; but Ann looked at the heavy cloud masses on the peaks yonder; they came stealing softly, smothering, white and heavy. Yet she thought there was about them something soothing; restful too. Something drowsy and calm and serene, as though they bade the weary fisherman to cease his labors and rest him for a while.

They crossed the bog, and plunged into thick spruce woods where roots lurked in the murky path to trip Ann's stumbling feet; they dropped down the steep trail for a mile or more, and then Ann heard the song of waters just ahead, and they emerged into a little open park beside the river. She saw that they were in a deep gorge; she caught a glimpse of a cabin of logs well chinked with moss and tight and all secure. Then Dave and Mac dropped their burdens, and Dave turned to her and cried: "We're here, sweet! Welcome to Partners' Pool!"

She smiled, for his pleasure's sake. Then while he and Mac put the bags away, she looked about her, appraising the surroundings here. The cabin promised comfort; there was built near-by a cooking hearth, roofed with bark against the rain, and a wigwam of bark where split salmon might hang in curing smoke for days. Ann sat down on the edge of the porch and her eyes drifted to and fro. At her feet the river ran. To her right, a rocky sluice of shallow golden water like fine wine poured down into a dark, deep pool a hundred yards or more in length which lay sleekly against the foot of the steep bluff on the other bank; and far below the pool other rapids sang.

Ann watched the river, and she brushed aside the flies that came to welcome her; and she saw, across the rapids above the pool, on a little level there, and well hidden among the trees, another cabin of logs, like this one, and as snugly built. She was surprised, because Dave had said they would be here—save for Mac's attendance—all alone; but Dave was indoors and she could not question him. She wondered whose this cabin was; and she remembered the matter of Mr. Fearing, and guessed a connection between these two mysteries.

Then a salmon leaped clear of the water, in the head of the pool, within twenty yards of where she sat; and she gasped at the bright glory of him, and his beauty, and his power. And a moment later, two men came up the shingle bank on this side of the water from the foot of the pool. One of them, who carried a gaff, looked at her sidewise, appraisingly; but the other gave her no glance at all.

This other was, she saw, an old man. His hair under the brim of his hat was white and thin; his chin had a white pallor. His frame was bowed, and his hands seemed feeble ones. He wore boots, and when he walked he lifted each one as though with a conscious effort. He carried a fifteen-foot greenheart rod, set with an ancient reel; but when he came beside the quick water here at the head of the pool, he made only three or four casts before surrendering the rod to the guide, who began to fish the water expertly.

The older man—this must be Mr. Fearing—sat down on a boulder by the stream; and Ann looked over her shoulder at the cabin where Dave and Mac were still engaged, and her eyes shone with a swift determination, and she descended to where the old man sat. She came close to him. He did not turn his head, but she said cheerfully:

"Good morning!" And when he did grudgingly look up at her, she explained, "I'm Mrs. Wooster."

He made a barking sound.

She said, "This is a beautiful pool, isn't it?"

"The pool's all right," he agreed.

"I expect it's a fine place to fish," she suggested. "I saw a fish jump here, a while ago."

"It's all right for one rod!" said Mr. Fearing briefly; and Ann drew back a little. Her color rose with a quick resentment. It was as though he had struck her.

"But there will be three of us fishing it now," she reminded him slowly.

He made that barking sound again. Then Dave came out on the porch behind her, and she saw him staring past her at the old man. Dave had again that frozen look, that look of a hurt child; so she went quickly toward him, to his side there, and he put his arm across her shoulder comfortingly.

The man yonder by the water did not turn his head; and Ann whispered to Dave, "He said there's only fishing here for one rod!"

Dave nodded ruefully. "Come inside, sweet," he bade her at last. "I'll tell you all about it, so you'll understand."

"I already understand that he's a rude old man," Ann said indignantly.

Dave smiled, almost sadly; and he shook his head. "He's a fisherman, Ann," he explained. "That's all. We're a strange, proud breed!"

So she heard the story of Partners' Pool. Dave began the telling while she changed her traveling clothes for garb better suited to these surroundings here; and he continued it while they ate the tender omelet which Mac confected over the smoking campfire. Sometimes Dave had to explain matters that were not clear to Ann, but she got at last the full measure of the tale.

Mr. Fearing and Dave's father—they were law partners in those days—discovered this pool together more than twenty years ago, and built this cabin here, and fished here together amicably for another eighteen years, without dispute or dissenting. There were two ways to fish the pool. A man might work the quick waters at the head, or the still tail of the pool where salmon sometimes liked to lie. Which was the better water depended on the weather day by day. So the two partners drew lots every morning to see which should have first choice of location; and if a man took the head of the pool for his early fishing, he must fish the foot in the evening.

Matters followed this routine equably and with no dispute for long—till a certain summer when a great salmon came upstream and lay in the tail of the pool, easily visible in the clear water, but not to be seduced by any fly at all. The two men were earnest for his capture; but the big fish ignored their every lure day after day.

On the seventh of July, Mr. Fearing drew for the morning fishing the head of the pool, and Dave's father fished the foot without moving the big salmon. In the natural course of events, Mr. Fearing would have had his chance at the fish that evening; but the day was warm, and the old man—his heart sometimes troubled him—found himself indisposed and too ill to come out. Mr. Wooster whipped with his flies the head of the pool where his evening province lay, but without success; and toward dark, yielding for a moment to insidious temptation, he sent one casual cast downstream into Mr. Fearing's territory—and hooked the great salmon, and landed him.

"Father shouldn't have done it," Dave confessed to Ann. "It was Mr. Fearing's water. Father was sorry; he apologized; he made what amends he could. But Mr. Fearing would not forgive him. They dissolved their law partnership; and the next year Mr. Fearing had the other cabin built, across the river there. Since then, they never came here at the same time; one would come early and the other late. Father was here in late July last year; so this would be his season now." His eyes clouded. "But Mr. Fearing always did prefer the early fishing, and he didn't expect me to come this year—so he's here in our time!"

Ann thought the whole matter absurd, ridiculous, childish; and she said so. But Dave shook his head. "Childish, maybe," he agreed. "But they were both fisherman, you see. You'll understand, after you've caught a salmon, dear."

She protested that she would never understand. "Mr. Fearing's too old to fish," she insisted. "He doesn't even fish himself; the guide is doing it for him."

Dave said reluctantly: "Why, yes. I don't suppose Mr. Fearing can cover ground, follow a fish downstream, or anything like that. He's pretty old, you see; and not very well. But he loves it, just the same. Wait till you've taken a salmon; you'll sympathize with him."

"It's your water," she argued. "He hasn't any right here."

"He has the right of priority," he told her patiently.

"The first man on the ground, you see. We've got to respect that."

She cried: "You mean you're going to let him hog the fishing? And—spoil our time here together! That scowling old—dog in the manger! He can't fish himself; it's time he gave younger people a chance to have some fun."

Dave grinned. "Oh, we'll make some arrangement," he promised. "And there are some pools down river."

He did, indeed, go to the old man that afternoon to seek to divide the pool; but he came back with a rueful grin to admit defeat.

"He won't make any bargain, Ann," he confessed. "So we'll have to let him have first choice, every day. He will take either end he wants, and we'll take the other." He added hurriedly, "Don't worry, we'll get our fishing just the same."

"I'm going to talk to him myself," Ann cried furiously. "If you're bound to let him have his own way, all right. We'll let him fish, as long as he handles the rod himself. But when he gets tired, instead of handing it over to his guide, we'll take our turn."

Dave shook his head patiently. "We can't do that," he told her. "He has a right to give his rod to the guide if he wants to." He urged appealingly: "Let the old man have his way, sweet. It means a lot to him. And—we'll have other years here together, you and I."

Ann in the end did allow herself to be silenced; but she was not persuaded. So, though she said no more, she thought many things; and there grew in her a stubborn and mischievous determination to upset, by and by, this ridiculous tyranny. But matters hung in abeyance for a while; for the fog blew over the mountain and the fish would not rise and the river sank deep between its banks. Mr. Fearing, wise in such matters, did not during these days fish at all; and Dave and Mac occupied the interval in teaching Ann the intricacies of the art. She learned the difference between the wet fly and the dry; she cast patiently, over and over, with the light rod Dave had bought for her; and she acquired the trick of seeing the salmon in the pools.

But she took no fish. Dave, using the dry fly, had better fortune; and Ann saw him hook and fight and land a salmon, and she began to catch the infection which possessed him. But for three or four days after their coming, she cast her flies in vain. Then one night they woke to the patter of rain on the roof; and Ann in her mosquito-netted cot heard Dave call softly:

"Awake, Ann?" And at her drowsy assent, "They'll be rising in the morning, sweet!"

She felt her sleepy pulses tingle at his tone.

The river rose; and Mr. Fearing seized on the quick waters at the pool's head and took four salmon in a morning. But Ann, at the foot of the pool with Mac to tutor her, cast fruitlessly. David had gone downstream to try his fortunes there; he came back at noon with one fish, and heard her ill success regretfully.

The river rose nine or ten inches, and in another day it fell again. That afternoon, while their rods were idle, Mac went scouting downstream, his accustomed eyes searching the ripples for shadows that were fish; and at suppertime he came to Dave with word that a big salmon had moved into the foot of the pool.

"How big?" Ann asked; and Mac said guardedly:

"Well, it's a big fish, Mrs. Wooster."

Dave laughed in quick delight. "Don't worry, Ann," he told her. "If Mac says it's big, it's big!"

Ann's eyes were shining. "I haven't caught one yet," she pointed out. "I might as well begin with the biggest. I'll catch him tomorrow."

She saw their glances interchange; and she asked, "Won't I?"

"Well," Dave explained, "we'll see what Mr. Fearing does."

Ann colored with a quick anger. "He's made me fish the foot of the pool for days, when there weren't any fish there. You mean to say he can drive me out just when I've got a chance————"

"He's an old man————" Dave urged.

"He's an old hog!" said Ann, and she went storming into the cabin. Dave found her there in tears; he tried to appease her, but she met his appeals with an icy dignity. And the young man was troubled, yet helpless to amend the matter here.

He and Mac had been right in their expectations. Mr. Fearing and his guide discovered the big fish; and Mr. Fearing next day, and day by day thereafter, fished the foot of the pool. They saw the monster now and then. Mac took Ann one still afternoon and pointed out to her the vast shadow where the great salmon lay.

"Dave could maybe get him on a dry fly," he said slowly. "Mr. Fearing only fishes the wet, and that won't move him; but I'd certainly like to see Dave try him on the dry."

Ann caught her breath in wonder at the proportions of the monster there, and she listened, and she held her peace. But she began to lay her plans. They were to come to fruition by and by.

There was a routine in their days; they rose early, fished the morning through, loafed the afternoon away, and fished from supper to full dark. Ann usually slept in the afternoon; but Mac and Dave were apt to depart on occasions of their own. They must pack supplies from the railroad, or try a near-by trout stream, or a hidden lake.

Ann did not go on these excursions. Since Dave had refused to stand his ground against Mr. Fearing's encroachments, she had held toward him a cool and pleasant friendliness, under which the young man sometimes winced. But she no longer openly reproached him. If he chose to submit to tyranny, that was his affair; she told him so, too sweetly, and would say nothing more.

Matters were in this state when upon a certain afternoon Mac and Mr. Fearing's guide departed to get a barrel and a supply of salt with which to preserve their fish; Dave went downstream to prospect the lower waters, and only Mr. Fearing and Ann were left here at Partners' Pool. Mr. Fearing always slept in the afternoon; so when Ann emerged from her cabin at about three and looked cautiously in that direction, he was nowhere to be seen. She proceeded unhindered with what she meant to do.

Ann had during her days here acquired a fair degree of skill in casting the fly. She meant this afternoon deliberately to encroach on Mr. Fearing's water—and with the dry fly, for Mac had said the big salmon might come to such a lure. Dave's spare rod was on the forks under the eaves of the veranda, the long leader doubled on the rod; and there was a Brown Hackle already attached. Ann knew the fly should be oiled; but she could not find the oil, and she decided oil was just one of the ritualistic formalities of the art, not strict necessity. She took the rod and descended to the foot of the pool.

The water shelved here to a considerable depth; and just before the current quickened for its dip over the rapids below, it flowed over three or four large rocks about which, in the gentle swirls and eddies which gave them rest from the pressure of the current, salmon liked to lie. Ann could see them even from the shore; through the confusing ripple of the water they were no more than shadows, but her eye had learned to distinguish the shadow of a fish from the shadow of a rock. She saw them where they lay.

She waded into the margin of the pool till there was room for her backcast; and as she had seen Dave do, she began to lengthen line while she kept it playing backward and forward through the air. Then the fly caught on the tip of the rod and she had laboriously to clear it and begin again. The fish lay scarcely thirty feet away and a little upstream from her, and she thought her fly would reach them.

So she launched the cast. The line ran well enough, but the long, light leader fell in a serpent's coil; only a faint wind at the last moment brought the fly clear, away from this coil and a little downstream. The whole tangle of it began to float with the slight current, over the rocks where the salmon lay.

Ann trembled with delight and looked up the pool toward Mr. Fearing's cabin, and made a face in that direction. She had no serious expectation of catching a fish; but at least she had made her gesture, registered her refusal to submit to Mr. Fearing's unreasonable tyranny. She wanted the old man to know this, and she was tempted to call to him to come and see.

But even as she looked upstream, out of the corner of her eye she saw something move near her fly; she heard a sharp, clapping sound. When she looked that way, the fly was gone; and a great shape was just turning in the water there.

More in astonishment than by design Ann lifted the light rod; but something at the other end of it refused to yield. And then with a great lunge and a spattering of shining drops, out of the water rose the form of a tremendous fish. He leaped majestically; he shook his noble head; he fell back into the water again.

Ann stood with the rod dangling in her hand, the line limp, staring and trembling at her own escape. Suppose she had hooked that leviathan! He might have chased her ashore, or dragged her in and drowned her! He was capable of anything! She was appalled at the sheer power revealed in the tremendous leap he made. Then she noticed that her line had floated downstream till it formed a semicircle on the water, but it hung there without floating farther. The hook must be caught on something!

So Ann began to reel in. She turned the handle twice or thrice, and then she paused, aghast at the fury she had evoked. The reel screamed, and the salmon proceeded to show his displeasure. He charged up the pool, and in that hundred-yard race he jumped three times. Once he leaped straight up till he was higher than Ann's head. He seemed to hang there, and there was a still fury in his contortions in the air. A moment later he was up again, dancing on his tail; then another run and a leap like an arrow's flight, a dozen feet from where he left the water to where he plunged down into it again.

Ann stared helplessly after him, while the reel shrilled in her hand. Then the reel was silent and the fish no longer jumped, and she looked at the reel and saw that it was almost empty of line. She began to wind it in, still with no thought of catching the salmon—she supposed, of course, the fish had broken free—but because Dave would not want to lose his line. She began to reel it in, and because it did not come easily she moved up the pool, taking up slack line as she went along. Once she had to wade out to clear the line from a rock, and she did this almost timidly, fearful that the angry salmon might seize the opportunity to do her a mischief. But he made no sign, and she recovered line till she was come to the head of the pool.

She realized then that the fish was still on; there was a faint vibration in the line, a pumping motion which even in its mildness was eloquent of power. She realized the fish was still on, and felt her own helplessness; and she felt very much alone, and looked all around—and saw Mr. Fearing standing on the gravel bar at the head of the pool, watching.

He was looking not at her but at the spot where the fish lay; and Ann felt her cheeks crimson like a child's detected in a fault. She was caught in the very act and crime—and just as the Ancient Mariner wore his albatross, so was the salmon fastened to her as a mute evidence of her guilt. With some vague impulse to be free of him she tugged hard at the line—and the fish went crazy with fury at this renewed intrusion on his dignity.

In this new rage he excelled his previous performance. He jumped twice in the quick water at the head of the pool; then he ran straight away from Ann and suddenly jumped at right angles so that the line hissed as it tore through the water. He returned toward her, and then raced away again, and this time when he jumped, he came down tail first and threw himself into the air again with a stroke of his tail before his body was immersed. The whole upper end of the pool was a froth of churned, tormented water for a while.

Mr. Fearing selected a boulder and sat down. He filled a pipe. He watched the fish with never a glance at Ann. He seemed so unconscious of her presence there that she began to be angry. Her jaw set stubbornly; and when the fish wished to rest, she renewed the strain upon the slender rod and teased him into a new burst of that magnificent rage which would tire him out in time.

She began to think for the first time that she might catch this fish. The possibility had not seriously occurred to her before. She tried to remember all Dave and Mac had told her. To keep a steady spring on the rod. If the tip rose, to reel in line till the strain made itself felt again. If the fish took line, to let the reel run free. To keep abreast of her fish, following along the shallows while he moved up and down the pool. And never to let him rest at all.

She remembered things Dave had told her about his tackle. The rod would not lift a ten-ounce weight off the floor; the leader would break at a four-pound pull; the reel would run at a tug of a few ounces. The fish yonder weighed she knew not how many pounds—twenty, thirty, possibly more. Yet with this fragile gear she must control him.

She found it impossible by and by to believe that this rod would not pull ten ounces; for her arms began to ache with the continued strain. The fish was quieter now. Little by little, he yielded line till Ann could see his heavy bulk in the clear water; then with one casual surge he took out the line it had taken her five minutes to gain. Again he yielded—to reassert his mastery whenever he chose.

She realized suddenly that he was drifting toward the foot of the pool. She thought this meant that he was tiring, and her own weariness was forgotten in this exultant prospect. Then she remembered that there was no one here to gaff her fish for her, so she must hold him till Dave or Mac returned.

She had forgotten Mr. Fearing yonder on his boulder, grim and silent. She remembered him now; but she would not ask his help, though her arms began to ache unbearably. She tugged at the rod, and the great salmon turned and ran downstream; he came to the very foot of the pool and jumped and landed in the first quick chute of the rapids; and she remembered that salmon sometimes went racing downstream and could not be stopped, and she ran after him. But the fish stopped in that first quick water till she came abreast of him, and then raced the length of the pool to the head again, at a steady, plugging pace.

So it was all to do over; and Ann looked at Mr. Fearing almost appealingly. He had moved downstream now; he was standing just beside her there. He must have moved, she guessed, when the fish started for the rapids; and she thought he wished to be near at hand to triumph in her defeat when the salmon broke clean away. She hated the old man with a weary hatred as she began to reel in line and follow the salmon up the pool.

It was nearly an hour since she had hooked this fish; it might have been eternity. Ann's arms ached as though she had been supporting a great weight for hours; her feet were sore from stumbling over boulders; her eyes burned from following the tiny thread of line. She thought she could not endure much more.

But the salmon was far from surrendering. As she reeled line and followed him up the pool, he began to drop back to meet her; she found herself suddenly abreast of him, and then above the fish again. He made short, stubborn runs, always downstream, and Ann held him as hard as she dared, and gave line when she must, and took line when she could.

They neared the head of the rapids, and Ann knew that for half a mile below there was a tumble of quick water, foaming over boulders half submerged or wholly so, where a fish must surely break away. She held the salmon hard, striving to turn him. But her very opposition spurred him into flight, he made a harder run; he fought to the very lip of the rapids.

And then she saw old Mr. Fearing go scrambling into midstream to intercept the salmon there; he took his post like Horatius at the bridge, in the head of the first chute; and when the fish came that way, the old man kicked and splashed till the salmon once more darted a few yards upstream. Ann felt a sudden warm gratitude and a belated understanding. What was it Dave had said? Mr. Fearing was a fisherman! She had trespassed on his water, she had hooked his fish; he must hate and despise her; yet for all that he would help her save the salmon, if he could!

He looked toward her now at last, and she smiled her gratefulness; but he shouted fiercely.

"Keep a strain on him, you little fool!"

Ann dutifully lifted her rod. It weighed six or seven ounces, Dave had said; but it seemed to her just then incredibly heavy. She put a strain on the fish; and he began once more to drift downstream.

Mr. Fearing was able to turn him a second time; but a minute later all his efforts failed. The great fish was very weary now; indifferent to alarms. It slid past Mr. Fearing's very shins, and in a boil of rushing water it started down the rift.

Mr. Fearing, the line looped between his thumb and finger, yet still running free, followed; and behind came Ann, stumbling over great boulders, her feet almost swept away at every step by the rush of the current, the reel buzzing steadily as the fish went farther and farther ahead of her.

In a little swirl he paused at last, and Ann came almost up with him, regaining her lost line; then he went on again. They moved in a sort of procession. First the sullen, weary fish; then, five or six yards behind, Mr. Fearing, guiding himself by keeping a light touch on the line, clearing it from entangling boulders, holding it away from snags and brush. And still farther behind, Ann. Once she stumbled to her knees and filled her rubber boots; but she scrambled to her feet and still came on, and when she could, she reeled in line. Sometimes the spool of the reel was almost empty; sometimes it was almost full before the fish took up his flight again.

It was at a moment when they advanced in open order that they met Dave returning upstream. He saw first Mr. Fearing, and then the fish splashing down a shallow run. Before he saw Ann at all, he had hurried out into the stream to try to turn the fish. But Mr. Fearing shouted:

"I'll follow him, you idiot! Watch your wife. Help her keep her feet!"

Dave looked upstream and saw poor Ann a hundred yards away, stumbling weakly toward them, trying to reel in line, wet to the waist, her hair disordered, her face blazing red with long exertion, her lips white with fatigue.

He raced to her side and he cried some question.

"I—hooked—the big one," she gasped.

"I think he's hooked you!" Dave corrected joyfully. "Tired? Let me take him for a while!"

"I'm going to land him if it kills me," she panted. "But you can keep me from falling down!"

So Dave became a fourth in this procession. He walked at Ann's heels, his hands under her shoulders to support and steady her. But he tried to hurry her, to overtake the running fish; and so disaster came.

What happened was that Ann stumbled; and Dave tried to catch her, and tripped over her feet, and so they both fell forward, Ann beneath and Dave atop her, into a foot of swift water. And they gasped and scrambled to their feet again, choking and laughing.

"But I've still got the rod!" Ann cried triumphantly.

Dave looked and shook his head. "Fish is gone, hon," he told her, and pointed at the empty reel. The line had broken where it was fast to the spool.

Dave saw her swift despair; and he said contritely: "That line's been on there four years. I never expected a fish to take it all out, or I'd have put a new one on!"

"He's gone?" Ann wailed. "Gone?"

"Got away," Dave admitted. "Yes, he's gone."

And Ann stared at the empty reel, and the useless rod; and then suddenly she knew how tired she was. Before Dave could catch her, she sat down helplessly in the very water there; the swift current boiled about her waist. She began whole-heartedly to cry.

No till Ann was rested and comforted did it occur to them that Mr. Fearing had not come back upstream; so Dave left her on the bank and went down to find the old man.

He was scarce gone when Mac appeared from the direction of the cabin to hunt for them, and discovered her, and heard the tale. When she had finished, the guide looked downstream thoughtfully.

"Hard work to follow a fish down this rift," he said, half to himself.

Ann nodded. "Mr. Fearing had to run like a boy," she agreed. "I can understand him better now, Mac. He shall fish where he likes, from now on."

But Mac only said, in a low tone, "Here comes Dave!"

She followed his glance and saw her husband picking his way up the rocky shore. Something made her silent while he approached them; when he drew near she saw that his lips were white. Then he came to where they were, and stood beside them, and they waited till he said at last, "He saved your fish, Ann! Held the line, and beached him in the next pool below!"

And Ann asked in a quick, hushed voice, "He's all right, isn't he?"

Dave, after a moment, nodded, and he smiled. "I think so," he agreed. "I never saw so much proud happiness in a man's face as there is in his—where he lies beside the great salmon there!"

Ann pressed her hands to her lips, and her throat ached. But Mac, standing there above her, smiled gravely; and his eyes swept a slow circle all around.

"He was mighty fond of all this," he said slowly. Then his glance rested on the mountains, where white cloud masses rolled; and after a moment he looked down at Ann.

"There comes the fog," he told her gently. "The old men always say that when the fog blows over the mountain, a man can hang up his rod for a while."

SIXTEEN

The Old Men's Pool

BEN AMES WILLIAMS

The Newfoundland Railroad runs on a narrow gauge, and the seats are proportionately restricted, and the aisle is narrow too. Nevertheless, the trains are companionable and accommodating conveyances. Thrice each week, when the *Caribou* docks at Port-aux-Basques, the Express takes aboard travelers and mail and freight, and starts on a journey of something more than twenty-four hours, in a great half-circle clear across the island; and thrice each week another Express returns to deliver traffic to the steamer about to sail. These are the only passenger trains, but there are freights besides.

And all these trains are neighborly. The tale, perhaps apocryphal, is told of a lady passenger who asked the conductor: "Do you know what those flowers were beside the track a few minutes ago?" And he said: "No, but I'll have the engineer back up so you can pick some and see."

Certainly all these trains—even the Express—will stop anywhere for the accommodation of fishermen; and there are many stations which are no more than signboards beside the track, with a meandering footpath leading away across the barrens to some spruce-clad slit in the mountains where a salmon river runs. When the train stops, everyone looks out of the window to see fishermen alight, cased rods in hand, their guides with corked gaffs and use-stained shoulder packs bulging with supplies and cooking dishes. Or it may be to see other fishermen come aboard, with great salmon heavy in a short sack that has been tied end to end for easier carrying. Sometimes horses pasturing at large wander on the tracks and canter ahead of the train for a mile or two while the engineer proceeds cautiously, waiting for them to get off the right of way, or perhaps stops so that the fireman may go forward and drive them to one side.

Once Frank and I were coming back to camp from Seven Mile Pool, and I heard the whistle sound, long, short, short; and I thought ignorantly that we would stop to pick up other fishermen. We did not, but a moment later I saw slide past our windows a faded signboard lettered with the legend:

THE OLD MEN'S POOL

The path beyond, leading toward the river, was badly overgrown and almost invisible; it was obviously seldom used nowadays. I wondered why the whistle blew.

"I thought we were going to stop," I said to Frank. But he shook his head. "No, that was a running blow!" he said. . . .

On another day I saw the Old Men's Pool itself. Down the river, when in spring the ice goes out, sweeps a battering ram, hundreds of tons of weight driven irresistibly on by the water banked behind. You may in summer see, twenty feet above the river's level, where from the trunks of trees ice has rasped the bark away; and the solid rock walls where the valley narrows to a gorge are planed by it and left smooth and bare, the naked rock veined with wandering lines of white where threads of marble run through the softer stuff.

And the scouring ice changes, from year to year, the contour of the river's bottom, scooping up boulders and gravel in one spot, only to deposit them farther downstream. Thus where there was a swift run of water last year, with fish nosing into the bold current, and—with a fine knowledge of the laws of flowing liquid which man had to build wind tunnels to acquire—resting in the burble above a boulder, or in the half-eddy where the current spills past the round rock's shoulder, you may now see only a shallow flat of gravel with water moving placidly, and no salmon near.

At one such spot, upon a certain day, as the boat, impelled by Frank's iron-shod pole, bore us downstream, I caught a glimpse of a cabin all ruin and decay, on the lofty bank above the water; and Frank to my question said:

"Yes." The word hissed softly as his slow tongue lingered on the final consonant. And he said: "Joe Denny built that cabin for Mr. Hamilton, when there used to be a good pool here. The pool's filled up and made again and filled up again in my time."

But Joe Denny was only a name, and Mr. Hamilton was no better, and I did not at the moment connect this ruined pool with that faded signboard by the track, and the engineer who whistled the running blow. But I would remember them when presently the tale came to be told.

It was another incident altogether which brought this matter at last to Frank's mind, and shaped the thing in words. Half a mile below the Overfalls Pool, the river turns to the right across ledges that stand on edge like a series of fences, their sharp crests rounded and smoothed by ice like the rims of cups across which the water thinly flows. But through each ledge there is a break deep enough even at low water to float a boat, if the boatman know his course and take a proper zigzag way from one opening to the next. Rivermen call this place the Gate and negotiate it warily.

It was near dark when we came down from the Overfalls toward our cabin a half-mile below the Gate, and there was no more than the shine on the water and the dark break of ripples to show the way; yet Frank, easing her with his pole, let us through without touching any ledge, and I said:

"Good going!"

"Seems like it's easier in the dark," he said. "When you can't see the trouble all around."

"Like driving a car on a bumpy road," I suggested. "It never seems so rough at night." And I told him about a certain pilot who on a cross-country jaunt after a festive night decided to land so that he might get his flask from the front cockpit. He could find no decent field, chose recklessly a restricted spot fenced and walled with trees, fishtailed in with a slip and a stall at the end, emptied his flask, and flew boldly out with no trouble at all!

"Yes," said Frank, with a soft sibilance. "If a man can't see the trouble all around, or if he's too drunk—or maybe too mad—to care, it's astonishing the things he can do and take no harm."

And with that half-chuckle I had long since come to recognize as the stir of wakened memory, he said: "Like the time Joe Denny ran the Little Falls of the Humber with Mr. Hamilton."

The names were faintly familiar, though for the moment the reason for this familiarity escaped me. Nevertheless, when we were back in camp, with a temperate noggin of Demerara rum in hand to banish the chill of evening, I asked questions. Frank spoke but briefly, and I had to cast back over the ground with many inquiries, probing and searching before the matter all was clear and plain.

Fergus Hamilton was his name, a New York man of means and leisure, both earned by his own efforts; a man used to command, and used to having his opinions received with respect and used to a certain deference. He came to fish the Little River and the Grand, and Joe Denny was his chance-allotted guide. Joe was the older by half a dozen years, and it was said of him that he had guided on more rivers than any man hereabouts. He was a driver and a worker; and—unusual among Newfoundlanders, whose many rivers are more apt than not to have an icy bite borrowed from the snow banks which even in July linger on the mountain flanks—he swam like an otter, as much at home under the water or in it as in his canoe upon its surface.

He taught Mr. Hamilton to cast a light and accurate fly, to fish the fly in many sweet seductive ways, to see the shadow of a moving fish in time to antici-pate and meet the strike, to play a salmon boldly at first and gently as the fish came near the gaff, to meet every wind condition—and winds forever scour these rivers—with an appropriate length and strength of cast, to roll his fly into an upstream wind so that it would point downstream on landing, to cast high with a following wind, so that the spent fly would settle lightly on. He taught him the whole lore and art of angling for salmon, which are the most mysterious and unpredictable of fish.

And between these two, not in one year but in many, a deep bond formed. Joe Denny was a widower, with one son named Mat who was an engineer on the railroad, and two others who were guides like their father; but Mr. Hamilton was a bachelor, a man alone. And year by year he returned to Newfoundland, and year by year Joe Denny was his guide. Sometimes they stayed in waters near at hand; sometimes, with an outfit assembled by Joe and financed by Mr. Hamilton, they went afield. Once they cruised along the south coast where small salmon are so plenty; and one mid-afternoon Mr. Hamilton hooked a fish which did not break the surface, and they played it by turns for three long hours and lost it at last and had never a glimpse of it, so that Joe Denny opined it must have been a seal, but Mr. Hamilton clung always to the belief that it had been a gigantic salmon of a record-breaking immensity.

And they fished the Torrent River, where salmon fought and scuffled to reach the fly, and the brief fruitful reaches of the Serpentine, and the great Humber from Deer Lake to the Falls, and many lesser and more easily accessible streams; and they made the acquaintance of an old dog salmon in Harry's River, forty pounds if he were an ounce, which would leap gloriously whenever a line dragged across his back, and which lay below the shoulder of the same ripple rock three summers in a row. In the third summer he took Mr. Hamilton's fly, and on his first run raced across the river, leaped high and dry on a gravel bar, flopped there for seconds that seemed minutes, while they stood helpless, fell back into the river again and broke the leader around a boulder and was gone, never to be seen more. But these two had their memories of him, and Joe Denny used sometimes to show—for proof of the tale—half a dozen tremendous scales which he had picked up afterward where the great fish floundered on the gravel bar.

And once they went to the Labrador and were blooded by the winged swarms of insects there and waded to their knees through schools of running salmon. And always they went alone; two men who welcomed no companion, and who by grace of years grew older. Till, arduous adventurings becoming a thought too wearisome, like sea captains weary of the sea, they settled down.

There was a pool on the Grand River which above all others Mr. Hamilton loved. Salmon came there fresh from the sea, bright as silver; and there Joe

Denny built a cabin, and there year by year they made headquarters from mid-June till the last week in July. Fishing for the mornings; long drowsy afternoons when no rod crossed the pool; fishing again from sunset to early dark. The traffic on the river, moving up and down in boats, might see Mr. Hamilton sitting on the screened porch, or thigh deep in the pool; and Joe Denny leaning motionless upon his gaff near by, or busy by the cooking hearth ashore. They were both old men now. The water they had chosen was by other rods left courteously free; and it came to be called the Old Men's Pool.

"It's all filled up with gravel now," said Frank to me. "You saw one day where it used to be, and the old cabin on the bank. It filled up the spring after Mr. Hamilton died. Never been any good again."

And I thought of an ancient clock in an ancient song which "stopped short, never to run again, when the old man died."

And Frank said: "Sometimes in the afternoon Joe would swim in the dead water toward the foot of the pool, but Mr. Hamilton never did. He couldn't swim."

So, year by year, though for shorter and shorter periods each day, the old men fished the Old Men's Pool.

For the most part, they dwelt in harmony, but once or twice they disagreed. In fishing, as in other matters, times change, and tackle too. Fergus Hamilton and Joe Denny were of that generation which believed that great fish must be taken with great rods, seventeen or eighteen feet long, fitted with leaders and flies to match. Such a rod, used all day in the wind, becomes a burden for strong young arms, and much more so for older thews.

Then someone discovered that a thirteen-foot rod with sufficient line, well handled, will kill any salmon; and Mr. Hamilton, persuaded against his prejudices by some New York acquaintance, brought one of these new rods to Newfoundland. Joe Denny looked at it with a malignant scorn, and for a fortnight refused even to set it up, and the two old men spent more time in argument than in fishing. But in the end Joe yielded, though grudgingly, and the lighter rod had a trial.

"It's no more than a switch to tickle 'em," said Joe Denny in a deep hostility.

"Aye, but it's easy on an old man's arms," Mr. Hamilton urged, almost pleadingly.

"A man too lazy to handle a proper rod has no place on the river," Joe said. Nevertheless, he saw that the new rod laid a light fly, and killed fish; and so was silenced.

Yet he never openly admitted his defeat; nor did Mr. Hamilton prod the raw wound to Joe's pride. Silence at the right time is good cement for the structure of a friendship, and these two were friends.

The new rod had another virtue too. It tired Mr. Hamilton so little that he felt young again. A batsman swings two or three bats as he goes to the plate, so that a single bat may feel no heavier than a wand in his hand when he flings the others away. It was so with the old man now. He fished longer hours, caught more fish, went back to New York rejuvenated—and the delusion of youth persisted so long that in March he wrote Joe Denny a letter.

"I want to go up the Humber again this year," he said. "To the Great Falls. I'll be on the boat that gets in on the twenty-third of June."

Joe wrote back in protest that it was a hard trip, that there might be logs in the river, that Humber fishing was not particularly good, that they would have to tent, that the flies would be bad.

"If you don't feel equal to it," Mr. Hamilton replied, chuckling as he wrote, and meaning this for a jest which Joe would understand and appreciate, "get a younger man to take me in."

Now, it is possible to say a thing with a smile and give no offense or hurt, but you cannot smile in a letter. Mr. Hamilton knew this, but he had forgotten it. So when he landed at Port-aux-Basques, he was surprised to see Joe Denny here to meet him in store clothes, wrinkled blue serge and a dusty derby hat.

And old Joe said, with a grim unsmiling countenance to meet Mr. Hamilton's greeting:

"Your outfit's in the baggage car, sir; and here's my son Dan to take care of you." He added, with the hurt bitter in his throat: "He's a younger man!"

So Mr. Hamilton knew what he had done; but for some things there can be no sufficient apology. Yet also he knew that Joe Denny would commit a double murder with mayhem before he let Dan Denny or any other man take his place. Therefore, he said loudly:

"Don't be a blithering jackass, you cranky old fool! Take off that fireman's hat and that undertaker's suit and get on the train." And to Dan, standing grinning by: "Go on home, youngster, and wait till you're a man!"

Dan was no youngster. He would never see forty again. But he only chuckled and said: "Aye, sir. It was the old man's idee!"

"He's cracked in his head," said Mr. Hamilton. "But a blooding by the black flies will cure him."

So the two old men got aboard the train, and Mr. Hamilton put on an urgent good humor and a loquacity quite out of character; but Joe would not be mollified so easily. He spoke, it is true, but gloomily and shortly; and by and by Mr. Hamilton mopped his brow and was silent, and the train plodded on its neighborly way, stopping here and there. Joe Denny's son Mat was the engineer of this particular train; and when in due time they alighted at Deer Lake, Joe still grim in serge and derby, Mat got down to see their outfit unloaded, and he said with a dry grin:

"The old man decide to try it himself, did he, Mr. Hamilton?"

Joe himself merely sighed, but his silence on the train had frayed Mr. Hamilton's temper, and the New York man flamed at the engineer in a low white wrath.

"Keep your tongue t' yourself, Mat!" he said forcibly, "or I'll stuff you into your own firebox."

And Mat chuckled and climbed back in his cab and left these two to finish their battle as they chose.

"You've not seen the Humber," Frank said to me, by way of parenthesis, as he told the tale. "But it's a bold river, and dangerous too. I went up once with a big party, and there was a New Brunswick guide along supposed to be the best canoeman in the province. His canoe got broadside on a rock in one of the little rapids and broke in two. Lost every piece of gear, bar a bag of bedding, and had a time of it to save the men.

"Oh, the Humber's no playground! You've got to know your way, whether it's up or down. There are some long deadwaters, but even in them you'll be first on one side and then the other, dodging ledges. And the runs are hard and heavy. You have to haul up through some of them, with a rope and men above pulling.

"And the Little Falls, the easy way is to carry around. There's a drop of as much as forty-fifty feet in not more than two hundred yards. At low water you can haul a canoe up through sometimes with a rope, and sometimes not. Coming down, you'd lower her through with a rope and someone holding back hard. You can't hold her with a pole. You come down a chute straight for a rock that looks as big as a house, and swing off at the last minute to go around it and then on down again, the water boiling like a pot, and rocks like teeth all around.

"Going up, it's pole most all the way; and coming down it's paddle and pole, pole and paddle. The hard places, you have to take the pole to hold her; and the Little Falls nobody ever runs, and there's three or four other places you have to ease her down."

He filled his pipe again, and having thus set the scene resumed the tale.

Frank said that Joe Denny, old man though he may have been, took Mr. Hamilton up the Humber from Deer Lake to the Big Falls. Call it twenty-five or thirty miles. They might have stayed the night at Deer Lake, and Mr. Hamilton so expected; but when the train was gone, Joe, without discussion, got the canoe into the water and loaded, and he stood grimly waiting. So Mr. Hamilton got in.

They slept that night beside the river, and at dawn went on. Joe carried around Little Falls, Mr. Hamilton helping as he could. But during that second day of sweating travel, Joe's frigid silence began somewhat to melt. By the time they reached their goal and had their gear ashore, things were, on the surface, as they had always been between these two; and Mr. Hamilton was humbly grateful for this much of forgiveness, and he called Joe to watch the salmon leaping in their efforts to breast the falls, and the two men applauded success and jeered failure as if these were human contestants whose antics they observed.

One great fish tried the barrier over and over, lifting his lumbering bulk out of water in clumsy leaps hopelessly inadequate. There were many failures, but none so abject as his. When, after supper, Joe launched the canoe for fishing, in the easier flow of water well below the falls the men could see the silver glint of many scales, rasped loose by bruising ledges, drifting in the river's bold current, drifting, drifting toward the sea.

And that night it rained and rose the water and penned them in their tent. Fishing was impossible. They had no cooking fly. Joe cooked in the rain, and they ate in the rain, and for the rest they sat all day huddled with their gear in the scant and restricted shelter the tent afforded. Their clothes were soggy and their blankets were soggy, and for two days it rained with a mild continuing persistence that raised the river three or four feet and made a torrent of it. And thereafter, even when the rain ceased, clouds and fog persisted, while they waited for the waters to fall.

Their tempers suffered; yet on the surface a certain serenity was still maintained.

Joe nursed his grudge, but did not air it; the other man read his mind and was angry at what he read, but would not broach the matter. Yet his tongue slipped once. While Joe was busy at the fire, Mr. Hamilton went to watch the jumping salmon; and returning, said:

"The old big one is still trying it! Hardly strength enough to jump clear of the water now! You'd think he'd know he was too old for the job!"

And Joe loudly clattered the frying pan on the rocks of the fireplace, so that Mr. Hamilton realized too late that he had opened the wound anew. But he thought that by another morning the waters would have fallen sufficiently to allow them to fish, and matters must be better then.

In the morning the sun did shine; they had good sport with lusty grilse of five or six pounds, and a salmon or two, and their humors improved, and at the nooning Mr. Hamilton said:

"Joe, why don't you set up one of the other rods and we'll both fish?" They were not using the gaff, freeing the played salmon, saving only a few grilse for the pan. And Joe agreed. But when presently they were on the river again, Joe with that old seventeen-foot rod which he preferred, Mr. Hamilton with the lighter gear, Joe was frowning gloomily. This time, though, he spoke.

"I see a short rod in your case," he said dourly. "What's that for—trout?"

Mr. Hamilton, sitting in the bow, was grateful that Joe could not see his face, crimson with a guilty shame.

"Why, no Joe," he confessed. "That's a dry-fly rod! Ten and a half feet long. They say it will handle anything that swims."

He heard Joe's snort behind him. "Dry fly!"

"They've proved killers, Joe," Mr. Hamilton argued, "when the salmon wouldn't touch a wet!"

"Ten foot long!" Joe grunted.

Mr. Hamilton tried to laugh. "You darned old mossback!" he cried. "You acted the same about this rod the first year. Remember? You're as hard to move as a mule!"

Silence. Silence behind him like a heavy cloud, persisting, oppressive, crushing. He fished under the weight of it for a long hour. If Joe would only argue, say something, curse, roar, explode, then, as if by a thundershower on a sultry afternoon, the air might be cleared.

But Joe said nothing at all.

The situation was explosive; the detonator might have been anything. It happened to be a fly, a Jock Scott tied on a No. 4 hook. Mr. Hamilton, fishing with a Montreal, hooked a piece of heavy drift moving half submerged and broke his leader. He swung the rod back so that the line came within Joe's reach for replacements, and Joe set to work.

But when the repairs were made, Mr. Hamilton looked at his fly and saw the Jock Scott there.

The thing, in his mood of the moment, irritated him out of all reason. Joe had advised a Jock Scott after lunch; Mr. Hamilton had insisted on the Montreal, and had since hooked and played and freed one salmon. He said explosively:

"Blast it, Joe, I don't want a Jock Scott! I want a Montreal!"

"Jock Scott's what we've always been using on the Humber of a sunny afternoon," said Joe inflexibly.

"Then it's time to try something else," said Mr. Hamilton, blind with wrath. "Every time you get hold of my leader you tie a Jock Scott onto it! You're a senile, stubborn jackass! The only way to get any sense into that granite head of yours is to crack it open with a canoe pole, and I'm a mind to do it!"

He twitched the Jock Scott off the leader and threw it over the side and swung his rod to Joe again.

"Put on a Montreal," he said curtly. "I'm sick of arguing with you!"

But for only answer he felt the canoe heave, and turned to see that Joe was taking the anchor in.

Mr. Hamilton was ashamed of his outburst and ashamed to say so. He said nothing.

Joe thrust the canoe ashore. He stepped out, not heeding the other man at all. With a stony countenance he collected his own few personal belongings—including the derby hat—and put them in the canoe.

Mr. Hamilton, during these proceedings, had sat on the shore without movement, not even watching. Joe finished, and he spoke at last.

"I'm going out," he said briefly. "You can suit yourself! Stay or go as you're a mind!"

Frank's own words best fit the rest of the tale. "And that's how come Joe Denny to run the Little Falls," he explained. "He told me about it himself that winter. He said he was mad clear through.

"Mr. Hamilton, when Joe said that, hadn't any choice but to come along; so he went to taking down the rods, and Joe packed the tent and gear, neither one of them speaking. By four o'clock or so they were ready, and Joe pushed her off and Mr. Hamilton got in front and Joe in back.

"Joe set down, and he told me he never left his seat till they got to Deer Lake."

Now, for downstream work in quick water a sensible man uses his pole, not only to pick his course but also his speed, lest his craft, with too much headway, escape from his control and run headlong to destruction. I knew this, and I asked:

"You mean that he never used his pole?"

"Never touched it all the way," Frank assured me. "Run everything he came to. Mind you, the water was high and heavy and fast. Being high, it covered some of the rocks, but there were plenty left. Joe ran it all, and I never heard tell of any other man, drunk or sober, crazy or in his senses, that done it.

"But Joe did. He said he was so stubborn mad that he never thought of being careful at first at all. And then he knew he was being a fool, and that made him madder than ever. He kept expecting Mr. Hamilton to say something about being careful, and he had his mind all made up to tell the old man if he didn't like the ride he was getting, he could go ashore and walk!

"But Mr. Hamilton never spoke a word all the way. He sat in front, his back to Joe, looking straight ahead; and he filled his pipe whenever it was empty and smoked it steady and slow. Joe said there was times they went so fast the smoke came back past Mr. Hamilton's ears like a pair of reins on a trotting horse; but the puffs came steady and regular just the same.

"Along the first of it, Joe expected they'd both be in the water the next lick; and he said he didn't care if they was. They came near the top of the Little Falls, and Joe was waiting for Mr. Hamilton to cry quits and want to go ashore, but the old man didn't. He just kept on smoking, as calm as if he was setting on the cabin porch down at Old Men's Pool. So Joe, mad at himself for being such a fool, swung her to hit the chute down the Little Falls.

"And about that time he remembered that Mr. Hamilton couldn't swim. Joe didn't mind being in the water any more than a salmon did, but Mr. Hamilton would have sunk like a stone. I tell you, any man starting to run the Little Falls, swimmer or no, he's got good cause to be afraid. But Mr. Hamilton never puffed his pipe any faster, nor turned his head, nor held on, nor even stiffened in his seat.

"They hit the chute and down they went, and Joe said, thinking that Mr. Hamilton couldn't swim, the sweat came out on him like a squeezed sponge. Halfway down you have to swing her hard. There's this great rock right in the way, and the river trying to pile you into it. Joe didn't know, after, whether he swung her with his paddle or the prayer he said; but next he knew, they were in the easier water below.

"So Joe looked at the back of Mr. Hamilton's head, and he loved that old man, and he told me he cried for as much as two miles of river, thinking what might have happened from his stubbornness and foolishness.

"And he took almighty care to hold her right side up from then on. But just the same, being proud of what he'd done, and kind of wanting to brag about it, the way a man will, he stuck to his paddle, never touched his pole. And by and by they was back to the landing.

"Joe stuck her nose ashore, and he was too weak to move. He just set there. But Mr. Hamilton stepped ashore and kind of stretched himself, being stiff from setting still so long. And he turned around to look at Joe, and he kind of grinned, and Joe stepped out into the water and came to land.

"Mr. Hamilton was the one to say what they both were thinking. Joe couldn't speak. His throat had kind of knotted up on him.

"'Joe,' Mr. Hamilton says, 'we're a couple of fools! Old fools, too! Both of us ought to know better!' And he grinned, and he says: 'But, Joe, you were right about the Jock Scott. That would have been the better fly!'

"And he stuck out his hand, and Joe hung onto it. That was all he could make out to do."

Frank was silent; and I asked: "So they came back to the Old Men's Pool?"

"Yes," he said softly. "And everything was smooth as cream from then on till Mr. Hamilton went home. Not a hard word spoke on either side."

He concluded: "Mr. Hamilton died that winter, but Joe wouldn't rightly believe it when the word came. He claimed it wasn't true. He was all of seventy and his head was pretty old. You couldn't make him believe it. The pool filled up when the ice went out that spring, same as it is now; but nothing would do Joe but he'd come down and get the cabin ready, case Mr. Hamilton did come.

"And Joe stayed at the cabin, and he'd be up at the railroad to meet every train, all that summer, looking for Mr. Hamilton. Next spring it was the same. He stayed down there in the cabin alone; but it was a hard walk up to the train, and that year he wouldn't always make it. If he didn't, and his boy Mat was the engineer, Mat would have the fireman whistle the running blow, so old Joe down't the cabin would hear, and know the train wasn't stopping, and not worry about meeting Mr. Hamilton, and rest easy in his mind.

"The other train crews took it up. Joe's been five-six years dead now, but it got to be a habit with them and they stick to it. Easing Joe Denny's mind so he'll rest easy. Yes, sir, every train that passes by still whistles the running blow for the Old Men's Pool!"

Writers' Biographies

Eugene V. Connett (1891–1969) founded The Derrydale Press and wrote six books on hunting, fishing, and boating, including *Wing Shooting and Angling* (1920), *Magic Hours* (1927), *Feathered Game from a Sporting Journal* (1929), and *Random Casts* (1939). For more details about his life and The Derrydale Press, see the Introduction.

S. Kip Farrington, one of the pioneers of deep-ocean fishing, was born in Orange, New Jersey, in 1904. He was for many years the saltwater columnist for *Field & Stream*. His books on deep-sea fishing include *Atlantic Game Fishing* (Derrydale, 1937), *Pacific Game Fishing* (1942), and *Fishing with Hemingway and Glassell* (1971). In 1952, while fishing off Cabo Blanco, Argentina, he caught a 1,135-pound black marlin, the first fish ever caught on a hook and line weighing more than 1,000 pounds. A stockbroker by vocation and a man of many enthusiasms who wrote books on duck hunting, railroads, hockey, ships, and soccer. For more on him, see "The Curmudgeon" in *Profiles in Saltwater Angling* (1973 and 1999), by George Reiger.

Roderick L. Haig-Brown was born in England in 1908 and as a boy fished the streams of his native Dorset. In 1927 he moved to British Columbia, where he worked as a logger, hunting and fishing guide, trapper, civil magistrate, and teacher. He wrote twenty-four books, many about the outdoors, including *Silver: The Life Story of an Atlantic Salmon* (1931), *A River Never Sleeps* (1946), *Fisherman's Spring* (1951), *Fisherman's Winter* (1954), *Fisherman's Summer* (1959), and *Fisherman's Fall* (1964). In 1975 a reviewer in *The New York Times Book Review* called him "the finest all-around angling writer this continent has yet produced." He died in 1976. For more on Haig-Brown, see two books by Arnold Gingrich: *The Joys of Trout* (1971) and *The Fishing in Print* (1977).

Van Campen Heilner was born in Philadelphia in 1899 and grew up fishing along the southern New Jersey shore. He wrote about saltwater fishing for *American Angler*, *Field & Stream* (where he was an associate editor), *Sports Afield*, and other publications. His favorite species was the channel bass (a.k.a. red drum and redfish), which he called "the bulldog of the sea." In the view of George Reiger, "Nowhere in angling literature is there a finer expression of the pleasures of surf fishing than in the writings of Van Campen Heilner." His books include *The Call of the Surf* (1920), *Adventures in Angling* (1922), and *Salt Water Fishing* (1937). He died in Madrid in 1970. For a brief biography, see "The Beachcomber" in *Profiles in Saltwater Angling* (1973 and 1999), by George Reiger.

Ernest Hemingway was born in 1899 in Oak Park, Illinois. His Nick Adams Stories, published in the early 1920s, drew in part on his boyhood experiences fishing for trout in Michigan. Fishing for trout in the Pyrenees and for marlin off Cuba figure, respectively, in his novels *The Sun Also Rises* (1926) and *The Old Man and the Sea* (1952). He won the Nobel Prize for Literature in 1955 and died in Idaho in 1961. For more on Hemingway the fisherman, see *Hemingway on Fishing* (2000), by Nick Lyons, and "The Literary Angler" in *Profiles in Saltwater Angling* (1973 and 1999), by George Reiger.

Charles Phair was born in Presque Isle, Maine, and was educated at Phillips Exeter Academy, in Massachusetts. His chief business was brokering fishing and hunting properties for wealthy sportsmen. He also imported salmon flies from the British Isles and created a popular trout pattern of his day, the Gees-Beau Streamer. The two-volume Derrydale edition of *Atlantic Salmon Fishing* was his only book. He died in 1943 in New York City, at age 68.

Edmund Ware Smith, who was born in 1900, wrote stories about life in the Maine woods for *Collier's*, *Esquire*, *Outdoor Life*, and other publications. His books included three published by Derrydale: *A Tomato Can Chronicle*, *Tall Tales and Short*, and *The One-Eyed Poacher of Privilege*, which chronicled the adventures of a Downeast ne'er-do-well named Jeff Coongate.

Howard T. Walden II was born in 1897. He served in the 35th Field Artillery during World War I and lived in Palisades, New York. He was a businessman who wrote avocationally. Along with two books for Derrydale, *Upstream & Down* (1938) and *Big Stony* (1940), his published works include *Freshwater Fishes of North America* (1964) and *Native Inheritance: The Story of Corn* (1966).

Ben Ames Williams was born in Mississippi in 1889, grew up in Ohio, and graduated from Dartmouth College in 1910. He and his family lived in Massachusetts and vacationed on a farm in Maine, the setting of many of his stories. He wrote for the *Saturday Evening Post* and other publications and was the author of more than thirty books, mostly fiction, and more than four hundred short stories. Two of them, *All the Brothers Were Valiant* (1919) and *Leave Her to Heaven* (1944) were made into movies. He died of a heart attack in February 1953 at age 63, while curling.

Hugh D. Wise graduated from the U.S. Military Academy in 1894 and served in the Infantry in the Spanish-American War and World War I. He retired as a colonel and in his later years became a deep-sea fisherman and authority on sharks. *Tigers of the Sea*, published by Derrydale in 1937, was his only book. He died in 1942, at age 70, in Princeton, New Jersey.

Derrydale Angling Anthology: Titles and Acknowledgments

The Channel Bass
Van Campen Heilner
Heilner's tribute to the channel bass (a.k.a. red drum and redfish) first appeared in *American Big Game Fishing* (1935), edited by Eugene V. Connett.

Marlin Off Cuba
Ernest Hemingway
From American *Big Game Fishing* (1935), edited by Eugene V. Connett.

Giant Bluefins of Jordan Bay, Nova Scotia
S. Kip Farrington
From *Atlantic Game Fishing* (1937). The original title was "Jordan Bay, Nova Scotia."

Montauk's Miracle Waters
S. Kip Farrington
From *Atlantic Game Fishing* (1937). The original title was "Eastern Long Island and Martha's Vineyard."

Fighting Sharks
Hugh D. Wise
From *Tigers of the Sea* (1937). The original title was "Fights Typical of Species."

Summer Steelhead
Roderick L. Haig-Brown
From *The Western Angler* (1939).

On the Water and in the Mail
Roderick L. Haig-Brown
From *The Western Angler* (1939).

Why Fly Fishing?
Eugene V. Connett
From *Random Casts* (1939).

And So It Goes
Eugene V. Connett
From *Random Casts* (1939).

The Selection of Salmon Guides
Charles Phair
From *Atlantic Salmon Fishing* (1937). The original title was "Selection of Guides."

The Spark Is Kindled
Howard T. Walden
From *Upstream & Down* (1938).

Sam Fario
Howard T. Walden
From *Big Stony* (1940).

Lost: Two Reputations
Edmund Ware Smith
From *A Tomato Can Chronicle* (1937).

Old Medical Bill
Edmund Ware Smith
From *Tall Tales and Short* (1938).

The Fog Blew Over the Mountain
Ben Ames Williams
From *The Happy End* (1939).

The Old Men's Pool
Ben Ames Williams
From *The Happy End* (1939).